FAM

Family belief systems, therapy and change

Family belief systems, therapy and change
A constructional approach

RUDI DALLOS

OPEN UNIVERSITY PRESS
Milton Keynes • Philadelphia

Open University Press
Celtic Court
22 Ballmoor
Buckingham MK18 1XW

and
1900 Frost Road, Suite 101
Bristol, PA 19007, USA

First Published 1991

British Library Cataloguing in Publication Data

Dallos, Rudi
    Family belief systems, therapy and change.
    1. Families. Interpersonal relationships – Psychological perspectives
    I. Title
    306.87

    ISBN 0–335–09493–7
    ISBN 0–335–09492–9(pbk)

Library of Congress Cataloging-in-Publication Data

Dallos, Rudi, 1948–
    Family belief systems, therapy and change/Rudi Dallos. p. cm.
    Includes bibliographical references and index.
    ISBN 0–335–09493–7   ISBN 0–335–09492–9 (pbk.)
    1. Family—United States—Psychological aspects. 2. Family psychotherapy.
3. Personal construct theory. I. Title.
    HQ536.D32 1990
    306.85—dc20   90–7326
                                                                     CIP

Typeset by Burns & Smith Limited, Derby
Printed in Great Britain by St Edmundsbury Press,
Bury St Edmunds, Suffolk

Contents

Preface

The aim of this book is to explore the intimate relationships in families from the standpoint of the people 'inside' them. We will be looking at the understandings, beliefs, explanations – the *constructs* that people use in order to manage their relationships in families. The term 'family' will be used as a shorthand to refer to groups of people who have been intimately involved with each other over an extended period of time. This includes one-parent families, reconstituted or step-families, couples without children, homosexual relationships and even communal structures. Of course this does not imply that these groups are all simply equivalent, but instead that they can all be usefully studied in terms of their systems of beliefs.

There is now a substantial body of literature about families from the 'outside'. In particular the concepts from systems theory have gained widespread application. Within time some of these concepts will, no doubt, permeate through to the language of the 'average' family. This has already happened with Freudian concepts which find expression in phrases such as 'defensive', 'death wish' and 'hangups'. So, what families think about and talk about to each other and share with researchers and therapists are therefore influenced by us, the 'merchants of ideas and theories'. Where there is overlap between the outside and inside perspectives, some comments will be made especially in terms of the interesting problems this poses for the therapist. For example, the children in one family coming for their second session requested if they could play that questioning game again (circular questioning). Also, in my experience many couples and families are a little disappointed if they don't 'have to' do something a bit strange like sculpting or psychodrama. Perhaps psychology and therapy are after all to some extent entertainments?

The embracing theme of this book is that in any given society and culture families construct their own social reality. There are of course a whole range of wider factors over which the 'average' family has little influence, for example the political system in operation and with it a wide range of structural and ideological factors which constrain the possible varieties of social realities that they can construct. In discussing this theme the content of this book covers a range of established theoretical and therapeutic approaches and as such does not claim to be particularly new. The major aim is to draw together in one volume a number of hitherto largely scattered and relatively independent varieties of constructional analysis.

This book is about change and therapy, and a fundamental question is to do with how people's beliefs are related to their problems and how to change their beliefs. Most forms of family therapy, and other therapies come to that, involve challenging either directly or indirectly the cherished assumptions that people hold about their problems and themselves. It will not be assumed in this book that people who come to therapy are misguided or wrong in how they see things. But we will consider in some detail what the *implications* are for some of the beliefs that people hold and how these can often serve to maintain their desperate and painful conditions. This idea that the way people think about themselves and their problems is a significant contributor to their problems is of course not new. It is at least as old as psychiatry itself. Nor is it a new idea that people have in some way to be 'tricked', cajoled, teased' away from their unhelpful beliefs.

> A man went to a doctor and told him that his wife was not bearing children. The physician saw the woman, took her pulse, and said: 'I cannot treat you for sterility because I have discovered that you will in any case die within forty days.' But she did not die at the time predicted.
>
> The husband took the matter up with the doctor, who said: 'Yes, I knew that. Now she will be fertile.'
>
> The husband asked how this had come about. The doctor told him: 'Your wife was too fat, and this was interfering with her fertility. I knew that the only thing which would put her off her food would be fear of dying. She is now, therefore, cured.'
>
> (Shah 1968: 61)

We might attempt to justify such use of trickery by suggesting that there is no way of disabusing the sufferer directly. Telling someone that their cherished disease is a disease is unlikely to help. Instead if people are to be helped, they must be tricked into changing their actions, which may consequently lead them to changed insights: 'If I am to help someone else to see that a false problem is false, I must pretend that I am taking his problem seriously. What I am actually taking seriously is his suffering, but he must be led to believe that it is what he considers as his problem' (Watts 1961).

There is of course a danger of adopting an arrogant position here – as if the therapist or guru 'knows better'. This issue is a central one though. Two key points are involved which any therapist must address. First, we often recognize that people have some fairly unhelpful if not downright damaging ways of seeing themselves, their friends, relations and life generally. Second, we are faced not only with the need to assess their beliefs and understandings, but with the task of developing the most effective and efficient techniques for assisting them towards more productive ways of seeing things.

We must be extremely wary, however, of assuming that therapy or counselling is always sufficient or even necessary when families appear to present problems. There may be a variety of economic, social and physical pressures which drive families into distress. Even when the problems appear to be caused by emotional difficulties or inability to think clearly or creatively in order to assist the family we need to consider the possibility that such 'psychological' short-comings are due to the family being immersed in a culture which is oppressing them. This is a great danger with humanistic psychologies, such as the ideas of George Kelly, which emphasize the ability of individuals to operate more successfully by rearranging how they see the world. And for some families therapy is only a palliative or, worse, insults them by failing to acknowledge the reality of the circumstances that they are in.

Racial, class and gender represents such basic realities. A black family may be helped to come to terms with the prejudice the children are likely to meet at school or when they start work, but this does not remove the prejudice. Likewise, a single-parent mother may be helped to cope with the problems of raising children on her own. This does not solve a vast array of problems such as lack of child-care support, low income and the loneliness that she is likely to continue to suffer. Attempts to assist families and change society go hand in hand. Critics of family therapy might argue that it is apolitical or simply maintains families in the status quo. In contrast some therapists, such as Minuchin, have argued that family therapy offers a form of 'soft revolution' in that it can empower families to be able to make a wider range of choices and be more capable of demanding social change.

Structure of the book

The book is concerned with not only personal belief systems but how families construct shared systems of beliefs which serve to guide the family members' perceived avenues of choices of actions and thoughts. The material is drawn from both clinical practice and research into families and also employs theories originally formulated in terms of individuals, namely personal construct theory and psychodynamic theory. This reflects my own involvement in this area as a clinical psychologist working with families and as a researcher.

The book starts by examining some images of the family and focuses on the concept of the family life-cycle model, which serves to bring together society's general consensus about what we expect family life and its development to be like. This lays the foundation of a dynamic view of families developed in Chapter 2, which emphasizes and reviews the contribution of cybernetic/systems theory-based models of families. An attempt is made to utilize and develop systems theory based models of the form and function of beliefs within families. The idea that beliefs may become patterned in an analogous way to patterns of actions is considered. Together the two chapters also attempt to lay the basis of an ecological model which integrates the individual, the family and society, particularly in terms of what family members believe society expects of them at various stages in their lives together.

Chapter 3 takes some time to review personal construct theory in order to offer an analysis of the individual within the system, and also to enable subsequent chapters to build on the tenets of construct theory so as to permit a more detailed and integrated analysis of family and personal belief systems. Chapter 4 examines work and approaches which have extended personal construct theory to explain not just individual beliefs and actions, but also group processes and shared construct systems. Chapters 5 and 6 then attempt to combine a construct theory approach with the systems theory concept of interdependent action. A key theme which is developed is that the processes in couples and families are guided by mutually interlocking cycles of beliefs and actions.

Chapter 7 offers a scheme for analysing and mapping family belief systems and emphasizes the symbiotic relationship between therapy and research in the idea of therapy as research and research as therpay. The conviction that exploration necessarily leads to some change is central to both personal construct theory and systems theory, and forms the backcloth to the final Chapters 8 and 9, which attempt to demonstrate the applications of the ideas discussed to therapy and theories of change. Tehniques such as reframing and paradoxical interventions are examined in terms of belief systems, and two detailed case studies are offered in Chapter 9.

Chapter I
Images of families and the family life cycle

I told Don Juan one instance of my father's behaviour that I thought would apply to the situation at hand. Almost immediately upon arriving on the farm my father would insist on taking a long walk with me at his side, so we could talk things over, and while we were talking he would make plans for us to go swimming, every day at six a.m. . . . At night he would set the alarm for five-thirty to have plenty of time, because at six sharp we had to be in the water. And when the alarm would go off in the morning, he would jump out of bed, put on his glasses, go to the window and look out. I had even memorised the following dialogue.

'Uhm . . . A bit cloudy today. Listen I'm going to lie down again just for five minutes O.K.? No more than five! I'm just going to stretch my muscles and fully wake up.'

He would invariably fall asleep again until ten, sometimes until noon. . . . I told him that my father was weak, and so was his world of ideal acts that he never performed. I was almost shouting . . . Don Juan did not say a word. He shook his head slowly in a rhythmical way. I felt terribly sad. Thinking of my father always gave me a consuming feeling. . . .

'If you think that you were so much stronger than he, why didn't you go swimming at six in the morning in his place?'

I told him that I could not believe that he was seriously asking me that. I had always thought that swimming at six in the morning was my father's business and not mine. . . .

'You are complaining', he said softly. 'You have been complaining all your life because you don't assume responsibility for your decisions. If you would have assumed responsibility for your father's idea of swimming at six in the morning, you would have swum, by yourself if necessary, or you would have told him to go to hell the first time that he opened his mouth after you knew his devices. But you didn't say anything. Therefore you were as weak as your father. . . .

'Wait, wait!' I said. 'You are twisting this around.'

(Castenada 1974)

As young children we probably take for granted many aspects of what a family is. It is literally familiar, like the air that we breathe, simply there. I remember with some awe my first experiences of visiting a young friend's home in Hungary and encountering a dramatic challenge to my assumptions. The colours were different, the smells, the noises and the way that people talked to each other. I was so in awe that, like many young children in this situation, I did not know what to say or do. Until this experience of the difference and contrasts between families, my assumptions about my own family were largely unconscious. When I returned home after the visit, my home looked quite different and I was never to experience it in quite the same accepting way that I had until then.

Later, of course, our understandings become much more overt, and we may attempt to demonstrate deliberately to the external world what kind of a family we see ourselves as and how we wish to be seen by others. We attempt to create something which is both normal and acceptable in our society but also something which is unique and personal. The idea that a family is 'creative' and is created by the people in it, as well as a social structure defined by society, is central to this book.

There is a legend from Africa of a husband and wife, arriving at a village in search of a new home. The couple engage in a mock quarrel at night to see if the other villagers would intervene. They left the village in the morning because no one came to arbitrate their conflict. Such interventions would occur, they thought, in a *good* village (Poster 1978). The African couple in the story demonstrate not only what kind of a family they want to create and to be, but further how they would like to interact with their community and what this community of families should be like.

Understandings of families: inside and outside perspectives

Whenever a therapist or researcher and a family meet, both will form impressions about how the other sees the world, including importantly what they think families are and should be. None of us has a monopoly on truth in this endeavour; families as much as therapists, psychologists, psychiatrists and social workers equally have the ability to construct meanings, to 'make sense' of the world around them and what is happening to them. A therapeutic encounter is similar to other forms of social encounter in that both parties are attempting to 'make sense' of each other, to figure each other out. Part of this may be that both therapist and family wonder whether 'their family' is like 'mine' and in what ways it is different. What do they believe in?

In the phrase 'make sense' perhaps lies the key theme of this book. We construct meanings to give us a sense of what is going on around us. The meanings do not simply reside 'out there' to be absorbed; people 'create' sense, they try to give meaning to the events they experience, to others' actions and to their own. The ability to create personal meaning, to respond and interact with the world and with each other but always with reference to a set of internal meanings (autopoiesis or self-creation), can be seen as the essential quality of living organisms: 'Living as a process, is a process of cognition. This statement is true for all organisms with or without a nervous system' (Maturana and Varela 1980: 8).

This is similar to George Kelly's (1955) proposition that each of us has a 'personal construct system' through which we view the world. This represents a form of internal cognitive organization or structure which is unique for each person. When we communicate with someone therefore, we should never assume that they have understood what we have said in the same way that we have understood it. Instead, what occurs is a two-way process of negotiation whereby we arrive at or create some shared meanings.

Arguing from a sociological rather than biological position, Berger and Kellner (1964) propose something very similar: 'Worlds are socially constructed and socially maintained. Their continuing reality, both objective . . . and subjective . . . , depends upon *specific* social processes, manely those processes that ongoingly reconstruct and maintain the particular world in question (25).

Beliefs

The word 'belief' is used widely and can offer a range of meanings. It can suggest religious beliefs or moral attitudes such as, 'I believe in God.' It can mean cognitions or what we take to be real – 'I believe X is a tree' – or accepting someone's statements: 'I believe he is telling the truth.' It can also mean predictions of future events – 'I believe it is going to rain.' The word belief also embodies two other important aspects. First, belief contains the idea of an enduring set of understandings and premises about what is taken to be true. Second, and related to the first, there is an emotional component or a set of assertions with an emotional basis about what 'should' be true. For example, I can have a belief that 'we are a happy family'. This contains the premiss that this statement is true and also an implication that this is desirable to me in some way. If this belief was challenged, I might feel anxious and try to defend it and even become angry if the attack on my belief was continued.

There are, of course, many other ways we could examine the concept of belief further, but it will be used in a deliberately general way to include other terms such as anticipations, constructs, attitudes and explanations. A broad way of summarizing these concepts is to say they all essentially refer to what a person 'believes to be going on'. It is difficult to find a more suitable term which captures the cognitive and emotive aspects of 'what a person thinks is going on'. Other terms such as constructs, anticipations and explanations will be employed to cover the same territory as the concept of belief. Bateson (1972) offers a definition which gets at the heart of what will be the concern here:

what is important is a body of habitual assumptions or premises implicit in the relationship between man and environment, and these premises may be true or false . . . premises which govern adaptation (or maladaptation) to the human and physical environment. In George Kelly's vocabulary, these are the rules by which an individual 'construes' his experience.

Bateson (1971) p.314

One important theme we will be exploring is that families serve to maintain or reinforce the kinds of beliefs held by the individual members. Above all else it could be argued that a central element in a family is a sense of belonging, of being a 'part' of a family. This sense of belonging, however, cannot simply be reduced to a biologically based instinct or predisposition. Instead, it appears to be largely a learned cognitive and emotional state. For example, children who have been brought up to believe that their step-parents are their 'real' parents will continue to accept this unless they are informed otherwise. Frequently, when such children discover the 'truth' there is a period of crisis of self-identity. Sometimes this can involve years of searching for their real parents. This behaviour and the emotional experiences associated with it seem to be based upon a reconstruction of their beliefs.

What fuels this desire or need to search for one's 'real' parents and ancestors? It is likely that cultural factors such as accepted images of what is 'normal' family life, the importance of family ties, 'blood is thicker than water', and the idea of inherited characteristics such as personality and looks are important. In effect, this constitutes a cultural premiss that our sense of identity 'is', and 'should' be, based upon our biological parents and ancestors. We are deeply influenced by the images of family life that our culture presents us with. The child's searching for its 'real' parents therefore represents a coupling of cultural and family definitions. If he has grown up with the culturally accepted definition of a family as consisting of two parents, himself and perhaps other siblings, he finds his model of family life shattered by this realization that his parents are not his 'real' parents. Furthermore, the cultural definition also contains a set of values that suggest that the nuclear family is the 'best' and that therefore he has been deprived in some way.

It is also important to remember that family relationships can transcend both place and time. As a result of the uprising in Hungary in 1956, I was separated from my father and sister for 34 years, but when we were eventually reunited we were 'familiar' to each other. The family grapevine had been able to cross continents and keep us all informed about each other. Some important discoveries about each other appeared, but we were far from strangers with little in common. I was quickly informed by my sister of the 'family secret,' which was that one of my relatives, a committed communist, left Hungary to escape not from the Russians but from the revolutionaries!

Definitions of the family

Families do not exist in a social vacuum, and the structure of any given family is partly determined by the particular culture in which it exists. Various writers on the family have emphasized that what we take to be the accepted image of the family, namely the nuclear family, is a relatively recent configuration exclusive to Western societies (Mead 1949, Poster 1978, Shorter 1975). Central to any definition of the family is the organization of the male and female roles. Anthropological studies of so-called primitive cultures (Mead 1949, Malinowski 1964) indicate interesting variations in these. One now famous example is that of the Tchambuli in New Guinea where the women were found to undertake functions that are regarded to be typical of males in our society, carrying out most of the physical work, whereas the men were frivolously occupied with making themselves look attractive and decorative. Numerous other variations have also been found, such as societies where the children are emotionally closer to their maternal uncles than their own fathers. In modern Western societies there have, of course, been some explicit attempts to reject the conventional nuclear family model, for example experiments with communes, the kibbutz structure, as well as a variety of step-family and single-parent configurations. Such variations serve to instruct us to be cautious about our assumptions concerning families and the variations we believe to be possible.

Legal and other quantitative definitions – for example in terms of family size – are important to the basic sketching of how families are structured. What is of paramount significance, though, is how families translate these societal definitions for themselves and the continuous processes of mutual adjustments and redefinitions that are required in order to manage family life. For example, leaving home is a fundamental issue because it raises a range of questions about the continuing viability of the family, its structure in terms of who will continue to be in it and how they will continue to interact. The implicit rules governing its existence may have to become explicit and open for debate and negotiation. As the children prepare to leave, decisions have to be made regarding how, and when, the children can leave. More broadly, 'leaving home' is in itself culturally constructed. There are differences between various cultures and sections of a culture. In Asian societies and agricultural communities in Britain, it may be quite acceptable for the children to continue to live at home even after marriage. Culture can be seen to lay down the broad brushstrokes of how things should happen in families, but each has to work out the details. Family members are often seen to grapple and disagree about their interpretations of the outside realities and question each other's grip on reality. For example, the children might accuse their parents of being old-fashioned and out of touch, while the parents might suggest that they have a more realistic and far-sighted perspective.

There are various models of family life, in its broadest sense, from which people to some extent are able to choose. Media representations still by and large offer an image of a nuclear configuration, even though statistically it is now a minority. The classic image of the nuclear family – father working and mother at home with their children – applies to only 5 per cent of households at any one time, and one in five children can expect to experience the divorce of their parents (Wallerstein and Kelly 1980). An important aspect of this is that a nuclear configuration is a model to which people are encouraged to aspire despite the fact that it is in fact impossible, as in the case of step-families, for them to achieve this. This seems strange when we bear in mind that, due largely to death of women at childbirth, step-families have been around for a long time. In Victorian society it was not at all unusual for a man or woman to have two, three or more marriages simply as a result of the death of their spouses. Yet despite this prevalence we have few available models explaining how to solve the complexities of step-family configurations. On the contrary, one of the most frequent problems that step-families present is the inability to abandon attempts to contort themselves into a nuclear family configuration (Wallerstein and Kelly 1980). Fairy stories serve as a powerful example of the way that images of family life are transmitted. The Grimm brothers' story of Snow White, for example, perpetuates a negative image of step-families, especially the classic stereotype of the 'wicked step-mother'. Erika DeAth (1984) expresses some of the contradictions that face step-families:

> Stepparents have traditionally had a 'bad press' in mythology, fiction and drama which is nowadays fuelled by the wide media coverage given to the rare cases of child abuse by stepparents. This negative image of the stepparent conflicts with the myth of the stepfamily as a 'normal' family and is compounded by the myth of 'instant love' or 'instant adjustment' which can arouse feelings of guilt, anger, panic and helplessness in adults and children. Society expects mothers to provide nurture and affection, leading many stepmothers into trying too hard to be the 'perfect' parent while fathers are expected to provide material and emotional support, guidance and authority in the management and discipline of children.

Our earlier distinction between 'inside' and 'outside' perspectives can be seen in terms of a distinction between *levels of analysis* emphasized by Bateson (1972). Anthropological and sociological explanations have concentrated on the societal or structural levels of analysis such as the 'functions' that families serve within a particular society. To take an example, some anthropoligical approaches have employed a functional framework and offered hypotheses about how the nature of the kinship ties, such as those between children and their maternal uncles, serve the function of enhancing social cohesiveness by helping to bind together the maternal and paternal sides of families and subsequently enhancing cohesiveness within the society as a whole (Malinowski 1964, Bateson 1972). Likewise various roles within families have been explained in relation to the functions that they serve for the society. Parsons and Bales (1956) suggested that the conventional male–female sex role division functions to maintain the two requirements of families: task centred – the men going out to work – and emotional/social – the women servicing the male workers. Alternatively, Marxists accounts have stressed the ways in which families serve to maintain the structural inequalities between classes in any society at a given point of history. Families are seen as passing on wealth and privilege through the generations and as operating as exclusive units serving to guarantee high levels of consumption of the products of capitalist economy and thereby guaranteeing high levels of profit.

Psychological explanations, in contrast, have emphasized the importance of families in terms of nurturing the child to enable a complete emotional development to occur, to provide a model of how to behave as an adult and to develop physical and social skills. Both levels of analysis, the psychological and the societal, are essential to an understanding of families. However, it will be argued that they are not sufficient in themselves to account for the diversity and uniqueness of family configurations in any society. What is also needed is an interpersonal or familial level of analysis. Bateson (1958) suggested this in his account of the processes in 'primitive' societies where ceremonies such as the Naven amongst the Latmul in New Guinea served to regulate and stabilize the potentially dangerously escalating conflicts between the sexes and helped to ensure the cohesiveness of the society. At the interpersonal level such ceremonies also served to provide a release for the potentially dangerous conflicts among the 'macho' males. Similarly observations of families in experimental and therapy situations show that the family is much more than simply a transmitter of the cultural values and norms. The essence of family life is that it is complex and changing and that unique situations and combinations of needs continually arise. Families therefore need to be able to act in creative ways to find solutions to their circumstances. Most of the book will be about this intermediate level of analysis: the dynamics and creative aspects of family life and how these are related to systems of understandings shared by the family members.

The family life cycle: ecological models

Families exist in environments which alter continuously and demand that families have the ability to make continual changes. A family is an *organic* entity which maintains some form of identity and structure whilst at the same time is continually evolving and changing. Apart from the day-to-day variations and adaptations necessary for family life, it is also evident that families may be faced at times with massive demands for change, such as when people arrive – births and marriages – and depart – leaving and death. There may also be external demands such as local social upheavals and major cultural changes. Duvall (1977) extended the idea of the individual life-cycle model to the idea of a family life cycle and outlined how families face a number of important developmental tasks. The implications of this model for the practice of family therapy were first set out by Jay Haley (1981) in his book describing the therapeutic techniques of Milton Erickson. He describes how Erickson discovered, in his extensive therapeutic work with individuals and families, that problems were often associated with critical periods of change and transition in families. For example, psychotic episodes were often concerned with late adolescence and the issue in the family of the young person about to leave to set up his or her own home. Haley describes the following stages as critical transitional stages for families:

1 The courtship period
2 Marriage and its consequences
3 Childbirth and dealing with the young
4 Middle marriage difficulties
5 Weaning parents from children
6 Retirement and old age

Erickson's concept of family development emphasized a life-long process of socialization, adjustment and learning within families. Hence families were not simply about socializing their children, although this is included in his stages 3, 4 and 5, but a reciprocal process whereby parents were also continually learning and adjusting to their children. Haley does not expand greatly on the subject, but he does make it clear that the model assumes that there are sets of values and norms inherent in Western society and that families are expected to comply with them. For example, he describes how young people 'need' to practise courtship skills in order to find a suitable mate. Interference with this learning process through family conflicts can detrimentally disrupt it and make problems for the young person since she is out of step with her peers.

Carter and McGoldrick (1980) have offered some elaborations of the family life-cycle model, proposing in particular that Haley and others tended to play down the influence of internal stressors resulting from transgenerational influences and developmental processes of the individuals in families. They propose a two-dimensional model (see Figure 1), which they describe as follows:

> The **vertical** flow in a system includes patterns of relating and functioning that are transmitted down the generations in a family. . . . It includes all the family attitudes, taboos, expectations, and loaded issues with which we grow up. One couple say that these aspects of our lives are like the hand that we are dealt: they are a given. What we do with them is the issue for us.
> The **horizontal** flow includes . . . both the predictable developmental stresses and those unpredictable events, 'the slings and arrows of outrageous fortune', that may disrupt the life cycle process.
> (Carter and McGoldrick 1980: 10)

The concept of the family life cycle has attracted critical attention, notably that it takes an overly normative view of family development and focuses on the nuclear family which, in its pure form, is not now the most common arrangement. The experience of step-families can be a muddling up and confusion of these stages. A 'new' couple may find itself in a

Figure 1 Developmental influences on the family

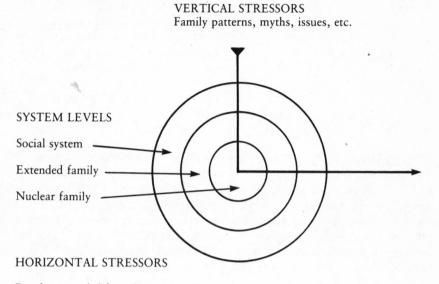

VERTICAL STRESSORS
Family patterns, myths, issues, etc.

SYSTEM LEVELS

Social system

Extended family

Nuclear family

HORIZONTAL STRESSORS

Developmental (life-cycle transitions)

External (war, untimely death, chronic illness, etc.)

courtship, romantic phase, but at the same time have to deal with adolescent offspring from the partner's previous marriage. There can also be a danger of ignoring the competing definitions in modern society regarding various forms of family life. It is possible that adults may choose to live in a single-parent arrangement or a commune, but these choices are less available to children; as Haley argues, their parents' 'eccentric' choices can have considerable ramifications such as rejection by their peers and becoming labelled in various ways.

However, the family life cycle offers a framework for considering some of the major issues that we want to discuss. It can be seen to contain a wide set of rules, norms and expectations about the family and even life outside the family. The crises associated with the various stages also point to the impact of ruptures between family beliefs and actions and those of the wider society. Parents may experience various forms of pressure if they 'cling' to an adolescent child too strongly. This is especially the case if the child exhibits problems, at which point the parents may receive advice from school, the doctor or social workers along the lines of allowing their child more independence in keeping with social norms. This is particularly illustrated by families coming from different cultural backgrounds, such as Asian families where a close and continuing involvement with the family is expected.

Young adults at the leaving-home transition can be seen as the family's 'research assistants'. They are usually spending more time away from home, sampling new social groups and thereby exploring and testing the relevance of the family's beliefs in a variety of outside settings. This naturally leads to some questioning of the family's accepted ways of seeing things. What works for the family situation and the established social networks around the family – work, school, friends and extended family – may need to be revised by the young people. For some families this questioning and challenging of the saliency and validity of their beliefs can be extremely threatening, especially if they are having to deal with other pressures.

The ways that families steer their way through the various stages of the life cycle are not simply capricious. One important source of direction comes from the family traditions going back several generations and in some cases hundreds of years. We can start to see this in episodes of storytelling in a family, such as a story about when uncle Dave left home and how things worked out for him. These anecdotes provide a store of experience generated by the traditions of family experimentation. These traditions have been conceptualized in terms of family scripts (Byng-Hall 1985) which serve to guide how successive generations of children come to regulate their family lives. A powerful example is provided in cases of families who have a tradition of calling in outside agencies at difficult times:

> The belief system of a family is formed by, and in turn sustains, its patterns of behaviour. For instance, take a family that throughout the generations has maintained its balance during a crisis by calling upon a social work agency to temporarily remove one of its members. This family may well be seen as conforming to a belief that expulsion of a member is the only solution to a crisis. The more the family believes that expulsion is the only solution, the more the family uses expulsion, and so on through the generations.
>
> (Burnham 1986: 21)

The family life-cycle model draws our attention to the interplay between the images offered by a society and the family's interpretation and internalization of them. The image is made more compelling by the fact that even if people aren't in a true nuclear family, that is with their own children, the structure of a heterosexual couple living together with children is still the most common form of family experience, and most of us will experience this for the greater part of our lives. However, this obscures the complexity of the roles and experiences that face many families. In a step-family in which both parents have been married before, have children from their previous partners and have their own children, there is at any given moment a variety of ways in which people can see themselves. Each parent may at times experience themselves as being in a single-parent family – with their children from the previous marriage – as a step-parent, as a nuclear family with their new joint children, and as a step-family. At different times one definition may predominate over the others or our experience may be confusing and fragmented. Needless to say, the experiences that we have are not simply personal but related to the demands of other members of the family.

It is also possible to see here different and complex sets of kinship relationships, such as ex-spouse's mother/father and new partner's parents as grandparents-in-law. We have very little in the way of concepts or even language with which to label these relationships. It can be argued that these changes have come about as a result of the growth of divorce, but this is not completely true since historically the high mortality of mothers at childbirth has given us a long legacy of step-parent configurations. It is arguable that the lack of development here is consistent with an ideological attempt to maintain the nuclear model as the image to be strived for. A widespread acceptance of alternatives may be seen as 'radical' and as a challenge to one of the foundations of Western and other societies:

> Attacks on the family are typical of revolutionary periods. Christ told his disciples to leave their parents and families and to follow him. The French, Russian, and Chinese revolutions all undermined the traditional family structure in those countries in an attempt to speed the progress toward a new social order. The Israeli kibbutz is another example of the same social process.
>
> (Minuchin 1974: 48)

Ceremony and ritual

In most societies the transitions involved in life-cycle stages are demarcated and assisted by various forms of ceremonies and rituals: the end of courtship and entry into marriage by the wedding ceremony, the birth of children by christening, bereavement by the funeral ceremony, not to mention various forms of graduation ceremonies, confirmations, retirement presentations and so on. Ceremonies and rituals play an important part in signalling change, perhaps erecting boundaries around a newly married couple or restating the relationship between the nuclear family and other parts of the extended family. The congregation of all the family members at ceremonies and rituals allows these redefinitions to be announced to all the members at one time, hence making it easier for them to become established. Palazzoli et al. (1978) make the point that ceremonies and rituals are a very powerful form of implicit communication. For example, those who stand closest to the couple in the wedding picture may at the same time be implicitly displaying and reaffirming, for all to see, the new nature of the family organization.

Haley (1981) has pointed out that in Western society the decline of ceremonies and rituals has recently led to a realization of their importance in facilitating transition between life-cycle stages. Greater freedom from formalities has produced greater confusion about the position of the grandparents, parents and so on. Likewise, we can speculate that perhaps the lack of a 'divorce ceremony' to mark the end of marriage explains in part the difficulty and pain experienced. Some ministers, especially in the USA,

Figure 2   The family life cycle

External and *Internal* demands for change

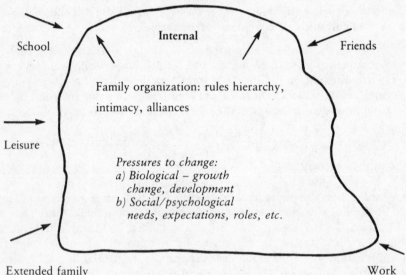

External

Cultural expectations

School

Internal

Friends

Family organization: rules hierarchy,

intimacy, alliances

Leisure

Pressures to change:
a) Biological – growth
change, development
b) Social/psychological
needs, expectations, roles, etc.

Extended family   Work

Family life-cycle stages: *transitions*

The External and Internal demands for change are *continuous* but become critical at transitional points in the family's life:

1 COURTSHIP	A family is under great
2 EARLY MARRIAGE	pressure at these stages
3 BIRTH OF CHILDREN	to change and reorganize
4 MIDDLE MARRIAGE	itself without
5 LEAVING HOME	disintegrating –
6 RETIREMENT AND OLD AGE	*ATTEMPTED SOLUTIONS*

have now started to offer divorce ceremonies. With these ideas in mind, family therapists such as Palazzoli *et al.* have developed the 'family ritual' as a therapeutic tool. In one example, to help a family through an unresolved bereavement, it was suggested to the family that they should meet together in the garden next Saturday afternoon, dig a hole, and plant a tree in memory of an unmourned child.

Above all, the examination of rituals and ceremonies shows us how families are inextricably connected to the wider social world. Our society contains ideas not only about how families should be, but how they should develop and change. In other words, the rituals and ceremonies provide 'rites of passage' not only for individuals but for the whole family. The family life cycle model suggests an image or norm of what people believe family life 'should' be like. Inherent in this image are beliefs about the form that the family should take; how a family should develop, solve problems, communicate with each other, how the members should feel about each other and when it is appropriate for children to leave and start a new family of their own. In a sense the concept of the family life cycle merely sets out formally a set of assumptions that people in a given society hold about family life. In the next chapter we will consider how the family life cycle complements an analysis of family life in terms of psychodynamic and the cybernetic models.

Chapter 2

Constructing patterns of shared experiences

If families are continually required to change, how is it that in some situations, especially in the context of therapy, families appear to operate in predictable and repetitive ways? We have started to consider the idea that people in families are engaged in the construction of a social reality. This can be seen to involve three related aspects: behaviour, beliefs and emotions. These are linked together so that families attempt to make sense of their world, to ascribe meanings to their own and to each other's actions and in doing so to construct a repertoire of choices. In this chapter we will look at each of these three aspects of patterning as a prelude for a more detailed analysis of family beliefs in subsequent chapters. To start with, a brief outline of cybernetic models – systems theory and ecological models – will be offered, followed by a sketch of some attempts to integrate them with concepts derived from psychodynamic theory.

Systems theory and ecological models

Some of the fundamental concepts that led to the development of the first systems theory models of family life came from Gregory Bateson's and Margaret Mead's anthropological studies in New Guinea. Initially interested in how various societies came to develop different types of gender roles and in the ways that ceremonies and rituals served to reinforce them, they also became interested in the dynamics and cybernetic properties of the societies and of groups. From their work they developed two notions of stability: on the one hand, how society and groups of people maintain a balanced state and, on the other, the tendency to show escalation or increasing instability (schizmogenesis). Later work on the communication processes in people displaying schizophrenic symptoms led one of Bateson's co-researchers, Don Jackson (1957), to articulate and develop the systems theory model of family life which focused on the first aspect of stability. As a practising psychiatrist Jackson observed that progress in his patients was frequently accompanied by the onset of deterioration in a member of their family or some other person intimately involved with them. Such observations led him to suggest that these oscillations could be described by employing the model of self-regulating systems. People in intimately involved groups were seen to be interdependent in terms of mutually influencing both each other's behaviour and their thoughts and feelings. Over a period of time, these interdependencies were seen as becoming patterned and to some extent predictable.

Linear versus circular causality

Paul Watzlawick and his colleagues distinguished between *linear* and *circular* causality in order to explain the repetitive patterns of interaction that can be found. This represented a fundamental shift from how relationship difficulties had previously been explained. Two simple examples are offered below to illustrate this idea. A circular view of problems stresses how the action of each person of the pair above influences the other, whose behaviour in turn influences them. This is radically different to linear explanations which emphasize how one person *does* something *to* another, for example, saying that Mary *makes* John angry. Each partner's behaviour in the examples below can be seen to be maintained by the actions of the other. So Mary's accusations or placation may serve to fuel John's angry behaviour, which in turn leads to more of the same from Mary. Likewise there is a move away from explanations couched in terms of invariant personality traits, such as George's level of insecurity. Whether he is more or less insecure than other people is less relevant than the fact that his level of insecurity is maintained by the interaction between him and Doris. Likewise Doris's level of detachment is maintained by George's behaviour.

This patterning and organization are equivalent to a setting of a boundary or limit regarding the deviations from its normal and expected pattern of organization that a family can allow. In systems theory this feature is described in terms of the concept of homeostasis.

An illustration of this basic model to a family system is shown in Figure 3. The model proposes that the family members act together in a concerted way so that over a period of time they display regularity. Over time a system functions so as to maintain a dynamic equilibrium; deviations from equilibrium are continually corrected. This whole process is called *homeostasis* and is analogous to the maintenance of room temperature at a constant level in a central heating or biological system. When we observe families in therapeutic or natural situations such as watching television together, out for a walk, playing on the beach and so on, we can easily

Figure 3   A systems theory model of tension in a family relating to a psychotic
cycle

LINEAR   CIRCULAR

                                                      angry

MARY *makes* JOHN *angry*   JOHN   MARY
- - - - - →

                                               accuses/placates

                                                      clings

GEORGE'S insecurity *makes* him cling to DORIS
- - - - - →   GEORGE   DORIS

                                          acts independent/detached

Increase or decrease
in tension

Bizarre
behaviour by
son
in family or   Level of
arguments between   tension
parents   *too high*
                                                     or *too low*

                            Perception of
                            tension by family

Figure 4 Circularity encapsulating a 'peripheral' father role

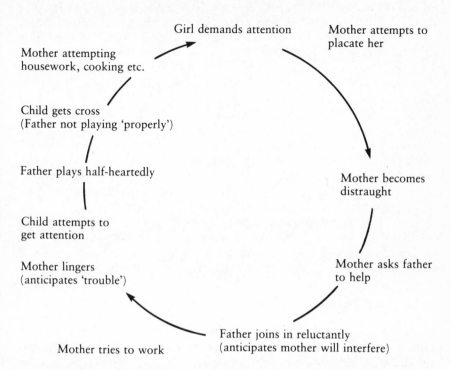

Girl demands attention

Mother attempts to placate her

Mother attempting housework, cooking etc.

Child gets cross (Father not playing 'properly')

Father plays half-heartedly

Mother becomes distraught

Child attempts to get attention

Mother lingers (anticipates 'trouble')

Mother asks father to help

Mother tries to work

Father joins in reluctantly (anticipates mother will interfere)

extract patterns of regularity in their behaviour. These repeated patterns are referred to as *circularities*. As an example a family might show the following pattern. The mother attempts to start cooking the dinner; the four-year old daughter starts to disrupt mother's cooking by making demands and attempting to join in the cooking; mother perseveres and tries to accommodate the child by giving her some simple tasks, but eventually becomes exasperated and asks father angrily to do something with her. Father reluctantly responds and takes the girl in the workshop with him where he is fixing something. Several minutes later the mother comes along to 'check' that everything is all right. She sees that the girl has not joined in with father's activities, gives her a hug and says, 'it's all right', she will manage her. Father, who was on the point of finding a little job for the girl, pretends not to be interested, and mother and the girl go off together. The behaviour of the family can be seen to be repetitive, and we can predict how they might interact in a variety of different situations such as bedtime, bathing, going to the park and so on.

The presence of these regularities in behaviour makes it look, to an outsider, *as if* the family are following a set of *rules* which seem to be necessary to maintain the family in the form of equilibrium (Jackson 1965). As observers we can see regularities in the actions of members of a family, and we can go on to *infer* a set of rules that might give rise to such regularities. These, are, however, only inferences in the minds of us as observers, and family members may not have any conscious awareness of such rules. There is an important distinction to be drawn here between *explicit* and *implicit rules*. An explicit rule can be a *family ruling* – such as a rule that children have to be in before eleven o'clock. Alternatively, there are implicit rules which we can attribute to the family but which are usually below the level of their conscious awareness. Such implicit rules may be so deeply buried in the history of the family and the members' individual unconsciousness that the rules cannot be described or discussed by the members even if the therapist tries to point out the regularities in behaviour. However, it is also the case that families do have some awareness of regularities in their behaviour. This may be a vague sense of 'here we go again' or a more clearly articulated sense of patterns: if the children continue to stay up and play games, they will get over-excited, start to fight, break something and mother will have to clear up.

The ability to detect and regulate or change patterns is related to the emotional aspects of family life. Family rows in particular display the feature of being highly stereotyped, but the participants' abilities to detect this is clouded by the emotions of anger, fear or sadness.

Content and process

Systems theory draws an important distinction between the *process* and *content* of family interactions. As an example we could observe a father and his four-year old son doing a painting together. We could focus on the content in terms of what they are painting; they might draw a house with a funny roof, a dark cloud over the house, mother going out in the car and the use of dark colours. Our analysis of the content could be that the picture represents troubled times for the family, the weak roof indicates an insecurity about coping with outside threats, mother going out a threat that she is dissatisfied and wants to leave, and so on.

At the same time we can look at the process and notice that the boy is lively, does most of the talking and makes the suggestions, that they touch each other very rarely, that father looks away distractedly and that they laugh infrequently. This gives a different kind of analysis which shows how the actions of the two are interrelated and form a pattern. The two types of analysis can complement each other but they are not identical. We cannot simply predict from the one what the other will show. The analysis of the content above might suggest that father and son would be close, as opposed to the process which suggests that they are not. We need considerably more information about the context and the family situation to be able to integrate the two types of analysis.

This distinction is important to bear in mind in therapeutic situations. A family may offer an area of content as the problem, and this is typically a particular symptom such as refusing to eat, school phobia or sexual problems – sexuality. This is the area or topic of discourse that the family is focusing on. However, it may be that the pattern or process of interaction in the family is similar even when they go on to discuss other areas. In a family with a girl displaying anorexic symptoms, there may be a pattern of disagreement between the parents about how to get her to eat. This same pattern of disagreement may also be revealed when they attempt to discuss her friendships and boyfriends, education, future and so on. Often whatever the topic, the disagreement may be terminated temporarily by a return to the 'favourite' topic of the symptoms, as if the only reason a decision cannot be reached is because of the symptoms.

Minuchin (1974) has provided some experimental evidence on the extent to which the physiological reactions of people in families are interdependent and related to structural disturbances. He developed a theory of psychosomatic illnesses – such as asthma, diabetes, anorexia nervosa – which suggested that these conditions could be aggravated by the emotional climate in the family. He demonstrated, for example, that blood sugar levels in children suffering with diabetes were directly related to the emotional conflict that was experimentally activated between the parents.

Ecosystemic models

Systems theory models tend to emphasize stability and resistance to change. This poses something of a paradox since it is clear that families need to be able to adapt and develop in order to cope with changing demands placed upon them both externally and internally, as we have seen in the concept of the family life cycle in the last chapter. Another way of seeing families, therefore, is as ecosystems. Ecosystems are continually changing and evolving but at the same time maintaining a *coherence* so that the changes in various parts 'fit' into an overall organization. Within such a perspective, a family coming for therapy is seen as an organized whole whose particular coherence includes a symptom – for example, anorexia in a daughter. The symptom is somehow necessary for the coherence of the family so that despite various demands from the environment for change in the family the symptom has persisted. However, in order to maintain the symptom the family may have had to contort itself in other areas in order to meet these environmental demands. However, in order to resist these changes in some area, it may have had to change considerably in others. The family with an anorexic girl may have resisted pressures to allow her to leave home, but they may have had to alter their lives in various ways such as frequent visits to hospital, staying up late with her, visiting therapists and doctors, or even some members abandoning jobs and careers. Such a system can be seen to display regularities when we focus on a particular part (for example, the symptoms), which may be described metaphorically as maintaining homeostasis. But when we look at the overall system, it is possible to see *any* pattern as fitting into a wider framework of change. Dell (1982) makes the point that when we focus on the constancy of one part of the total system, we run the risk of ignoring change in the rest of the system:

For example, an alcoholic or a heroin addict introduces certain constancies into his or her physiology by keeping constant the level of drug in his or her system. As a result the rest of the addict's physiology adjusts to come in line with the constancy. The longer the constancy is maintained, the more the rest of the system shifts.

The move towards regarding families as ecosystems has implications for the relationship with the therapist and the supervision team. Instead of simply focusing on the family, there is a recognition that the family and the therapist also form a larger system. It is therefore necessary to include an assessment of the connections between these two systems. Furthermore, the focus moves away from one of the therapists doing things to the family or 'giving' them interventions to one of promoting movements or perturbations in the family-therapist system and watching for the effects. Put simply, the emphasis of therapy becomes less directive and more mutually exploratory. This is similar to a piece of ethnographic research where the researcher is sensitive to the ways in which her presence inevitably influences what she observes.

Patternings of beliefs

When we talk to people about their families or when we first talk to a family in a therapy situation, it is easy to feel overwhelmed by the amount they have to say. Gradually we can start to detect patterns in the stories that are offered so that we might, for example, notice that the father generally tends to talk in a pessimistic tone whatever aspect of their life he is covering. We also might find that some of the same words and phrases are used repeatedly. For example, the mother may repeatedly refer to people being worried, frightened and upset. A useful exercise is initially to listen simply for the words and phrases that are used to describe events in the family. These can reveal patterns in how the explanations and understandings in a family unfold. The case of Louise, a young mother who was referred to the psychology department complaining of depressive symptoms, serves as an example.

During the course of the first interview it was observed that whenever Louise engaged in a bout of pessimistic talk, this was followed by attempts by her husband, and occasionally the therapist, to offer reassurances such as telling her she would get over it, that things were not so bad, to look at all the things she could do and what a lovely child she had. Following these reassurances she appeared to become more, rather than less, depressed and offered even more reasons why she was a hopeless case. Several repetitions of this were enough to demonstrate the futility of this approach, and a more realistic tactic of accepting some of her self-attributed shortcomings produced a more positive change in her behaviour and demeanour. At this point a second process started to emerge. Upon detecting signs of improvement, her husband started to make demands and recounted incidents which served to remind her of just how difficult she was to live with. This seemed to have the effect of deflating her and ensuring that she returned to displaying her expected depression.

The use of concept of circularity here provides a powerful way of describing the mechanisms whereby problems may be unwittingly maintained despite the obvious distress that all the members of the family may be experiencing. However, the description of the circularity tends to be limited to the analysis of behaviour, and we now need to consider the following propositions that will form the basis of the rest of the chapter:

1 The understandings in families are patterned and shared in an analogous way to their patterns of behaviour.
2 The understandings can be seen to consist of a limited number of shared constructs or dimensions of understanding.
3 The members of a family may use a variety of terms, and these carry subjective meanings for them, sometimes not immediately accessible to outside observers.
4 They may employ a variety of different terms which effectively cover the same range of events. In other words the basis of their understandings or belief system may 'boil down' to a few major or 'core' constructs or dimensions.

Sluzki (1983) has suggested the analogy of a film to relate the patterns, dynamics and beliefs of family life. The still gives a picture of the *structure* at the moment and the moving picture a sense of the dynamics or *process*. He adds that the structure of a family, its boundaries, hierarchies and subsystems, are dialectically related to the processes or dynamics of the family. At any moment of time we must necessarily define the processes as reflecting a particular structure. The family's beliefs system operates at a higher level in that it serves to regulate the processes and the structures:

> In the case of the family, interactions are always framed by a rich, rather stable symbolic context, specific to the human condition, that reminds the participants how reality should be constructed and creates, anchors, and reminds of, family rules. In fact, each member of a family, is defined as such as a member of a particular family, because he or she shares with the rest a rather specific way of organising reality, an ideology. The family member's sense of belonging to a collective derives from the experience of consonance emanating from shared reality-organising constructs.
>
> (Sluzki 1983: 472)

This view does not simply imply that families are in continual agreement, far from it as we all know. It does imply, though, that they do share some beliefs, often implicitly, about what is worth agreeing or disagreeing about. To take an example, a family may hold a set of beliefs that it is important and valuable to be fully educated, widely read and interested in academic and cultural matters. Coupled with this they may regard people who avoid education as ignorant or to be pitied because of their lack of intelligence.

Now it is unlikely that every person in the family will whole-heartedly endorse such a set of beliefs. However, it is likely that education will be a highly salient issue for all of the members. In fact the topic of education may act as a sort of a cue or trigger which activates a range of family processes. An adolescent in this family, for example, may know that he can exert considerable power and disruption by threatening to drop out of school and take a menial job. It can represent the area in which various struggles are conducted. Likewise for an anorexic girl, the key topic which carries the underlying family conflicts may be food and health. The beliefs do not simply determine the family processes or dynamics, but are in turn maintained by the behaviour that follows from them.

Communication and punctuation

Cybernetic models of families are based on the idea that members are continuously engaged in communication. The concept of a system is based on the idea of balance or patterns being achieved through information in terms of error-correcting feedback. A broad view of communication is adopted as shown in the following definition:

> First of all there is a property of behaviour that could hardly be more basic and is, therefore, often overlooked: behaviour has no opposite. In other words, there is no such thing as nonbehaviour or, to put it even more simply: one cannot *not* behave. Now, if it is accepted that all behaviour in an interactional situation has message value, i.e. is communication, it follows that no matter how one may try, one cannot *not* communicate. Activity or inactivity, words or silence all have message value: they influence others and these others, in turn, cannot *not* respond to these communications and are thus themselves communicating. It should be clearly understood that the mere absence of talking or of taking notice of each other is no exception to what has just been asserted. The man in a crowded lunch counter who looks straight ahead, or the airplane passenger who sits with his eyes closed, are both communicating that they do not want to communicate to anybody or to be spoken to, and their neighbours usually 'get this message' and respond appropriately by leaving them alone. This, obviously, is just as much an interchange of communication as an animated discussion.
>
> (Watzlawick *et al.* 1967)

Any behaviour in the presence of others can be seen to be potentially a communication. And for communication to occur there must be both a sender and a receiver. Just how an action is interpreted depends not only on the disposition of the sender or the receiver but on the interchange between them. The meaning of the communication is seen as arising from a process of negotiation involving a further exchange or meta-communication (see also Harre 1979, Pearce and Cronen 1980). This idea of a negotiation of meaning will be discussed later in this chapter.

Watzlawick and his colleagues see communication as a never-ending/never-beginning flow. They argue that it is always possible when we search for a starting point to point to some previous antecedents which served as a potential communication. Also, they take a broad view of communication, regarding it as multifaceted including non-verbal as well as verbal actions. This in itself is a well-established distinction which social psychologists have empasized. Argyle (1969), for example, stresses the importance of non-verbal communication in the moment-to-moment management of social interactions. Much of this work has taken ethological studies as its basis. Social interaction in a variety of species is clearly regulated by various forms of behavioural signalling as well as sounds. In particular, studies of animal communication show that one of its essential functions is to establish the nature of the relationship between participants or members of a community. Especially important in this is the establishment of the dominance hierarchy or pecking order.

Non-verbal communication conveys information about feelings and emotions, and the report part of a message can be relatively ambiguous without this information to clarify the intention. As an example, the message 'I don't like you' can be said with a very seductive, cheeky kind of manner that conveys just the opposite. Alternatively, it can be said in a belligerent way implying I am going to punch you on the nose. The n.v.c. or command predominantly conveys either a negative or a positive emotional tone and information about the intensity of feelings. A mother might say to her son, 'you don't seem very enthusiastic' or 'you seem a bit fed up' or 'my God what's the matter', depending largely on the non-verbal way that he has communicated something to her. Usually when people sense that others are distraught they may avoid verbalization for a while and simply offer sympathy on a non-verbal level.

Punctuation

Communication and beliefs are interdependent particularly in the sense that what we experience the other person to be communicating is partly determined by what we 'expect' to hear. Furthermore these expectations or self-fulfilling prophecies can become mutually interlocking as has been elegantly articulated by Paul Watzlawick and his colleagues (1967). They suggested that cycles of interaction in relationships could be understood in terms of the punctuations that people made of the circularities. As in the examples above, once a pattern is established it is virtually meaningless to attempt to define who started it. Nevertheless this is precisely what people do. For example, in a busy bar we need to divide up the buzz of interactions taking place into sequences such as catching the barman's eye or an apology for a push. Problems can arise when people react without awareness of the previous antecedents, for example someone else pushed the man who pushed the man leading to the spilt drink. Punctuation involves not only dividing up a cycle in a particular way, but also inferring causes and reasons about why people are acting. In some situations the mutual punctuations may be in agreement; for example a couple may be in agreement that they are making love. There may still be some differences in how each interprets the other's motives.

There may also be cases where people are interacting on the basis of profoundly incorrect assumptions about each other's punctuations. An illustration is given by Watzlawick where two psychiatrists unknown to the other were asked to assess a middle-aged man suspected of suffering from a delusional psychosis. The main feature of this was that he thought that he was a famous psychiatrist. Suitably briefed the two psychiatrists were put in the room and proceeded to interview each other. It took some time before one of them started to become suspicious, not because of the other's behaviour, but because he remembered having heard of a 'real' Doctor Don Jackson and started to 'smell a fish', so to speak.

In established relationships, however, such sequences become more complex and less trivial. Each partner segments the circularity into a linear and potentially self-fulfilling sequence. This can be illustrated by the following classic example:

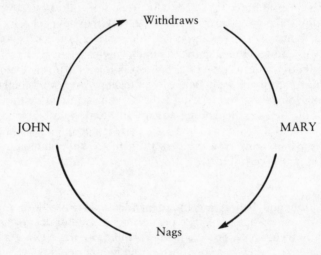

This cycle is mutually maintained in that Mary may perceive John's behaviour at a moment in time, perhaps reading the paper, watching television, leaving the room, as indicating that he is *withdrawing*, ignoring her and so on. This perception subsequently leads her to make some indirect attempts to contact him such as asking him to do some jobs around the house or where he is going. More than likely these will be made in a slightly tense tone since what will follow is already anticipated. John may then construe Mary's actions as indicating that she is *nagging* or trying to get at him. Since he doesn't like this and thinks she shouldn't go on at him, he withdraws further. Mary might then become angry and really nag him and he may obstinately withdraw further. By now each partner may think that their perceptions have been *confirmed*. Yes, Mary feels she was right, he was withdrawing. Likewise John thinks he was right, she was trying to nag him – again. Bateson explains the tendency to engage in punctuations which focus on individual responsibility as follows:

> In the punctuation of human interaction, adjectives which purport to describe individual character are really not strictly applicable to the individual but rather to describe transactions between the individual and his material and human environment. No man is 'resourceful' or 'dependent' or 'fatalistic' in a vacuum. His charater, whatever it be, is not his but is rather a characteristic of what goes on between him and something (or somebody) else.
>
> (Bateson, 1972)

The cycle can in this way become self-validating. It can be extremely hard for either partner to see what contribution they are making to the cycle. Also, a fact that many individualistic or insight-orientated therapies don't take into account is that unilateral insight might not help. In the above example, if Mary goes for therapy and comes to be aware of this sequence between them, her attempts at explaining it to John may be seen as further nagging! Likewise an insight from John about this might be regarded by Mary as further evidence of his 'smart ass, detached, uninvolved, over-rational' withdrawing! As we saw earlier, it was precisely this kind of observation of the negative effects of some attempts at unilateral change or individual therapy that led Jackson to develop the systems theory model. Similar complaints are often made by people who attend various forms of workshops and growth groups. Their partners are often 'difficult' or 'resentful' rather than receptive to the recounting of the stimulating experiences that they have had. There are, of course, complex reasons for this phenomenon, but partly it is to do with the fact that the partner's behaviour is likely to be interpreted within the previous framework established by the couple.

Such sequences are by no means restricted to marital relationships. For example, a similar situation can be seen in parent–child relationships.

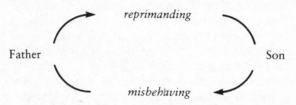

In this cycle the father may punctuate the cycle as his having to reprimand the boy continually for his frequent misdemeanours. However, the son may punctuate it as his misbehaving in order to get back at his father for continually reprimanding him. Watzlawick goes on to suggest that such 'struggles' over the definition of the relationship and each other's actions are at the base of marital and other problems. The idea of unilateral control is pervasive. Bateson (1972) and Palazzoli *et al.* (1978) suggest that this tendency is deeply embedded, is cultural, is inherent in our language and thereby constrains us to think in terms of 'linear' punctuations:

> The dichotomization which we are forced to use by the very nature of language, requiring a 'before' and 'after', a subject and object (in the sense of he who performs the action and he who receives the action), implies a postulate of cause and effect, and in consequence a moral definition.
>
> (Palazzoli *et al.* (1976: 53)

One feature of Palazzoli's therapy and other systems theory therapies is to teach families, usually indirectly, to regard their interactions in terms of circular rather than linear causal sequences. We will return to these therapeutic implications later.

Recent evidence from social psychological research has emerged which offers some elaborations of these ideas; it has been suggested that people typically make attributions about their own and other people's behaviour in terms of 'dispositional' or 'situational' factors (Kelley 1967, Nisbett *et al.* 1973) For example, the couple above may be making dispositional attributions in that they see each other as that kind of person – withdrawing or nagging. The alternative is to employ 'situational' explanations, such as that the other is tired, has has a hard day and so on. A further finding is that different types of information are available regarding our own and the other person's actions. For example, when couples were able to see a video replay of their interaction from the other's visual viewpoint, this led to more attributions being made of the relationship being directed by their own contributions and not simply as responding to the other (Storms 1973).

Though interesting, these approaches have tended to take a static rather than dynamic view of relationships, and have only recently started to examine how such attributions operate in a continually shifting, negotiational way between participants. Also, most of the research comes from laboratory based studies of short-term relationships, and we need to remember that families have shared histories of interaction and do know quite a lot about each other. More than this they have constructed the explanations that each person holds about themselves. Children, for example, are frequently told what kind of children they are: 'good – bad', 'noisy – quiet,' 'clever – slow'. Some work has investigated how attributions operate in long-term relationships. Generally findings indicate that attributions can be employed *strategically*. For example, a husband may use situational factors to explain why he does not want to do the garden – having a hard time at work – and at another time he may use dispositional ones such as its not the kind of activity he likes, if his wife has already exposed his situational 'excuses' (Scanzoni and Palonka 1980). Perhaps the most important finding, not unexpectedly, is that disturbed relationships are associated with negative dispositional attributions, such as 'he is intolerant and aggressive just like his father' or 'she is cold and prudish just like her mother'.

Meta-perspectives and imputations

R.D. Laing *et al.* (1966) have proposed that it is important to assess not only how people punctuate a cycle of interaction and what attributions they make, but how they think the other(s) do this. In part this involves a spiral of perceptions about each other:

How I see you
How I think you see me
How I think, you think, I see you

Laing terms these recursive, spiralling perspectives *meta-perspectives* Through an analysis of them he traces various forms of impossible relationship struggles or knots:

Daughter: Well, why did I attack you? Perhaps I was looking for something, I lacked affection, maybe it was greed for affection.
Mother: You wouldn't have any of that. You always think it's soppy.
Daughter: Well, when did you offer it to me?
Mother: Well, for instance if I was to want to kiss you, you'd say 'Don't be soppy.'
Daughter: But I've never known you to let me kiss you.

The causal attributions operate at a hierarchy of levels: The daughter makes attributions about her own behaviour as a response to situational factors – lack of affection. Mother responds by making an attribution about the reasons for her daughter's actions in dispositional terms – she doesn't like soppiness. She goes on to suggest that if she was to offer affection her daughter wouldn't correctly recognize her intentions as offering affection but would instead see it as soppiness. Finally, the girl responds by challenging her mother's explanations by saying that not only does she not offer affection but she does not 'let' the daughter kiss her.

Laing develops his analysis further by offering some ideas about how understandings and beliefs develop in families. He identified a process of induction whereby, for example, children in the family may be implicitly and subtly 'instructed' into certain beliefs about the world and about themselves:

Mother: (To five year old) Are you going to get up and dance?
Daughter: No I don't want to.
Mother: (Looking to grandmother and smiling) She's shy. There's no need to be shy. Granny wants to see you dance. Come on.

Daughter: I can't do it properly.
Mother: Come on. Don't be frightened.

Young children and people displaying problems are frequently involved in such interactions whereby the events are punctuated 'for them' by another, and attributions about why they are acting are sometimes subtly, sometimes not so subtly, inducted into them. Frequent repetitions of such attributions are likely, especially with young children, to be accepted and to become part of their self-concept.

An important aspect of this is the extent to which our expectations lead to *self-fulfilling* effects (Rosenthal and Jacobson 1968, Watzlawick 1984). Frequently we may hold implicit expectations or make interpretations during an interaction which are only partly conscious but which predispose us to act in certain ways. These reactions can have a powerful effect on how the interaction proceeds, since we may alter our behaviour in subtle ways and thereby help to produce our expectations.

Negotiation, episodes and rules

Both the patterning of family actions and the perceptions of the actions can be seen to be regulated by sets of *rules*. It is also possible to think of families as engaged in broader sweeps of actions. Harre and Secord (1972) suggest that people structure their interactions in terms of *episodes*, which they define as any part of human life, involving one or more people, in which some internal structure can be determined. The emphasis is on subjectivity in that the actions determine what constitutes an episode and what it is. Pieces of interaction come to be defined in certain ways, such as 'having tea', 'doing business' or 'attempting a seduction'. It is up to the participants to negotiate a definition of the episode. Again, it is important to point out that this is not necessarily a conscious process. In retrospect the participants may reflect about what went on and even consider alternative ways that they could have acted. The feeling after the event of 'if only I'd said . . . or done . . .' is probably familiar to most of us. It is even possible that some of the most memorable speeches attributed to the great figures of history are actually what they wished they had said later, rather than what they did actually say at the time.

Pearce and Cronen (1980) have extended the analysis of episodes by identifying three main types:

● *Episodes 1* – consist of patterns of meanings and behaviours which are culturally sanctioned and which exist independently of any particular individual or group. These are public symbols necessary for meanings to be shared and seem identical to the concept of 'significant symbols' which have traditionally been studied by anthropologists and sociologists. They include social rituals, ceremonies, rites of passage or ritualized ways of dealings with social situations such as greetings, deference, and humour and sarcasm. These in a sense represent the fabric of any culture. They are employed in numerous ways, not least as reference points for comedy and drama which often revolve around confusions, disruptions and fragmentations of such episodes. They even form the basis of dreams and nightmares, for example the groom who is late for the wedding or the actor who forgets his lines.

● *Episodes 2* – consist of patterns of meanings and behaviours in the minds of individuals and are similar to the discussion of images and plans (Miller *et al.* 1960) or definitions of situations. These are private symbols which express individuals' understandings of the forms of social interaction in which they participate. To the extent that a person's episodes 2 resemble society's episodes 1, the person will be able to converse easily, understand others and be understood. If the episodes 2 are very idiosyncratic, the person will have problems coordinating his actions with others.

It is important to note that there are many cases of people who have creative and artistically idiosyncratic ways of punctuating events into episodes, but their work may become popular and acclaimed to the extent that their idiosyncrasies become part of the cultural heritage.

● *Episodes 3* – consist of the communicators' interpretations of the actual sequence of messages which they jointly produce. This is the idea of episodes as co-enacted or mutually created (Cicourel 1967, Garfinkel 1967). However, to give meaning to these co-creations we have to refer to both episodes 1 and 2 at the same time.

As an analogy it is possible to see the coordination of joint construction of episodes as similar to the playing of a group of jazz, rock or 'primitive' musicians where there is extensive improvisation. The musicians may have very little in the way of preset ideas about what they are going to play, but they do have some *shared* knowledge of musical conventions, for example a twelve-bar blues sequence, ragtime patterns, various evergreen melodies, well-known riffs or passages and chord sequences. It is possible to generate some very pleasant music by referring to this shared knowledge and the use of some simple strategies. The players can take turns to lead to the others so that one person sets up the initial key and rhythm; they can use call and reply sequences, mimicking or echoing on different sequences and harmonizing. Coordination is achieved when the players successfully contract with each other to enact particular episodes. The players don't have to be in any amicable agreement as long as there is some shared understanding. Eric Clapton, for example, described some of his concerts with the Cream as a 'war on stage' with each of them trying to outplay and test the others with new and more frenzied improvisations.

The early phases of conversations can easily be seen as similar kinds of negotiations in which each person requests the others to enact his preferred episode 2 at that time. These requests may be rejected or accepted, usually with counter-requests. Once a request is accepted, each knows what the others expect and what is expected, assuming that their understanding of the rules of the episode are similar. Of course, this may not always be the case, so that one person may profess to know more about how an episode *is* conducted or how long it should go on for and what it should change into.

A simple example of a negotiation is the following:

Sue: Hey, did you hear what's happening about my application?
Mother: No what did you hear?
Sue: No, I was asking you, I thought you had heard!
Mother: Oh yes, well they said you had been placed on the waiting list.

In the above Sue appeared to want to initiate an episode of question and answer with her mother, who instead interpreted Sue's initial remark as a cue for a sequence of newscasting or listening to Sue's news. A brief sequence of adjustment is carried out to bring the interaction into a shared, agreed episode of question and answer. Part of the process of negotiation here involves what has earlier been referred to as meta-communication: communication about communication. There is a simple example of this when Sue says, 'No, I was asking you'. She is making a statement about the meaning of her previous communication. In relationships such as families, people may spend considerable time talking about what they 'really' meant to say. However, in some families there appear to be powerful rules proscribing such communication. Pearce and Cronen (1980) indicate that people interact on the basis of predictions about whether they are in agreement or not about the nature of the episodes that they are in. An example in a family might be that the parents regard the conversation they are having with their adolescent son as an episode of providing helpful advice about his future. The son, on the other hand, might regard it as an episode of 'being hauled over the coals', again, by his parents. They propose that there are a number of possible states of agreement and disagreement.

1 Predicted agreement is confirmed.
2 Predicted agreement is discomfirmed.
3 Predicted disagreement is confirmed.
4 Predicted disagreement is disconfirmed.

These predictions are based on the immediate social context, cultural rules and, most importantly, the participants' shared previous experience. They go on to distinguish three major types of strategies that are employed to manage these interactions:

● *Casting* – one person trying to manipulate the other into his preferred episode 2, for example to act as a submissive admirer. This is similar to McCall and Simmons' (1966) model of alter-casting and to Bateson's concept of complementary relationships that will be discussed in Chapter 5. The person is in the position of leading and initiating the action.

● *Mirroring* – attempting to discover what the other wants and then trying to fit into this. This resembles Bateson's concept of complementarity with the person adopting a submissive and following position.

● *Negotiation* – some negotiation is involved in the above strategies, but here there is a more equitable form of negotiation in that the interaction proceeds on the basis of such strategies as inviting the other to take part in an episode, bargaining, creating shared experiences or by open meta-communication about what episodes might be enacted.

Enigmatic episodes

Some interactions have an enigmatic quality where people are not sure what is going on. There are two main possibilities here. First, situations where a particular piece of behaviour can be interpreted equally well in two or more ways. An example of this was a couple where the husband had occasionally been violent towards his wife. The couple frequently found that there were 'tense' silences between them. The wife interpreted this silence as a sign that her husband was about to burst out into violence – an enactment of an episode of wife abuse. On the other hand, the husband interpreted the silence as a sign of contempt from his wife – that she did not think he was worth talking to. Second, a particular explanation may fit two or more different sequences of behaviour. Often the people occupying the 'sick' slot in a family are faced with this. Gazing intently into the mirror, laughing, touching every third railing and rambling talk when 'alone' (out of sight but within earshot) might all be construed as demonstrations of mental illness or as ordinary silliness depending upon what we expect. In themselves they don't contain enough information to be explained definitively.

These accounts start to provide a basis for an analysis of how people construct their social realities in families. Though helpful, there is a danger that a focus on taxonomies of negotiations obscures the unique and complex ways that interactions in families are managed. A number of issues arise in connection with this and the previous discussions:

1 Frequently couples and families seem to be unable to resolve the differences about how parts of their lives should be defined.
2 The actions of people in families have a quality of being mutually maintaining, as we have seen in the discussion of circularities. These circularities seem in some cases to serve to fuel and entrench the disagreements between them.
3 Most of the work on analysis of episodes seems to have concentrated on couples or dyads, and this ignores the possibility that the constructions of each participant are embedded and maintained by other systems. An example might be a son who, when he visits his mother, frequently hears negative evaluations of his wife, such as that she is making a 'fool' of him and not 'looking after him'. He may attempt to defend her to his mother and offer different interpretations, but on returning home finds that he is seeing episodes through his mother's eyes and distrusting his wife's

actions to the point of seeing their interactions as episodes of her getting the better of him, making a fool of him or exploiting him.

So far, then, we see that systems theory offers a view of families as engaged in the negotiation of rules which govern their interactions. It is also proposed that these rules are negotiated through the process of continuous and inevitable communication between the members of a family. The endless flow of communication is divided up into meaningful segments or punctuations. These punctuations in essence represent the members' beliefs about what they think is going on and why. The work on episodes and meta-communication assists this model by suggesting that people in families are intimately connected in the wider cultural reality and have a knowledge of a culturally defined episodes which operate as a grammar of interactional rules.

Patternings of emotions

Systems theory-based models offer a picture of families as engaged in the construction of patterns of behaviour and beliefs. Essentially this implies that they are engaged in jointly building a shared reality. The question arises about the circumstances whereby families build constructions which appear to differ significantly from consensual versions of reality. Another way of saying this is that they can be employed in the construction of *unreality*. This can take various forms such as denying what is to others patently true, projecting inaccurate feelings on to others or constructing myths. These processes can be seen to be related to the emotional life of families. Psychodynamic theories offer a useful starting point for an analysis of such contortion of beliefs. Central to Freud's psychodynamic model is the idea that cognitions and the rational processes are directed by emotional forces: 'ego in the service of the id'. Freud proposed that a variety of defence mechanisms operate such as denial, projection, repression and projection, whereby unpleasant emotions attached to certain memories and thoughts are blocked from consciousness. In other words, if reality is unacceptable then we can attempt to distort it into something which is less unacceptable or push it out of our mind. The main implications are that a consideration of family beliefs requires some consideration of how the beliefs are related to the family's emotional life.

For Freud the basic model of family life revolved around the concept of the Oedipal triangle. A central task for the family was to tame or socialize the child's lust for its mother. This tension continually threatens to destroy family life. At the same time Freud saw the family as the buttress against 'barbarism' in its taming of the incestual lust and the conflict between father and son through the process of repression. The primary mechanism for the taming of the conflict he saw to be the process of identification: the son modifies his hostility towards, and jealously of, his father by identifying with him – becoming 'like him'. This process conveniently facilitates the process of socialization in that the boy introjects his father's morality through the process of attempting to resolve the 'guilt' engendered in him by his feelings of hostility towards his father. Also, by becoming more like father, he might hope to become more attractive to mother and subsequently other women who perhaps resemble his mother. The theory has some weaknesses in explaining the processes of psycho-sexual development for girls (Mitchell 1971) and makes little mention of the role of the rest of the family, siblings, grandparents, etc., who often play an important role.

Freud's account offered a way of connecting the emotional and cognitive aspects of individual and family experiences. A number of his followers developed the analysis of cognitive processes – 'ego psychology'. Important contributors here were Melanie Klein (1945) and Fairbairn (1952). They suggested that initially infants develop through a process of dichotomous differentiations of their world. These are largely emotional reactions in terms of 'good' and 'bad'. Initially the focus for the child is the mother's breasts, which are experienced as good or bad depending on whether the child's experience was one of satisfaction or frustration. The young child is not able to differentiate itself from its mother so the total experience of mother–child is internalized as a 'good' or 'bad' object. Subsequently this total experience is 'projected' on to the mother as the person who 'caused' the feelings without any awareness that the feelings came partly from oneself.

In later life and especially in family relations this process of projecting the internally absorbed and unresolved feelings about the parent can produce powerful transference effects. For example, the feelings may be projected on to a wife so that she is continually seen as being just like his mother. This is despite the fact that the man initially selected his wife because, consciously or unconsciously, he experienced her as like his mother. Consequently it may be difficult for the relationship to develop since this transference prevents information about his wife's differences to his mother from being recognized. These ideas have been employed by Winch (1958) to suggest that there is a complementary process in partner selection whereby couples unconsciously select each other because they match each other's intro-jections of their parents.

A number of other theorists have also been concerned with inter-generational traditions of resolving emotional conflicts. Boszromenyi-Nagy (1973) suggested that families could be seen as operating in terms of 'invisible loyalties' transmitted through the generations. Families were seen as keeping a kind of unconscious ledger, a sort of emotional accounts book, of who owes what to whom in terms of loyalties and affections. No matter when an injustice occurred, there would be a retributive move at some later point, although not necessarily involving the original debtor. As an example, a mother who was angry at being rejected might try to compensate by giving total devotion to her own children. The daughter in turn would be expected, in the language of a balance of payments, to re-establish family justice by giving the mother all that her mother did not give her. Unexpected negative feelings on the daughter's part could be explained by an excessive contribution to this unconscious accounting that is expected of her.

Likewise Bowen (1960) suggested that the basis for many forms of symptoms was the inability of a person to separate from his family and fully to become an individual. This can be compounded through the generations so that children are there to meet a parent's emotional needs, and subsequently a child exhibits a psychosis which is related to such an overinvolvement with a parent, usually the mother. The main direction for therapy suggested by this model is to help untangle and disengage the person from this overinvolvement, primarily by helping them to see that they are in an enmeshed situation and 'working through' the emotions invested in it. Training in Bowenian family therapy requires therapists to work through any tensions with their own family in order for them to become fully and clearly disengaged from their own parents, thus avoiding the risk of placing their unintended counter-projections on to clients. This resembles Freud's insistence on the importance of self-analysis as part of training as a psychotherapist.

Some of these concepts unfortunately involve an unnecessary tendency to pathologize processes such as mate selection. However, one of the important contributions of psychodynamic theories is to emphasize the importance of the role of emotions and cognitions. One area where this is particularly important is in the analysis of mismatches between the family's version of events and external versions of reality.

Constructing systems of unreality

An important integration of systems and psychodynamic explanations was developed by Ferreira (1963), who suggested that unconscious fantasies and conflicts operated not only at the level of the individual but also as a collective unconscious fantasy or 'family myth'. Aspects of a family's past, especially traumatic or distressing events experienced by the parents, grandparents or even more distant relatives, can become shrouded in defensive myths which serve to cover up memories too painful for them to accept. This can involve not only denial but the fabrication of stories or myths, a sort of Orwellian rewriting of history. Such myths, however, can become debilitating when they serve continually to falsify and mystify experience in the family, leading to spirals of denial and fabrication.

> The term 'family myth' refers to a series of fairly well-integrated beliefs shared by all the family members, concerning each other and their mutual positions in the family life, beliefs that go unchallenged by everyone involved in spite of the reality distortions which they may conspicuously imply. . . . The family myth describes the roles and attributions of family members in their transactions with each other

which, although false and mirage-like, are accepted by everyone as something sacred and taboo that no one would dare to investigate, much less challenge.

(Ferreira 1963: 457)

The function of family myths is to preserve the family homeostasis, to avoid the possibilities of disruption or disintegration of the family or of relationships within it. It represents a response to real or perceived threats to the viability of the family. It can be seen to represent to the family what a defence mechanism is to the individual.

Seemingly, the family myth is called into play whenever certain tensions reach predetermined thresholds among the family members and in some way, real or fantasized, threaten to disrupt ongoing relationships. Then, the family myth functions like the thermostat that is kicked into action by the 'temperature' in the family. Like other homeostatic mechanisms, the myth prevents the family system from damaging, perhaps destroying itself. It has therefore the quality of a 'safety valve', that is, a *survival* valve.

(Ferreira 1963: 462)

An important point about family myths is that there is little awareness of any distortion of reality in the family. This is very like Freud's concept of defence mechanisms such as denial, projection and repression. Considerable emotional energy is invested in keeping up the myth, and attempts to expose it are met with great resistance.

Ferreira's work marks an extremely important bridge between systems theory and psychodynamic accounts of families. It starts to offer a way of looking at processes in families which includes not only an analysis of behaviour but also an integration of beliefs and emotions. The theoretical stand that will be adopted here is that emotions and beliefs are inevitably interlinked. Emotions are connected to cognitions and vice versa. In other words, an emotion is about something, it requires some cognitive discriminations of events. I may feel angry *about* something a colleague said to me, or sad *about* the loss of a friend. The connection between the emotions and cognitions is a dialectical one. Likewise I may perceive a certain physiological state in my body and give a meaning to it. In short, cognitions lead to emotions and emotions lead to cognitions. Which is predominant is not a question we have time to explore here. However, it is worth mentioning a series of studies by Schachter and Singer (1962) which explored the possibility that emotions are socially constructed. In one study subjects were injected with an epinephrine, a drug which causes general arousal. Some subjects were told to expect to be aroused by it and others were not. They were then asked to fill out a questionnaire in the presence of another 'subject', in fact an accomplice of the experimenter, who acted either in a bizarre and euphoric way or angrily. The results indicated that people who did not know what the effects of the drug would be claimed to feel euphoric or angry depending upon which type of accomplice they had been with. Those who knew what effects to expect generally reported less feelings of anger and euphoria.

This provides some important clues to the processes in families where attributions are typically made by other members about each other's feelings. Young children are especially open to the influence of others in interpreting their own emotional states. In fact it is important that parents accurately detect when a child appears to be hungry or wanting affection. Meanings or interpretations of one's own and each other's emotions, like the beliefs regarding other aspects of family life, can be seen to be mutually constructed. This is not to say, of course, that physiological changes in moods are not important, but rather the labels assigned to these changes are constructed within a family, and these meanings, as Ferreira suggest, serve to maintain the stability of the family system.

Myths are seen as social constructions which serve to avoid the family having to confront painful tensions and conflicts which are perceived as potentially threatening the viability of the family. Another way of putting this is that myths may emerge as a tactic to maintain the family homeostasis, or coherence, in the face of requirements for change. It is salutary to note that the idea of a constructed unreality was first presented by two French psychiatrists more than a hundred years ago in the famous paper 'Folie a deux' (Lasegue and Falret 1877). They first describe the so-called patient and then go on as follows:

> The above description belongs to the insane person, the agent who provokes the situation in 'delire a deu'. His associate is a much more complicated person to define and yet careful research will teach one to recognise the laws which are obeyed by the second party in communicated insanity. . . . Once the tacit contract that ties both lunatics is almost settled, the problem is not only to examine the influence of the insane in the supposedly sane man, but also the opposite, the influence of the rational on the deluded one, and to show how through mutual compromises, the differences are eliminated.

As we have seen, Ferreira has extended a similar notion to the processes in families with the concept of the family myth. Underlying the account by Ferreira is the notion that the family is an ecosystem in that it is embedded within and is required to adjust and integrate with other systems. A family myth, such as that 'we are a happy family' or that a step-parent loves his son even more than his own, may be driven by an attempt to conform to socially acceptable values. Of course, not only the family but society can create a model of family life which is based on a shaky foundation of myths in the form of unrealizable expectations. One of the periods when families are confronted with the need for change – and consequently some reappraisal of what they are and should be as a family – is at the time of major transitional stages in the life cycle. A family might perceive, sometimes correctly, that the demands for change are too threatening or contradictory. One solution then, might be to turn away from reality or to attempt to maintain a version of reality which was reasonably appropriate in a previous stage of the family's life-cycle but now serves to deny the reality of the changes and developments which have occurred. Pollner and Wikler (1985) present an example of such a process of denial in family:

> The family . . . was initially encountered at a large psychiatric institute to which they had turned in their search for a remedy for five and a half year-old Mary's unusual behaviour. Family members stated that Mary was a verbal and intelligent child who malingered and refused to speak in public in order to embarrass the family. Extensive clinical examination revealed Mary to be severely retarded and unable to perform at anywhere near the level of confidence claimed by her parents and two older sibs . . . Initial viewings of the videotapes suggested that family members' transactions were permeated by subtle, almost artful, practices that could function to create the image of Mary as an intelligent child.

The authors describe six strategies whereby the family operate in a concerted way to attribute intelligence to Mary's actions. The attributions in effect ascribe 'agency' and purpose to her actions which to outside observers was blatantly missing. From a family life-cycle perspective this can be seen in terms of an inability to come to terms with the fact that Mary would not develop as expected. The recognition that a child is seriously handicapped has been likened to a process of bereavement for a family (Black 1987). There is a need to face up to the pain that the child will not develop as expected and that this will involve some possible difficulties for the family. Most importantly it destroys the belief that they are a 'normal, happy, trouble-free family. The authors note and describe a number of strategies employed to distort the reality of their situation:

● *Framing* – this involved the construction of a frame such as a game of 'catch' wherein virtually any activity that Mary displayed could be attributed with intelligent meaning. If she stood passively and let the ball drop out of her hands, it could be framed as deliberately dropping the ball or not wanting to play.
● *Postscripting* – was the reverse in the sense of giving meaning to Mary's actions after the event. The family tracked any action that she might perform and weaved a meaningful story on to it as if she was acting in a goal-directed way. For example, at one point Mary's sister dropped a block on the floor while Mary was banging a block on the table. As Mary sat down her sister said, 'O.K. let's find that block.'
● *Semantic crediting* – here a range of reflexive behaviour responses such as a startled reaction to a noise were integrated by the family with simultaneous verbal requests to Mary. Though she was in fact responding to the non-verbal stimuli, the family interpreted her response as showing a comprehension of verbal instructions.

● *Puppeteering* – in some instances rather than wait for Mary to do something as a basis for the implementation of an attributional strategy, the family might subtly manipulate her physically towards an object. This would be accompanied by a verbal instruction and touch or positioning themselves so that she was forced to move in a particular direction. The result could appear and would be credited as Mary making deliberate planned actions.

● *Putting words into Mary's mouth* – this involved the construction of a dialogue or episode wherein each utterance such as a gurgle emitted by Mary was interpreted by one member of the family at a time. As an example, in one sequence she was encouraged to talk by asking her to say her name and age for $5. Her following gurgles were interpretated for her as 'she's bargaining for more money'.

● *Explaining in the bright direction* – despite the previous strategies it was possible that at times Mary's behaviour was obviously inadequate. Such inadequacies were explained away by an overriding incorrigible belief that she was 'intelligent' and so therefore these were lapses explained as being due to her 'not wanting to play', 'teasing,' 'pretending' or 'malingering'.

The practices in the family served to maintain the myth that she was 'intelligent' and that there was nothing wrong with her. The process can be seen as the family's attempt to deal with the process of 'mourning' described by Black (1987) in families when they come to recognize that their child is severely handicapped. The family's behaviour was in some ways appropriate for the treatment of a child below two years of age, which was roughly the level of Mary's actual functioning, so rather than constructing a false belief system *de novo*, they can be seen to be attempting to hold on to a previously appropriate frame that no longer tallied with the external reality.

This analysis goes some way towards offering a picture of the interlinking between the actions, beliefs and emotional aspects of family life. It is possible that when a family is unable to cope with the combination of emotional demands, demands for organizational change and demands for the revision of beliefs inherent with a life-cycle transition, it may try to manage by the construction of various myths such as that one of them is the 'damaged' or 'sick'. This represents a myth such as that 'we are all O.K. except for the fact that one of us is ill, sick, or crazy,' and were it not for the stresses and strains involved with 'looking after' the patient, they could all lead happy and fulfilled lives. Alternatively, as above, they may attempt to deny that one of them is in fact handicapped by constructing a facade of normality.

Chapter 3

Personal construct systems

In this chapter I want to outline the fundamental approaches that will form the basis for the discussion of family belief systems in the following chapters. The major concepts will be drawn from the work of George Kelly. At first sight this may appear somewhat paradoxical since Kelly's approach focuses on the intra-psychic processes of *individuals* rather than groups of people such as families. However, Kelly was insistent that his was predominantly a social theory which was concerned to explain social behaviour. He attempted to explain how our beliefs, understandings, explanations and expectations guide our dealings with the people that we encounter in our social lives.

Some time, therefore, will be taken here to outline Kelly's (1955) theory in detail. This is necessary in order to prepare the ground for the extension of some of his ideas in the following chapters to an analysis of family systems. Kelly's ideas have gained currency with psychologists, especially in Britain, but his theory has had less impact in related areas such as sociology, family theory and family therapy.

To start with, it is important to draw attention to a change in terminology that this chapter signals. From here on, the term *construct* will be employed extensively as an alternative way of talking about beliefs. Kelly gives a technical definition of a 'construct' which specifies most importantly that it is a *bipolar* categorization. By this he means that when I use the word 'bad', by implication I am contrasting it to the concept 'good.' This idea of bipolarity pervades our language in the West and is also embodied in Eastern philosophies, for example in the *yin–yang* symbol. Kelly makes explicit what is often taken implicitly when we talk about a belief in that the belief implies its opposite – what we don't believe in.

Kelly termed his philosophical position 'constructive alternativism'. This view derives from Kant's position that although we can argue that there is a reality out there, we can only know it in terms of our own experience of it. However, the experiences that we have are 'real' and valid objects of study and investigation in themselves. Kelly, of course, is not alone in holding this view. He stated that we see the world 'out there' through our personal beliefs or what he calls personal constructs. Hence, everyone's reality is unique and different from other people's, at least to some extent. However, by this he was not implying a 'relativistic' position that we simply 'invent' reality and that any version is as good as any other. He proposed that there was a 'real' world out there. However, we can only know it through our own senses and our own constructs and preconceptions. At the same time some interpretations are more adequate than others in a variety of ways, such as predicting the future actions of others and understanding how others see things. In other words our beliefs have real *consequences*. If I believe I am at the top of a house, there is a real consequence if I walk out of the window. Furthermore I might believe, perhaps if I have taken a substantial dose of LSD, that I could fly off the ledge. Others might even agree with me so that we have a socially agreed belief which exists and is in itself also real. However, my belief will be disproved when I hit the ground and break my legs or worse. This is central to Kelly's view. How we construe the world around us and even within our own skin, come to that, has consequences in terms of how we act (see Figure 5). Kelly's theory, therefore, stresses that each of us is *active* in our perception of the world (see also Goffman 1971, Berger and Luckman 1973, Harre and Secord 1972, Rogers 1955). He also stresses that our beliefs and our actions are dialectically related or interdependent.

Figure 5   Interdependence of Construing and Action

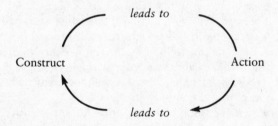

Construct – My wife will be *angry* when I walk in through
the door.

Action – Enter the house and immediately *apologize*
or start to *criticize* the state of the house,
etc.

Whatever the choice of action taken on the basis of the construct starts to construct the interaction that will follow.

A second important focus is that the world, especially our social world, is seen as continually changing. Obviously, physical features of our environment like mountains and buildings may not appear to change that much or very rapidly, though of course our perceptions of them may. But our social world is much more likely to be changing. Likewise our understanding of this world is, at least potentially, able to change. In fact for Kelly our understanding or constructs about our world is synonymous with the concept of *personality*. He did not see people in terms of static, unchanging personality types but as continually adapting and evolving. He offered a tongue in cheek definition of the 'reliability' concept of stating that 'reliability is a measure of a test's insensitivity to measure change in people' (Kelly 1955).

Anticipation and replication

Kelly suggested that all of us are like scientists in the sense that we are concerned with *anticipating* events in the world. We form hypotheses and build theories about the world which are more or less useful to us in predicting what is likely to happen. A good scientist, however, is prepared to discard her theory for a new one in the light of new contradictory evidence. Furthermore he argued, like Kuhn (1970), that science develops not simply by the dogged accumulation of facts and cataloguing of experiments, but by the process of generating new insights and ways of looking at the subject matter. We can act only from a whole or meaningful picture of the world which we attempt to create, as opposed to simply deducing or building up a picture from isolated facts. Once we have created a picture we can then change, improve, extend and elaborate it. The overall picture, though, is what guides our activity; it directs where we try to look for further evidence.

In the case of our social worlds this becomes even more critical. People do not usually change unpredictably from moment to moment, but certainly they do change a bit most of the time and sometimes quite a lot. Even if we propose that people have stable personalities which change very little, we would have to admit that friendships change, people grow older and take up different interests, relationships develop and disintegrate. Each of us in a sense also creates the people that we interact with, especially, as we will consider later, in long-term relationships such as the family, by the way that we act towards them. In families continual changes in people's beliefs about each other are required to keep up with the unfolding of their developmental cycle. Major changes in how people regard each other are required at the point of transitions such as the leaving home stage when a passage from a 'child' to an 'adult' status is acted out.

Kelly's metaphor of 'man the scientist' suggests, therefore, that each of us conducts his or her social life in ways similar to a scientist. We hold a set of beliefs and explanations which we use to help us to 'predict' or 'anticipate' the future actions of acquaintances and new people with whom we will come into contact. Some of these beliefs may be very general or loose. For example, I may hold a belief that 'it is a tough competitive world out there and one had better be prepared to fight if we don't want people to be forever putting one over on us.' Or our constructs may be quite specific, such as Jane is a *homely* kind of person or Peter and Mary have a *possessive* relationship. The important point is that these constructs help us to make decisions about how to act towards others. We can then *test* our constructs by seeing how well or badly they help us to anticipate the situations that we enter into. For example, if Jane is not too impressed with the household orientated presents she was given for her birthday and starts to talk about how she is planning to sell the house and start to travel, we might be tempted to revise our constructs about her. This is obviously appropriate with specific constructs. Some constructs, though, may be couched in vague and general terms and are consequently harder to test and therefore more resistant to change. A construction of the world along the lines of 'it's a jungle out there' does not lend itself to easy falsification, and this may go some way to explaining the persistence of analogous political positions. A similar line of argument can be applied to scientific theories; for example, the premises of psychodynamic theory are notoriously unspecific and difficult to test.

At the same time Kelly emphasizes the need for continuity in his focus on the idea that we anticipate the world in terms of the *replication* of events. Life would become extremely chaotic if we did not have any resistance to giving up our constructs in the face of limited samples of evidence. We might also abandon too readily some useful ways of seeing things. Many analogies with the operation of the natural sciences hold here. Sometimes we are too resistant and try to ignore, discredit or even falsify the evidence available to us. A special case of falsification which is extremely significant is when we discredit the evidence of our own senses, for example because we have been led to think that we are 'having a breakdown' or 'going mad'.

Kelly's theory emphasizes the idea that our social worlds are changing and that our constructs need to evolve continually to adapt to these changes. At the same time our constructs also provide us with a sense of continuity and predictability. We predict the future by expecting a measure of *replication* of past events. When I return home I expect my house and wife and children to be pretty much the same as when I last saw them. Probably most of us expect our interactions with others to be predictable in the sense of being 'like' the interactions we had previously. Constructs therefore provide a bridge and continuity between the *past*, *present* and the *future*. This is an essential contribution of Kelly's work in drawing our attention to the way that our beliefs link our existence over time. In families, as in other aspects of social life, we frequently hear people talking about past events in attempts to explain current and future behaviour. As we will see, it is more fruitful to think about how our beliefs held about past events construct our future and present behaviour, than it is to think about the past events as 'in themselves' determining what happens:

Each adult carries within him, ready for awakening or even on the tip of his tongue, his own memories of childhood, and these in cooperation with the impulses of the child provide the dynamics for which each new generation must live. . . . As the father watches his five-year-old-son posturing with a spear, sending an arrow straight to its mark, bidding for the mother's breast or being pushed away as too old for such indulgence, he lives again his own feelings when he at the same age was treated in the same way.

(Mead 1949: 117, 130)

The following is an outline of some of Kelly's major concepts set out in faith with his own style in terms of a systematic set of corollaries which elaborate his theoretical position.

The *dichotomy* corollary: a person's construction system is composed of a finite set of dichotomous constructs.

This states that people generally divide their understandings of the world into bipolar terms or categories for example:

Friendly – Hostile
Sick – Well
Nagging – Easy going

An important point is that the meaning of a construct is defined by the 'constrast' between the two poles. Kelly alerts us to this in the statement of his philosophical position. He argues that a concept such as 'freedom' is given meaning by contrast to the concept 'determinism'. In clinical situations it is typical to hear a client talk about one pole of a construct such as 'depressed' without it being clear what the contrast is for the person. It can be a mistake to assume that the client, his spouse, children, friends and the therapist all see the opposite of this pole in the same way. For example, the client may see the opposite of depressed as being able to tell certain people to leave him alone or to be able to sleep without medication. His wife may see it as him doing more around the house and not being so irritating. The therapist may see it as an improved score on a depression inventory or change in his transference relationship with him!

Fundamental postulate: a person's processes are psychologically channelled by the ways in which he anticipates events.

By this he meant that everything that we do, feel or think results from our attempts to understand what is going on in our world. Kelly includes our constructs about ourselves, our thoughts and emotions as well as constructs about other people.

The construction corollary: a person anticipates events by construing their replications.

By replication Kelly here meant that we seek out similarities and differences in our world between certain events and experiences. We expect things not to change all that much from day to day. Whenever we use a construct we are essentially identifying some *difference* in our environment. If I see someone as 'manipulative', then I have in fact discriminated some aspect of their behaviour which is different and similar to other people that I know. Subsequently I form some kind of an image of what this behaviour consists of and expect to see it more or less replicated the next time I meet the person.

Range corollary: a construct is convenient for the anticipation of a finite set of events only.

This makes the important point that a construct divides the world in three ways: things which are like the similarity pole such as people who are depressed, things which are like the contrast pole such as people who are not depressed, and things which are irrelevant to this construct such as teapots, trees and flowers. In other words some things are outside the 'range of convenience' of the construct. We see the edges of the range of convenience when we start to debate whether the construct applies to a class of objects. We might debate whether mammals or fish also experience depression.

Organization corollary: each person characteristically evolves, for his convenience in anticipating events, a construction system embracing ordinal relationships between constructs.

Each person's construct system is regarded a being organized in a hierarchical way. Evaluative constructs such as 'good–bad' tend to be at the top or to subsume others. As an example we can consider a common construct system, or part of one held by a member of a family where one person is seen to be displaying problems.

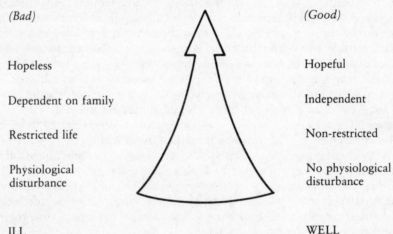

(Bad)	*(Good)*
Hopeless	Hopeful
Dependent on family	Independent
Restricted life	Non-restricted
Physiological disturbance	No physiological disturbance
ILL	WELL

Kelly noted that our beliefs are organized into such hierarchical linkages of implications. The structure can be seen to represent the person's value system or core assumptions about the world and this organisation is resistant to excessively rapid change or replacement. He noted further that a variety of emotional reactions such as anxiety, hostility and panic could occur when the organization of a system of constructs is challenged. A useful technique called *laddering* has been developed by Hinkle (1965) in order to explore the implications and organization of our constructs. A person is simply asked which of the two poles in a construct she would prefer to see herself on, for example well–ill. Assuming she chooses the pole 'well', she is asked why she chose this. This produces a further construct, e.g. I prefer to not to have a physiological disturbance. Why? Because I don't want to have a restricted life. Why? Because I want to be independent. Why? Because I want to feel hopeful about life, etc. You might like to try this exercise on yourself.

The implications are not strictly logical or always easily translatable into an ascending or descending pattern of implications since a person might say that being independent implies being well, so being independent is superordinate or higher in the hierarchy. However, he could answer that being well does not necessarily imply that one is independent. It is possible, though, to see being well as superordinate in that it implies the capacity to be independent if one chooses. The notion of levels of meaning and recursive loops will be discussed further in Chapter 5.

Fragmentation corollary: a person may successively employ a variety of construction subsystems which are inferentially incompatible with each other.

This corollary helps to explain the 'inconsistencies' that we often find in ourselves and others. Kelly gave the example of people with compulsion neuroses. Such people would try very hard to put events in their life into neat, tidy pigeonholes. Unfortunately this will tend to result in apparent inconsistencies for them whenever they encounter periods of rapid change in their life circumstances. Kelly was keen to point out that we can form constructs about our own construction processes, which is what seems to be implied by the idea of insight. Hence, in this case the person is likely to notice his own 'inconsistency', and since his superordinate constructs are to do with striving for order and consistency, he will find this state very difficult to tolerate.

A number of writers (Festinger 1954) have noted how people may attempt to reconcile inconsistencies in their construing processes. For example, having chosen my wife I might avoid people who do not like her and might say negative things about her. Faced with inconsistent information people will tend to attempt a variety of measures such as ignoring the inconsistent information, dismissing or belittling it, or actively seeking positive information in support of the quality of their make of car and so on. More will be said about this later when the construing processes of groups of people are discussed. In families it is particularly important. For example, children may find themselves in an untenable position where they try to remain faithful to two parents who don't get on and are encouraging them to take sides.

The *individuality* corollary: Persons differ from each other in their construction of events.

Kelly here suggested that people are essentially unique and develop their own ways of seeing their world. This applies even when two people apparently have the 'same' experience but interpret it in quite different ways. I might experience a cold wind as exhilarating and clearing out the cobwebs, whereas my friend might construe it as painful and certain to lead to illness. In families these differences can be extremely powerful. In one family the parents had dramatically different construings of 'silences' between them. The man interpreted silence as an indication of his wife's contempt for him, whereas she saw it as the 'calm before the storm' of his imminent bad temper and violent behaviour.

Experience corollary: a person's construction system varies as he successively construes the replication of events.

This follows from the philosophical premise that 'we can never step into the same river twice'. If we construe someone as friendly on the first occasion of our meeting, we might find that he is a bit grumpy the next time. In other words people naturally vary and change at least a bit. We probably won't completely revise our experience of him as a result of this, but we might qualify it slightly – perhaps he was tired or had a conflict at home – so he is still 'friendly' but also a bit 'moody' or 'troubled'.

In relation to family life this corollary is especially interesting. People in families come to know a great deal about each other through past experiences, knowledge of each other's current circumstances and so on. Consequently the situation can easily occur whereby they become extremely blind to any changes in each other's behaviour. This may be associated with feeling stuck and depressive feelings that can occur in a marriage that feels 'stale'. It is important to recognize also that the process is doubly complicated because people in families provide a large part of the context for each other within which the construing occurs. So if I see my spouse as unchanging, it is easy to forget that my behaviour may be prompting her into the typical behavioural patterns upon which I base my construction of her.

Modulation corollary: the variations of a person's construction system are limited by the permeability of the constructs within whose range of convenience the variants lie.

The experience corollary suggests that experience 'rubs in' some change. However, for development to occur further we must also have available some constructs which are flexible or permeable enough, permit some chinks of light through the door, to allow us to entertain new ways of seeing events. Kelly gives the example of the constructs 'mature–immature' which may be able to subsume my previous constructs, for example, 'fear–domination' and 'contempt–respect'. The former may now be seen as a more childish/immature way of looking at things and the latter as more adult/mature. An example from family life was a young man displaying schizophrenic symptoms who was typically seen by his parents as *sick vs well* and *awkward vs helpful*. These construings allowed for very little development and change in the family. Subsequently it was suggested that his behaviour could be seen in terms of a more permeable construct, *adult vs childish*. At times he might act like a seven year old and at others like his true age. Also, the construct implies development and growth rather than a potentially impermeable label such as sick or awkward.

Choice corollary: a person chooses for himself that alternative in a dichotomized construct through which he anticipates the greater possibility for extension and definition of his system.

This embodies Kelly's philosophy of psychological development. It is similar to Piaget's (1977) view that we are by nature curious and striving to understand and predict our world in more effective ways. However, this is not merely a casual exercise but is essential for our social survival. On the surface people often appear to act as if this was not the case, such as when it seems obvious that a person should choose to avoid arguing with his wife, and start to think of some more productive ways of being together, but perversely seems to continue arguing. However, it may be that for him to do so might imply 'weakness', 'being dominated' or 'like his father was', so that for him to adjust these constructs and avoid arguing might pose the threat that his constructs would be less, rather than more, elaborated.

This is similar to Rogers's (1955) idea of 'the organism seeking growth' or the work suggesting that people have a preference for cognitive complexity. In fact most of the experimental literature suggests that there are major differences between people, with some appearing to prefer a simple view of the world and others a more complex one. Most likely this preference is associated with different social experiences: modelling, use of language and educational attitudes in a family. It is important to be cautious here in assuming that by extension of the construct system Kelly simply means verbal insight and 'the more complex the better'. Some families may not share this view and it is possible for a therapist to suggest to a couple or a family that they should talk to each other more. This can ignore the possibility that perhaps they disagree on the value of 'taking' or even that one of them regards talking as 'unnecessarily stirring things up' and may prefer to make some changes by 'doing' in the first instance rather than 'talking'. As Kelly emphasizes, new behaviour can also lead to new construings.

An important aspect of Kelly's theory is the construct of *validation*. This derives from his fundamental view that we are in the business of continually testing our hypotheses. If our anticipations are proved correct, then we tend to hold on to our construing. However, if the reverse has occurred, then we may need to change or alter our constructs in some way. Usually we are unlikely to completely throw them away; instead as the organization corollary suggests, we replace the constructs most closely associated with the event by some others at our disposal. If our spouse becomes suddenly extremely happy, we do not totally change our construct about them, but instead we are likely to look for some causes in recent events or, failing that, perhaps start to worry about some disturbance. If a range of external causal explanations appear untenable, we might start to admit that they are perhaps more mysterious and unpredictable than we had thought.

Possibly the most important aspect of Kelly's theory is that of *reflexivity*: people are able to reflect not only on their world but also on their own thinking and about their own feelings. He saw psychologists and psychological theories as bound by this same idea. In other words my theory should be relevant to my own life, and the theory should also be capable of incorporating my activity of building psychological theories. In the case of repertory grid testing, Kelly did not see the positions in terms of expert and subject but as two people engaged in a process of mutual discovery. Obviously the psychologists will initially play more of a role of a guide, but the testing process involves continual discussion, questioning and exploration. In fact the psychologist must necessarily examine or at least recognize the presence of their own construct system in how she interprets the other's constructs. She successively tests her hypotheses with the other person to reach an agreed interpretation of the constructs. Out of this joint process of 'co-research' there are inevitably new insights and some alterations in the constructs system. This was Kelly's aim. He insisted that the process of testing necessarily promoted some change and did not expect to see exactly the same grid emerge the next time round.

Emotionality and change

One criticism that has been levelled at personal construct theory is that it is a rather cold, cognitive approach which ignores the emotions. Human experience appears to be reduced to the study of rationality and cognitions. This clearly is a very serious criticism for a theory which took as a prime aim that of assisting therapeutic change to occur. It is certainly true that Kelly could have given more attention to exploring this area and perhaps most importantly to offering some links between his theory and psychodynamic theory in particular.

For Kelly the emotions were closely bound up, as we would expect, with his concept of motivation. For him the basis of motivation was the 'urge' to seek elaboration of our construct system. To paraphrase Descartes, Kelly suggested that 'I research therefore I am'. Kelly adopted an operational position regarding emotions. He suggested that it was essential when talking about a concept such as anxiety, just what 'operations' we would have to carry out to determine its presence. He was not simply adopting a behaviourist position but rather was making an attempt at clarification regarding emotional concepts. In fact somewhat cryptically Kelly defined psychopathy in relation to behaviourism: 'A psychopath is someone who *really* believes in behaviourism.' He went on to offer the following definitions of the emotions.

● *Threat* – threat is the awareness of an imminent comprehensive change in a person's core constructs. This implies that the person is experiencing a sort of 'gnawing' awareness of some major change. It is possible that positive news, such as the thought of passing an important examination, can pose a threat just as can the possibility of failure.

- *Fear* – fear is the awareness of an imminent incidental change in one's core structures. Basically this implies a more specific experience such as a fear of rejection or ridicule. There are obvious overlaps between threat and fear, for example a fear of rejection might underly a more general threat to one's self-esteem and self-concept.

- *Anxiety* – anxiety is the awareness that the events with which one is confronted lie mostly outside the range of convenience of one's construct system. Essentially this is exemplified by a sense of not knowing what is expected or what will happen. An operation provokes anxiety because the person does not know what will happen. It can be reassuring simply to be told what procedures will be involved, who will be present and so on, in order that the person can develop some ways of construing the event in terms of details that he is familiar with. Anxiety often seems to involve 'flights of fancy' or imagining the worst, and this can be seen as a too rapid attempt to extend the construct system.

- *Guilt* – guilt is the awareness of dislodgement of the self from one's core role structure. One way of seeing this is that a person feels guilty when his self-esteem is threatened, by the fact that he has or will act in a way that is inconsistent with how he would like to be. This introduces indirectly the possibility that the 'ideal self' in this case is based upon socially defined and subjectively internalized values such as honest, brave, civilized and fair.

- *Aggressiveness* – aggressiveness is the active elaboration of one's perceptual field. This sounds rather bland when we consider the range of possible actions that can be classed as aggressive. However, it does emphasize the important point that people may resort to aggression as a way of attempting to avoid the threat and anxiety experienced when parts of their construct system are challenged. In family arguments this often seems to be indicated. A couple may be repeatedly accusing each other of acting in a particular way, with each disagreeing with the construction. An example might be a father accusing his son that he is 'lazy' and the boy retaliating that he doesn't wish to join in with his father's activities because they are 'boring'.

- *Hostility* – hostility is the continued effort to extort validational evidence in favour of a type of social prediction which has already been recognized as a failure. Underlying this definition seems to be the idea that the person is in a sense admitting that she doesn't understand the other or recognize them as being like them. This seems somewhat counter-intuitive in that we might typically think that a person is hostile towards another simply because he doesn't like them but may in fact understand them quite well. At the same time, this, as Kelly suggests, is tinged with a recognition that the person does not know how to deal with the other. In other words, I may not like someone but I may not be hostile to them as long as I can find some way of effectively dealing with them. It is debatable whether there are some circumstances whether hostility might not be an appropriate – as opposed to an inappropriate – stance such as appropriate assertiveness or anger at an injustice!

It is important to note that all Kelly's definitions include the idea of a process rather than a state. The picture is of a person attempting to deal with the demands and fluctuations of their world. He saw problems as associated with attempts to resist this natural process of change. Also, the definitions here can be linked to the account given in Chapter 2 of Schachter's work, which indicates an interaction between experiences of arousal which are physiologically produced and the awareness of these experiences. A form of escalation or 'runaway' can occur in which making an attribution of the type, 'I am anxious', can serve to heighten the physiological arousal, which results in an increased sense of 'anxiety'.

Kelly generated numerous excellent ideas about how people attempted to resist or avoid change. His views were not imbued with notions of pathology, but simply attempts to describe the processes involved in feeling stuck. One of his central notions was that people experience difficulty because of excessive attempts to maintain 'consistency'. This idea is also found in Festinger's work (1954) where he suggests that people have a 'drive' to maintain consistency and experience emotional tensions if they are subjected to situations where they experience inconsistency. Likewise, Kelly suggested a particular area of difficulty is when we experience a contrast between our 'real' self and our 'ideal' self – what we would like to be like. For example, I may find myself in situations where I yell at people or tell lies but I want to see myself as a non-violent and honest person. He argued that 'inconsistency' is a personal issue in that what may be inconsistent to me may not be inconsistent to you. Perhaps this is at the basis of some of the remarks that we make about others acting in a 'hypocritical' way. Their actions are 'hypocritical' from our construct system but perhaps not theirs. Kelly added that the feelings associated with inconsistency were greatest when our core constructs about ourselves were challenged.

Types of constructs

In addition to the corollaries Kelly detailed some meta-constructs regarding the types of constructs people might use and their implications for their behaviour. These describe different types of construing processes which have implications for how easy or difficult it may be for the person to revise her constructs. Kelly described two types of 'rigid' constructs – pre-emptive and constellatory – as opposed to 'flexible' constructs – permeable and propositional.

Pre-emptive construing – this is a pattern whereby the constructs operate in a black or white way. In a relationship the man may see his wife as vindictive and *nothing but* vindictive. This represents a sort of holding the person 'hostage' to this one way of seeing them and denying that there is any other way to see them. In relationships this sort of construing may be reciprocated so that wife, in the above example, may likewise come to see him as abusive and nothing but abusive. Typically the construct will be applied very rigidly to a wide range of events without any allowance for any exceptions or alternative ways of seeing a piece of behaviour. Pre-emptive construing has a quality of pushing the other person into a particular slot 'whether they like it or not'. In marital struggles, for example, adjectives and adverbs like very, always, never are frequently employed: 'you always do that', 'you never listen to what I have to say' and so on.

Man – wife is 'vindictive' and *nothing but . . .*
Woman – man is 'abusive' and *nothing but . . .*

Constellatory constructs – this relates to pre-emptive construing above, but involves a collection or cluster of constructs which are repeatedly used together. Examples are found in cases of prejudice or the use of stereotypes such as that women are non-rational, emotional, home-centred, etc. The constellation is a kind of a ready-to-use package which does not allow for alternative implications between constructs and has the effect of denying some of the conflicting evidence available.

Women – non-rational *and* emotional *and* home-centred *and . . .*

Permeability – in order to allow change it is suggested that constructs had to be *permeable* or open enough to allow new information in and change to occur. He suggested that constructs which were 'propositional' were able to allow this to happen. These constructs had the quality of scientific hypotheses about them. For example, my construct could be qualified by adjectives like sometimes, usually and so on. This is not simply vagueness but an openness to incorporate new information.

Propositional constructs – these are characterized by a form of pragmatic quality, the construct having the status of a working hypothesis. In relationships this might be seen in terms of a man seeing a number of possible ways of explaining his wife's actions. For example, if she was short with him he might construe it as perhaps she was tired, had a hard time at work, pre-menstrual tension, etc., rather than just 'the bitch is out to get me, again'. I will return to this issue in the next chapter where we will see that it may be more appropriate to view these processes as *interpersonal* rather than simply *personal* phenomena.

Man – my wife is *sometimes* 'vindictive', *sometimes* she is just 'tired',
        sometimes she has had a 'hard day', etc. . . .

Finally, Kelly also suggested a similar dimension of '*loose vs tight*' for describing the person's overal construct system. Overly constricted or tight construing occurs when constructs are used which only cover a very limited range of events; hence the risk of disconfirmation of the constructs are limited. In other words, we can attempt to become more and more certain about fewer and fewer things. In contrast a construct system can be so loose and vague that it becomes virtually impossible to falsify or test it effectively. Research by Bannister (1960) compared construct systems of people diagnosed as suffering from schizophrenic disorders and others. Photographs of people were used in order to elicit constructs. The findings suggested that those diagnosed as having schizophrenic symptoms showed much lower correlations between their constructs and that the patterns of constructs changed and appeared unstable over time. The results discriminated between 'thought disordered' schizophrenics who demonstrated this 'looseness' and other schizophrenics who did not. A related set of studies (Salmon *et al.* 1967) indicated that this was not a general tendency which applied to all construing. When asked to form constructs of ordinary objects, the thought disordered schizophrenics were only slightly less organized than 'normal' people. However, they were considerably more disorganized when it came to forming constructs about people. Their problems and confusion appeared to relate to their social world, a finding which supports the work of Bateson (1972) and others in their theory of a family-based etiology, especially the concept of doublebinds, in families with schizophrenic members.

Assessment: repertory grids and ethnographic methods

In addition to the comprehensive model that Kelly developed, he also designed an extremely useful and convenient test. The repertory grid test is a flexible scheme for examining a person's constructs about particular areas of their life. For example, if we want to examine how someone sees their family and friends, we gather together the various people that we are interested in and list them as *elements* of the grid. We then randomly select three of these elements, for example my mother, friend and sister, and ask how two of these are seen as similar to and different from the third (see example of grid below). The person is told that what is wanted is their idea of the most important differences between these people.

Table 1   An example of a repertory grid with family members as elements

Construct	*Elements*							Construct
	Self	*Mother*	*Father*	*Brother*	*Sister*	*Friend*	*Ideal-self*	
Male	2	4	2	2	5	3	1	Female
Open	2	1	2	3	3	3	3	Defensive
Stoic	2	4	2	2	5	2	1	Emotional

(Numbers represent ratings for each element/person on each construct e.g. male (1) ... female (5))

Ethnomethodological/descriptive methods
Prior to developing grid methods Kelly employed a variety of informal

descriptive and observational methods. One of these was simply to ask people to provide a self-description which was subsequently analysed to reveal the constructs employed and their organization. In addition he also employed *inductive* methods such as observing people's behaviour and aspects of the social situation they were in. For example, the way a family behaves together, such as loud and critical remarks, might imply that the construct *angry–passive* is important to them. Likewise whether they display their children's drawings on the walls at home might imply that they do or do not value their children's activities, creativity and so on.

This observational, inductive approach forms the basis for the application of Kelly's ideas in the context of family research and therapy, rather than the more formal use of grids which do not allow us to examine the operation of constructs in the context of the family dynamics. The next chapter will examine Kelly's ideas about social processes which were covered by his two remaining corollaries: the sociality and commonality corollaries. This will lead us into an analysis of how people understand each other, what beliefs they have about each other's beliefs and how they may come to develop shared ways of seeing events. Rather than focusing at how individuals create their own views of the world, we will be looking at how people in families create these jointly, at times attempting to induct others into their beliefs, as parents may do to their children, and at other times jointly negotiating new ways of seeing events.

Chapter 4

Shared construct systems

The last chapter has given an overview of the contribution of PCT to an analysis of personal constructions. We now want to move the focus from an analysis of individual construings to an exploration of *shared* construings. This of course is the core issue of the book. The question is whether and in what ways it is legitimate to talk about a shared social reality rather than simply an assemblage of individual constructs within the family. In Chapter 1 the same point was made regarding the behaviour of the members of a family: namely that it is more appropriate to describe many features of family life as being regulated by a set of *rules* which specify the behaviour of the family as a unit rather than individuals within it (Jackson 1965). Looking back at the systems theory-based model of family action proposed by Jackson, we can see that his concept of rules contains two aspects. On the one hand, a family rule is *constitutive* in that it defines how we are to regard a particular action, for example the emotional atmosphere in the family as 'too tense'. Second, the rule contains a *regulative* aspect in that it defines what is to be done about the state of affairs perceived, for example to act in ways that will reduce or increase the level of tension. This is similar to Kelly's definition of a construct: it is not only a perception but serves to guide our course of action. Furthermore the construct and action flowing from it are dialectically related in that the consequences of the action are in turn construed and form the basis for subsequent action.

Commonality and sociality

The exposition of Kelly's theory so far has focused on individual processes. However, he formulated two further corollaries which deal specifically with interpersonal or social action.

Commonality corollary: to the extent that one person employs a construction of experience which is similar to that employed by another, their processes are psychologically similar to those of the other person.

This stresses that people are similar not simply because they have experienced similar events, nor because they appear to be behaving in the same way, nor because they use the same language or verbal labels to describe events, but rather because they construe events in the same way. This means that they interpret events, discriminate between events and interpret the implication of events in the same way. For example, in a family being vegetarian might be interpreted as 'good', 'healthy' and implying that one should avoid eating meat on all occasions and that lapsing or eating meat should be something to feel 'bad' about.

Sociality corollary: to the extent that one person construes the construction process of another, they may play a role in a social process involving the other person.

This suggests that for two people to interact effectively does not require them to be similar, but does require that they have some constructs about how the other sees things. In effect this is saying that we need to have some degree of empathy or at least a rudimentary theory about how the other might be seeing things. As an example, a father and his young son will have a different construct system. The child will be concerned with and interested in different aspects of the world to the father. Yet they will be able to form constructs about each other which will enable them to interact. The father might construe that his son is interested in constructing large and complex buildings out of Lego. However, it is unlikely that it will be an equally important part of his construct system. They will have some constructs about how each of them thinks the other sees this activity and be able to interact quite amicably by playing the game together or, alternatively, acknowledge their differences in interest. It is important to note here that problems may be associated with situations where one person makes demands about what the other 'should' think (thought control) about a particular issue, based on an assumption about what the other 'does' think. This might be an example of an impermeable and pre-emptive kind of sociality construct which assumes that the implication of what the other person has said or done can *only* imply that they see things in a particular way. For example, a husband might think that his wife believes in putting herself first and that all her actions imply this and only this.

In his commonality and sociality corollaries we have the idea that people share some agreement about how they see their circumstances and that they hold construings about each other's construings. We will consider work, such as Heyman and Shaw's (1978) studies, which details some of the difficulties that may arise when people make incorrect assumptions or meta-perspectives about the other person's assumptions. Laing (1969) also described some of the implicative spirals or knots that can occur in relationships.

The sociality and commonality corollaries might suggest that it is only possible for people to have, at best, an approximate sharing of their constructs, since my constructs are a result of my unique set of experiences and my personal *constructions* of these experiences. Even if two people share the same events, for example watch a film together, Kelly would argue, not unreasonably perhaps, that they do not necessarily construe it in the same way. Kelly argues further that even if we use the same *words* to describe an event that we have experienced together, we may not mean the same thing by them. Wittengstein (1951) argued similarly that we should not assume that we mean the same thing when we use the same words as someone else. Some possible solutions to this issue are offered in the suggestion that we approach commonality when we use the same constructs and within a similarly organized construct system; in other words, if the constructs we use have similar implications and are equally important to us. For example, a couple may agree, having watched Woody Allen's film *Manhattan* together, that it is a comedy about the complexities of relationships and that this is an important subject to explore which touches aspects of our own life. Furthermore, it might hold similar implications for them such as it is useful to be able to have a sense of humour about these issues or we have been through something similar ourselves.

Duck (1975) proposes that the development of commonality is a central aspect of the development of relationships and the formation of friendships. People select each other based upon perceived commonalities of dress, interests, political attitudes, musical tastes, etc. The level of commonality desired is seen to change as the relationship develops from an initial concern based upon constructs about superficial physical features to more psychological constructs about temperament, attitudes, interests and interactional style. This seems to be analogous to the development of construing in children in that they appear initially to employ physical constructs such as hair colour and size to form anticipations. Gradually children learn to elaborate these anticipations by employing verbal labels to make finer disciminations and anticipations.

What is significant here is that Kelly and most subsequent PCT theorists seem to have ignored the possibility that constructs are *constructed* and *constrained* within a social reality. At a broad level Kelly accepts that we share a basic cultural commonality in terms of our language, values conventions and so on. Even here, though, he views the individual as being potentially free to reconstrue this *real world* in alternative ways. In fact this is the core of his theory: constructive alternativism. Certainly this may be potentially true and it does offer a positive approach to the question of therapeutic change.

Studies on conformity

One criticism of Kelly here is that he underestimated the power of groups to *create* and *enforce* a social reality. Some of the early studies on conformity such as Asch (1956) demonstrated the power of groups to create distortions in people's constructions. In an experiment the false reports of a group of the experimenter's confederates were found to influence people's basic cognitive judgements regarding the length of lines. When interviewed following the experiment and asked whether they had felt any pressure to conform, some went so far as to deny that they had been pressured in any way and defended the distorted and incorrect judgements that they had made. These studies brought people together for a relatively brief period of time of an hour or so, but there still appeared to have been some important changes in beliefs towards a group norm. Generalizing these findings to families, schools, work and other long-term situations of social influence, it is possible to imagine the potentially damaging effects of imposing or inducing negative social experiences such as denials of a person's attempts to form consistent perceptions of reality.

Further work, such as Sherif's (1966) studies, adds support to this idea and suggests that not only conformity but specific ideas and feelings can be promoted. In one study competitive and aggressive feelings were promoted between groups of boys at summer camps in the USA. Following an initial period during which the boys were allowed to choose and form friends, they were then separated into two groups. Care was taken to put friends into different groups. After a period of isolation from each other and the encouragement of competitive feelings towards the other groups, they were placed in competitive situations against each other. This procedure was found to lead to the development of considerable hostility between the two groups, even to the extent of previous friends becoming antagonistic towards each other. Various refinements and elaborations have been carried out since the early work to suggest, for example, that groups have a tendency to polarize (Moscovici and Zavalloni 1969) rather than simply conform and that in some contexts the group behaviour becomes riskier (Stoner 1961). However, the important point is that an analysis of such groups required a Gestalt (Lewin 1958) approach, a focus on the group and not simply individual features leading to attitude change.

Such studies suggest that groups have considerable power to produce distortions of reality and negative feelings of aggression. It is not simply the case that people have made any errors in their construction of the world. It is more accurate to say that they have responded appropriately to inconsistencies or real negative aspects of the social reality. Kelly instead seems to make the assumption that in some situations people *get it wrong*; they misunderstand the situation or interpret it in an unfortunate and unhelpful way:

> We can . . . see clients as people who are unable decisively to test out and elaborate their personal theories, their understandings of themselves and their interpersonal worlds. Their construing may have become circular, so that they are endlessly testing and retesting the same hypotheses and are unable to accept the implications of the data which they collect. They may have moved into the kind of chaos where the constructions are so vague and loose that they cannot provide

expectations clear enough to test and they simply flow back and forth around the same issues.

(Bannister and Fransella 1986)

This statement carries the assumption that people can, if not *get it wrong*, at least see things in an *ineffective* way. The purpose here is not to detract from Kelly's major contribution but to consider in this chapter attempts that have been made to extend his work in this respect. The example from Bateson of the young man in the double-bind situation is illustrative here. From a Kellian position we might be tempted to say that the young man has in some way *got it wrong*. Bannister (1960) examined the construct systems of people diagnosed as suffering with schizophrenic symptoms and concluded that they typically had excessively loose construct systems which underlay their inconsistent behaviours. It is possible to present an alternative explanation along the lines that perhaps the young man in Bateson's classic example has more or less *got it right*! There *is* something strange going on. His mother is communicating in an incomprehensible way. He may also be behaving appropriately in terms of a shared family belief about what to do when she communicates in this way. He can be seen to be acting appropriately in terms of interpreting the contradictions in his social reality but at the same time *self-destructively*. Bateson provides an anecdote to illustrate this idea of fit between behaviour and contexts. In one experiment people were asked to try to work out a sequence of codes on a simplified keyboard by typing in combinations. They were told that if they came up with a correct combination they would gain a point. In fact this was a non-contingency experiment so that the points were awarded randomly. The aim was to see how long people would continue to try to guess the combinations and whether there was a tendency to generate more and more complex combinations. One subject, diagnosed to be suffering from paranoid schizophrenic symptoms, attempted this task, and in comparison to 'normal' subjects abandoned it very rapidly saying, 'It doesn't matter a damn what keys you press, there is a guy behind the screen who just gives a point when he feels like it!' Bateson went on to develop this idea in his model of the double-bind, which proposed that people are subjected to 'real' contradictory experiences. Research and therapy with a variety of families containing a person presenting problems support a view that their problems are associated with a 'faulty' social reality and not simply a faulty personal construction by one or more members (Haley 1971, Minuchin 1974). Bizarre ways of acting and thinking tend to be shared to some extent by other family members, and there may also be 'real' contradictions and confusions in the community that the family are in and between the professionals with whom they come into contact.

Families as acting upon people

Kelly's definition of constructs embodies the idea that they contain two parts: *constitutive* – what a particular action means – and *regulative* – what is to be done about it (see also Harre and Secord 1972 and Pearce and Cronen 1980). In Kelly's view a construct contains a prescription not only about what an event means but also about what course of action this suggests. This is the core of the implication of the construct. A central point here is that the experience of the family reality is not a passive but a dialectical and active process. The constructed family reality *acts* upon and regulates the construing processes of each of its members. The example below illustrates the active nature of this process. This two-way process underlies some of the patterns of escalation described by family therapists. The case of the Drake family illustrates such an escalating process, which nearly sabotaged any attempts at working with them. The family was presented with a range of problems but repeatedly focused on the 'delinquent' son David as the main issue. The following illustrates the start of my first interview with Mr and Mrs Drake (separated) and David:

Therapist:	(Explains set-up and use of video tape to record the session. The family makes very little attempt to discuss whether it is all right or not.) 'Nice to meet you all'. . . . (social introductions . . .) Could you tell me a little bit about the problems at the moment?
Mr Drake:	Well, we don't really have any problems, it's just David and my wife really . . .
David:	I don't understand why we have to have this camera . . . I used to be proud of my family . . . we don't know who's watching. . . . I've got a criminal record . . .
Mr and Mrs Drake:	Don't be so silly David. . . . The doctor explained to us . . . it's confidential . . .don't be so silly . . .
David:	Silly, I'm not being silly (starts to shout and gets up to leave). . . . I'm not staying here.
Mr and Mrs Drake:	Stop it, David, you are being stupid . . . sit down.
Therapist:	O.K. can I make a suggestion? David, I suggest that you be the *censor* here today. If anybody says anything that you think might incriminate you or them, just say so and we will stop and rub it out from the video. Is that acceptable to you? You are in charge of seeing to that, O.K.?
David:	(Mumbled and rapidly sat down and proceeded to join in the session without further fuss.)

Members of families, and people generally in social interactions, actively regulate each other's construings. We make inferences about what the other person is thinking and actively make attempts to alter this. In the example above, the social reality of the family revolves around the belief that David is the cause of the problems and that he is troublesome. This belief is used to ascribe meaning to his actions such as that he is being 'silly' and 'stupid', when he could be seen to have been prompted by his parents' silence to ask some relevant questions in an attempt to protect them and himself and ensure the confidentiality of the interview. The social reality also operates on a more general level in that it can be seen to map out certain areas of concern. In the family above, there had been extensive involvement with a wide range of agencies – doctors, social workers, probation officers, psychologists, psychiatrists and health visitors – to the extent that intrusion into the life of the family was a major issue. Consistent with this was a sense of failure about themselves as a family and a feeling that they could not and had not been able to solve their own problems. The solution was to call in a professional whenever problems arose. David's comments made a lot of sense within this context, and the consequent denial of this issue by the parents or passive acceptance of further interference could be seen as drawing an appropriate angry response from him. Rather than getting it all 'wrong', his comments were possibly about getting it 'too right'.

There is further evidence from a number of sources that families actively regulate people's experiences. The work of Brazelton (1974) describes how parents *impute* meaning to their child's action. For example, a mother responds to her child *as if* his action was deliberate and meaningful:

Baby: (Makes movements with his arms which brush against her
         necklace.)
Mother: 'That's a clever boy you, do you want the necklace, it's
         pretty, isn't it?' (Makes eye contact with the baby and smiles
         at him.)
Baby: (Smiles at her face.)
Mother: 'Yes, you do, don't you?' (Tickles and kisses him.)

Kelly discussed in his sociality corollary the idea that a social interaction occurs if the participants have a construction of the other person's construct system adequate enough to allow interaction to take place. In the above example we can see that the mother ascribes an intentionality to the child's behaviour which may facilitate his development and eventual autonomy. However, at this stage it is questionable whether he or she was in any significant sense acting *deliberately*. Watzlawick *et al.* (1967), as we saw earlier, described social interaction in terms of a never-ending-never-beginning sequence of communications that the participants *punctuate* in order to make sense of what is going on. Fundamental to this was that people make an assumption that what the other is saying is meaningful. However, sometimes the reverse is assumed, that the communication is *not* meaningful, for example in transactions characterized by schizophrenia. The communication of such people is typically *disqualified*, that is, interpreted and responded to *as if* it was crazy or meaningless. Goffman (1971) describes such processes in the context of psychiatric hospitals where, for example, a patient's attempts to maintain a sense of self-identity by collecting odd pieces of paper, photographs, objects such as buttons and coins can be taken to imply obsessive and mad behaviour. Bateson (1972) and Watzlawick *et al.* (1967) make similar points about the pervasive influence that contexts have on the definitions of behaviour – the person must be mad because he is in a mental hospital.

The central issue is that families have an immense power to construct the experience and beliefs of their members. There are important links here between psychodynamic and systems theory perspectives: the notion of projection that was discussed earlier is an instance of how our early experiences can be mapped on to our later relationships. Laing (1969) takes this further by suggesting that in all families a process of induction occurs whereby people are in a sense coerced into accepting and internalizing (introjecting) what other people want them to think and believe:

> Hypnosis may be an experimental model of a naturally occurring phenomenon in many families. In the family situation, however, the hypnotists (the parents) are already hypnotized (by their parents) and are carrying out their instructions, by bringing up . . . in such a way, which includes not realizing that one is carrying out instructions; since one instruction is not to think one is instructed. This state is easily induced by hypnosis.

Laing goes on to describe how the family can be considered both at the level of what goes on, behaviour, and in terms of what is experienced. The experience is in one sense personal but at another level is shared by the family members:

> The most common situation I encounter in families is when what I think is going on bears almost no resemblance to what anyone in the family experiences or thinks is happening, whether or not it coincides with common sense.

In his view each person in the family has a set of beliefs about the family and the relations inside it. However, these beliefs are at the same time projected out on to the family relationships. There is a spiral of influence with, as he suggests, various core assumptions that are held in common but may not even be conscious. The effects of such *inductions* are illustrated in the Brown family where Erik, an 18-year-old boy, had previously taken an overdose of sleeping pills. The following fortnight the family attended for an interview. Mr and Mrs Brown came with Erik and his older and younger sisters.

Therapist: Can you tell me a little bit about the other children? Did any of them have problems with potty training?

Mother: No, the girls were as good as gold. I just took the nappies off Mary when she was six months and that was it, she was perfect. . . .

Therapist: What about Erik? What was he like?

Mother: Oh yes, Erik was a problem. In fact he had a bed-wetting problem from the day he was born.

In this sequence we can see that the young man was fitted into a slot that was prepared for him perhaps even before he was born. We would not be surprised if his subsequent experience and the constructs he developed about himself were negative. Broadly we can summarize some of the main issues here by suggesting that families present a set of constructs to the individual members both in terms of the expressed beliefs in the family and by the behaviours or transactions in the family.

Such a view has considerable implications, incidentally, for much of developmental psychology. Erik Erikson, for example, described in his concept of the epigenetic cycle a set of experiential stages that people pass through from childhood to adulthood. For the young child he suggested there are the stages of trust versus mistrust, initiative versus shame, identity versus confusion, etc. Like Kelly there is a sense in his accounts of the child *getting it wrong* somehow. But what if instead, as our illustrations above suggest, people are responding appropriately to the realities of their family situation? So in a case of a young child who develops feelings of mistrust, we might consider the possibility that:

1. The interactions in the family are characterized by lack of trust, guilt, anxiety and parental conflicts. The conflicts may at times be specifically on the issue of how to deal with the child's potty training.
2. The child's *correct* construing of the nature of these relationships, especially the negative aspects, may be validated by what the child hears his parents saying about each other and their relationship.
3. Further, as Laing suggests, the same process of conflict and distrust may be exemplified in how the parents disqualify the child's explanations or attempts to construe his reality.

Alternatively, of course, it is possible that 'positive' experiences can be constructed in the same way.

In the case of the Brown family Erik was not allowed to comment on the conflict between his parents or to challenge the interpretation of his bed-wetting. Mrs Brown, who appeared to hold the position of 'family historian', told the story of how Mr Brown had also in his childhood wet the bed, ceased when his father went away in the army but then reverted to bed-wetting when he returned. She added the theory that this was 'possibly' a sign of rebellion because he did not like his father. By implication, therefore, Erik's bed-wetting was also to be seen as a form of rebellious behaviour. The story was well known to all of the members of the family, and Erik confirmed that he had heard it before.

Shared construct systems: research evidence

Two studies will be described here before we move to an examination of shared belief systems within a therapeutic context. The first was carried out by Karnst and Groutt (1977) and examined the constructs of a set of people living in a commune called The Brotherhood of the Spirit set up in the late

1960s in New England. The commune was quite large with 240 members in total. Apart from the usual reasons for joining such as dissatisfaction with conventional forms of life, the members held a number of powerful shared beliefs. They held a broadly Buddhist religious belief in reincarnation and karma, and various members felt themselves to be the living reincarnations of famous historical figures such as John the Baptist and English kings as well as 'common' people from the past, Vikings and so on. Music was also a central issue and they had a rock band that they felt was a pure channel of their energies. The authors' description, though sympathetic, and my attempt here no doubt immediately present this group as rather strange. This may, of course, be partly due to the fact in the 1960s there was a strong tendency for young people to present themselves deliberately as strange in order to 'make a point' to their family and to society generally. However, the relevance of this study is in illustrating how the beliefs in a close group may be regarded as shared and also as containing individual implications.

The method of the study consisted of participant observation with the researchers living in the commune and becoming immersed in their way of life. They also employed interviews and developed a form of repertory grid elicitation. The sample interviewed consisted of the observed leaders of the group, new and old members, and marginal or 'drop out' members. The repertory grid elicitation consisted of a comparison of the commune with other communes and comparisons between members of the commune using a form of triadic elicitation: how are two of these three different from the third? Think of as many ways as you can. The researchers noted here an important shared construct, which was that the commune members despised psychological research and consequently they had to adapt their methods somewhat to appear more easy going and 'laid back'.

The initial individual analysis produced some interesting results. The group 'leader' Mark, for example, was seen as experiencing an element of guilt regarding 'ego trips', especially the pursuit of power or specific personal goals. On the one hand, he strongly fostered the belief shared by the commune that they should accept the principles of the group and have faith in him as their guide. In the event of people expressing doubts, they were asked to leave and think things over until they had made up their minds. This represented a clarification of boundaries – to be *in* or *out* of the group. This, like the blatant attempt of the bond to become famous and project the image of superstars, was incompatible with a belief in spirituality. The authors go on to suggest that Mark's guilt was resolved or reframed using two of the group constructs – real vs illusion and spiritual vs material. When members outside the commune described some of their activities as 'ego trips', the members dismissed this by claiming that they missed the spiritual significance of their intentions. On the other hand, the commune member's 'real' experience was different to this. Neither of these constructs was one of Mark's core personal constructs, but he was able to draw upon them in order to resolve his guilt. The authors suggest that this may be an important function of shared constructs – that they permit alternative constructions when people experience guilt in the sense of Kelly's notion of being dislodged from one's core role constructs.

This idea complements our earlier discussion of Jackson's idea that social values can be summoned by family members in a tactical way to exert leverage on the others to restore the status quo. Here an analogous process can be seen to operate whereby a socially constructed reality or a rehearsed 'public' position can be put forward and used to ward off criticism. Partly this can be seen as a form of safety in numbers or a diffusion of responsibility. Calling upon a shared reality allows the person to avoid the threat to his personal construct system as long as she has made some separation from the group. In other words, the person does not feel that she would 'sink with the ship' if the shared group construct system becomes threatened.

The authors then went on to produce an analysis of the shared constructs held by the group along the following lines:

Spiritual	Material
Brotherhood	The world
Real and natural	Illusion
Positivity	Negativity
Feeling high	Feeling low
Mind	Brain/intellectual
Letting go	Holding on

Karnst and Groutt describe the ways in which these constructs functioned to regulate the daily interactions within the group. Members would tell each other to 'let go' or accuse each other of 'holding on'; 'positivity' was used as 'a kind of "weather" term used to describe the general atmosphere of the day'. The authors state that the construct 'spiritual vs material' was hierarchically the most important, along with 'brotherhood' and 'real', as ways of defining the group in contrast to the outside world.

Broadly the construct system here reflects the kinds of constructs that family therapists have found useful in describing families: namely constructs to do with a clarification of the *boundary* between the group and the outside world, and those to do with the nature of the *internal relationships*, emotional tone of the group, intimacy and so on. It is possible, of course, that the researchers here imposed their own constructs to some extent on their interpretation of the core constructs for the group.

The next stage of the research was particularly interesting in that they then attempted to relate these inferred group construings to the actual constructs used by members of the commune. They were looking for the extent to which the members 'spontaneously' used similar personal constructs and the degree of shared construing and apparent agreement amongst them. (This analysis was based on observations rather than repertory grid elicitation.) They found that for the first construct, 'Brotherhood vs the world', seven out of the eight members interviewed used some form of this construct to compare and contrast friends from the past, family, outsiders and commune members. There was found to be considerable agreement regarding the positive side of the construct but not regarding the contrast pole.

Table 2 Personal constructs held by each member in relation to the shared group construct Brotherhood vs the world

Member	Brotherhood vs	The world
A	Those who stand with me	Those who deceive
B	Insider	Outsider
C	Close friendship	Merely together
D	Evidence of total belief	Holding back
E	Companionship	Solitude
F	–	–
G	Communicate with easily	Communicate only with difficulty
H	Companionship	Sexual relationship

Source: Karnst and Groutt 1977: 83.

This general pattern was repeated with the other core constructs with some interesting variations. For example, in relation to the construct 'spiritual vs material', seven of the eight members employed similar constructs with negative contrast poles – illusion, superficial, intellectual, etc. One member regarded the brotherhood's notions of spirituality as giving a false sense of security as opposed to real security. She later withdrew from the commune 'with a certain amount of contempt'.

The authors concluded that there was a need to distinguish between a 'public' shared commonality and the more 'private' implications that constructs held for each person in the commune. Second, they pointed out that there was a 'one-sided' commonality whereby there was general agreement about the emergent side of a construct pole but not the implied pole. They were *not* generally aware of such differences in the meanings of the constructs, and the members generally assumed a greater level of agreement amongst themselves than the authors observed. This clarifies further how, because of the somewhat ambiguous nature of the 'public' construct system, the members were able to use it in different ways to fit their particular needs. This corresponds to Kelly's distinction between 'tight' and 'loose' construct systems. A degree of ambiguity permits the constructs to have a wide range of applicability and reduces the likelihood that members will feel that the system is not relevant to their needs.

An informal participant study of a British commune in Devon reveals similar processes. In this commune the core constructs appeared to be:

Vegetarian (vegies)	Non-vegetarian
Moral	Immoral
Sharing	Selfish
Drop-out	Realistic

Idealistic	Sensible
Intolerant	Tolerant
Middle class	Working class
Family based	Single
Serious	Hedonistic
Rural (self-sufficient)	Urban

One of the core constructs was vegetarian vs non-vegetarian. This served to divide the commune into two camps, and for a time the division threatened to destroy the community, with the vegetarians calling the meat-eaters 'pigs' and the meat-eaters calling them 'self-righteous'. This dimension seemed to be employed in a constellatory way, implying a range of other constructs so that the vegetarians were also 'into' sharing the child-minding, dropping out of the rat race, encouraging self-sufficiency and generally being more 'serious'. There were, of course, in actuality massive overlaps between the two camps so that some of the non-vegetarians were on this side of the construct poles. The division between the two sides was reflected in two constructs which fuelled the division and in turn increasingly restricted the diversity of construing. The vegies saw the meat-eaters as 'immoral', which also meant insensitive, lacking ideology and being selfish. The meat-eaters developed a pre-emptive construct 'intolerant' as a defence to the 'guilt trip' laid on them by the vegies. To demonstrate that they were 'intolerant', they increased and made more blatant their amount of meat-eating, which of course produced increased rebukes and moral lectures.

Traditionally it is assumed that communes represent an alternative to family life for those who are disaffected with families from their own experiences, either in childhood or as adults. The commune in this sense represented a microcosm in that several family units coexisted along with people who were either single or single parents. This led to conflicts of interest between the good of the commune and the good of the family units. One practical implication of this was that not all members were equally willing if at all, to carry out child-minding tasks. Hence the community did not inevitably provide the release from the conventional family roles that it was envisaged might occur. These and other similar expectations were not universally shared and rose to the surface as the commune developed. In effect a similar developmental pattern to families could be seen in that following an early heady period or 'romance,' the realities and differences started to emerge and tensions developed which led to some members leaving and others renegotiating their expectations. As with the formation of a relationship, the members did have some models regarding the kind of commune they aspired to be, based on information about others from books and visits. One of the guiding constructs embodying these anticipations was that of tolerant vs intolerant. There was a general sense initially that excessive 'ideologies' could disrupt the commune and a *laissez-faire* approach was more appropriate. This was, however, the public image, whereas in fact the commune had a middle-class, moralistic bias with the members having a broadly socialist outlook, a negative view of drugs and sexual promiscuity, and a commitment to remaining integrated with, rather then opting out of, society. This was embraced by the construct 'sensible' vs 'idealistic'.

Finally, the members also held constructs about their relationships with each other. The division between the vegies and meat-eaters was obviously noted, as were attempts at give and take. Broadly these occurred in terms of the vegies agreeing to lay off moralizing so much and the meat-eaters not flaunting their carnivore habits. Most importantly some constructs about change and development of the commune also started to emerge, such as the idea that their initial problems were 'like a marriage' and they would reach some compromises and a middle ground. Apart from these internal dynamics, there was also a concern with the linkage with the outside world. Many of the members kept up outside jobs and used the commune as a commuting base. However, there was still a shared goal for the commune to provide external work, for instance to function as a conference centre and to provide educational programmes of various sorts. Initially this was difficult and engendered a sense of failure just as it would in a conventional marriage. Increased success in this area led to an easing of some of the internal problems.

Turning now specifically to families and their shared construct systems, Reiss (1980) has conducted a detailed set of studies examining the relationship between the nature of the construct systems employed by families and their abilities to solve 'problems' in an experimental, laboratory-type situation. His studies have indicated that when families are confronted with their problem-solving tasks, such as detecting patterns in complex stimulus arrays, they differed considerably in how effectively they worked together. The styles of problem solving ranged from co-operative to uncooperative. They found that families differed in how they perceived the laboratory task and the situation they found themselves to be in. Some families were highly suspicious, felt that the task was unsolvable and attempted to get away as quickly as possible. In contrast, some families regarded it as fun and proceeded to work together effectively and creatively. Reiss goes on to suggest that these problem-solving styles indicate each family's view of the world:

> We argue that the family's reaction to us, the research staff, is not idiosyncratic but is an example or an indicator of their usual or typical view of any novel social group or situation. For example, a family that views us with mistrust and pessimism. Likewise a family that feels it can decipher the underlying patterns in the materials we present to them is likely to approach most novel situations with similar confidence. In other words, we propose that a family's problem-solving style arises from its assumptions about the nature of the social process or group in which the problem is embedded. Moreover, we are arguing that a family is relatively stable from situation to

situation. Thus, its problem-solving style is likely to reflect its *typical* or *enduring* assumptions about how such social groups might function.

(Reiss 1980: 240)

One study will be described here which required families to compare and contrast themselves with other families. They employed Kelly's notions that constructs develop by this process of comparisons and contrasts. The investigation included families which contained an adolescent who had been admitted to a psychiatric hospital. As a result of visiting and other contacts, many of these families knew each other. The procedure consisted of asking the families to sort a large set of photographs of families attending the clinic into the six families that they knew the best. They were then asked to discuss the six families (including themselves) and to generate a construct representing the most characteristic aspect of each.

The following dimensions were employed to analyse the family:

- *Synchrony* – the observation of the *process* whereby families discussed the issues and the extent of co-operation between them.
- *Depth* – a measure of the extent to which their constructs were meaningful and rich in implications as opposed to superficial.
- *Variety* – the range of constructs that were generated whilst the family were discussing and attempting to generate the main dimensions to describe the other families.

Included was an analysis of the extent to which each member of the family employed an underlying family or *shared* dimension. This was the proportion of statements that expressed perception of some core or shared family constructs.

Following this elicitation each family was given a set of photographs showing each member of all six of the families (about 30 photos), and they were asked to sort the photographs into two equal piles for each end of the six constructs that they had generated. This enabled an analysis of the *structure* of the families construct systems by examining correlations between the constructs.

Their results indicated that the co-operation shown by family members in producing the constructs reflected their overall abilities on the problem-solving tasks. They did not find significant differences in the number of constructs produced by the different families. However, they did find that families who were more able at problem solving had a more integrated, that is clearly structured and differentiated, system. They also found, perhaps surprisingly, that in most of the families all members made a significant contribution with each member contributing at least one dimension. There was no clear evidence of *control* by a key person in the families, but there was evidence that the low problem-solving group used more *command*-type communications than questions.

The studies by Reiss (1980) suggests that families do hold and are able to articulate shared dimensions. They also propose a developmental model of how family construct systems may mature and evolve:

Some families mature in the sense that the relationships amongst the members become more complex and subtle. For example, as children become adolescents they perceive and accommodate to an increasingly complex appreciation of their parents. As relationships of this kind flower, individuals become increasingly sensitive to each other's view including, presumably, their views on other families. The mutual appreciation involves, among other features, the continuing integration and reintegration of each individual's view into a common set of understandings and conceptions. The structural conceptions of other families, which many high-configuration families showed in our study, may serve as the simplest example of such common conceptions. By contrast, 'immature' families – ones that are less adaptive or healthy – may fail to reconcile the varying perceptions and conceptions of its members.

(Reiss 1980: 254)

This is very similar to what Kelly has to say regarding the development of individual construct systems. He argues that there is a progression from concrete, simple constructions to more sophisticated and propositional systems which allow people to deal with a greater variety of novel situations and problems.

These studies give broad support to the idea that families can usefully be construed as having a shared set of beliefs or constructs. Unfortunately neither of them attempted to look specifically at the extent to which individual members actually agreed in their use of the dimensions, e.g. what level of correlation existed between each individual's use of the dimensions in ranking other people and their families. We now describe two studies which have attempted to do this. The first, by Watson (1970), examines construct processes in a therapeutic group. The second, by (Ryle 1975; Ryle and Lipshitz (1975) looks at the extent to which couples had shared, common agreements about their construing of their relationship.

Watson gave a repertory grid to members of a therapeutic group. Each of the ten people in the group and the two therapists were given a grid consisting of the twelve members of the group as elements and twelve supplied constructs. The latter were chosen on the basis of representing important group dimensions: like me, like I would like to be, like my father/mother, affectionate, sexually attractive, like a child, jealous, unfriendly, depressed, angry and frightened. Each member of the group rated every other member, and themselves, on the constructs. The scores were then correlated in order to assess the extent of agreement in the group. Generally this indicated that the people in the group were in agreement in their use of the constructs on the group members. The agreement on ten of the twelve constructs was statistically significant.

There was also broad agreement in the group who were the people on the extreme ends of each constructs, such as who was most disliked. These were Miss A and Mr Z, who were also seen as most disturbed. (The two therapists were seen as most 'all right'!) The scores indicated that there was evidence of a shared construing in the group. They also revealed and clarified important aspects of the group's dynamics. For example, Mr Z was functioning as a group scapegoat.

It was possible to assess the degree of *commonality* of the constructs used by examining the agreement between the ratings for different people in the group. For example, there was considerable agreement between the therapists and the patients regarding the terms depressed and frightened. Only for one construct, angry, was there a significant difference between the therapists' and patients' use of the constructs.

Watson's analysis also included comparisons between the way members of the group used their constructs (construct correlations). So when Miss A used the construct 'like my mother', this correlated with other people's use of the constructs frightened and unfriendly. Watson suggested that this woman's way of comparing people with her mother had become an important construct for the group, not just for her. However, she did not see her mother as depressed and frightened. Watson was able to extrapolate from such findings to analyse how shared constructs operated in the group, and he revealed such patterns of denial not only at the individual but also at the group level. Most members of the group saw this woman in the terms that she had 'taught' the group about her mother – as unfriendly. One exception to this was one of the therapists who liked Miss A and did not accept the tendency of the group to accept the implied resemblance to her mother. This raised an important issue: shared constructs can be seen to set out the discourse or terms of discourse for a group or a family. Even when members do not unanimously agree on what position each member occupies on the dimension or construct pole, they are still likely to accept the importance of the construct dimension.

A related study by Ryle and Lipshitz (1975) has developed from work with couples in therapy. A central issue for Ryle is how each partner sees the relationship and how each thinks that the other sees the relationship – *meta-perspective*. This bears a resemblance to Laing's ideas of meta-perspectives. His work is based in objects relations theory so that a focus of concern was the extent to which a couple's construings of each other are similar to, or transferences from, their relationships with their parents. Ryle's approach is to employ relationships as elements for his grid, such as husband in relation to wife, wife in relation to husband, and husband in relation to his mother. Constructs are then elicited about the differences between the relationships. The couple are also asked to fill in another grid in terms of how they think that their partner would fill it in. This gives an assessment of the extent to which they understand or can predict how the other regards these relationships.

In this way Ryle's analysis permits an examination of *commonality* – the similarities and differences in how couples saw their relationships. It also reveals *sociality* – the nature of the construct they have about how the other person construes the relationship. His studies suggest that not only are there frequent differences in commonality or agreement about how they see things, but there are often significant discrepancies in terms of how each partner thinks the other sees the relationship. In one study Ryle suggested that accurate prediction of the other partner's grid correlated positively with indices of mental health (1975).

In exploring the construings of couples encountering difficulties, he found that there was a tendency to see their partners in the same terms that they saw their parents. For example, in one couple Ryle found that the wife, Barbara, saw herself in relation to her husband (Ernest) in a similar way to that with her parents. She saw herself as more distrusting and hostile towards her parents and them as more affectionate to her. In other words, she saw herself as more to 'blame' in that she is nastier to her husband than he is to her. However, she saw the relationship between her parents as the opposite of her marriage in that her father was more hostile to her mother. Ernest, on the other hand, saw Barbara as domineering to him and himself as being submissive to her. This is the reverse of the relationship with his parents, who he saw as domineering and himself as hostile to his father.

Ryle suggests that this example demonstrates how the two sets of construings:

Barbara's – confused feelings towards her parents
Ernest's – fears about becoming like or challenging his father

are associated with her dominance and his submissiveness towards her. He suggested that the constructs about themselves in relation to their parents and the constructs about the kind of relationship between their parents were regulating the couple's current relationship with each other. This suggests, as indicated in Chapter 3, that constructs can bridge the experiences we have in the past, the present and our future expectations. Here the constructs from and about the families of origin bridged time to construct the type of relationship the couple had constructed between them.

These studies offer some support for the view that families have shared construct systems and that it is possible to examine the nature and extent of their agreements. What is missing is an account of how the constructional processes are related to how they act as individuals and as parts of the family patterns or 'dance'. In order to explore this question we will look, in the following chapters, at constructs in *action*. We will examine the dialectical process of family life: the way in which the constructions and the social reality of how people act are related and are interdependent.

Chapter 5

Family processes and
constructs: dyads

In the previous chapter we considered how families and other groups of closely involved people can be seen as creating shared construct systems. What we want to look at more closely now is how the dynamics or processes of mutual actions in such groups are related to the constructs employed. A more detailed analysis will be offered here, and continued in the remaining chapters, of the dialectical relationship between processes in couples and families and their construct systems. The focus in this chapter will be on dyads for the following reasons. First, this broadly follows the story line of the family life cycle in that the formation of a couple can be seen as the natural starting point for a family. Second, the core of a family can be seen to be the relationship of the couple, and out of this flows the development of the rest of the family. Having developed some concepts to describe and explain the processes in couples, we can go on to consider to what extent this needs to be extended when considering larger groups.

The concept of the family life cycle will be employed continually as a backcloth to draw our attention to the location of the couple and the family within the wider cultural system. More specifically it helps to reveal the 'tasks' that face a couple, and subsequently a family, in its initial formation, and thereby helps to clarify the relationship between these demands and the construct systems that families evolve to meet them.

Formation of a couple

Jackson (1965b) painted the following scenario as an example of some of the possible interactional ingredients that may go into an initial encounter:

Boy meets girl on their first date. Take any aspect of the many behaviours involved; say, he arrives a little late. Suppose further that she delays her entrance (consciously or not) by exactly the amount of time he kept her waiting. He gets the message that she will not tolerate his keeping her waiting. At the same time, though, he cannot be sure whether this is just her mood tonight, or coincidence, or characteristic of her. If they are exceptional persons, they might discuss this 'interchange', which would be a step towards resolution or change. But, whether they verbalise it or not, real change would require several repetitions of the corrected behaviour. That is, if he were really unavoidably detained the first time, he would have to be on time the next several times to 'prove' this. So suppose they still have this question, undiscussed, and unresolved. In the course of the evening, he decides they should go to a movie, and while she agrees, she picks the movie. He could decide he must treat her as an equal and start practising equality; she responds by treating him equally, that is, she does not overdo it and push him around. Within a few dates, they could have something which could last a lifetime – although of course we cannot prove this. Mate selection must be in large part the matching of certain expected behaviours (and self-definition) in certain crucial areas.

Central to Jackson's picture is the concept of an exchange of information at both explicit and implicit levels. The available literature on empirical studies of relationship formation supports Jackson's idea. Duck (1975) has developed the idea of the growing relationship as a sort of 'filtering process' in which each person is seen to be conducting a series of experiments or explorations in terms of disclosing bits of information about themselves and making similar inquiries about the other person. From these probes they attempt to establish the amount of similarity that there is between them in terms of interests, attitudes and aspirations. The nature of the information sought varies as the relationship develops. At the start of the relationship the information may be fairly general, consisting of disclosures about similar tastes in music, leisure interest and friends. As the couple progress the information searched for may move to more specific issues such as political attitudes, life aspirations, sexual attitudes, expression of emotions and more personal details of each other's life experiences.

In these disclosures we can see in operation the core constructs carried from each person's own family. There will be other influences as well, but their families are where the substantial parts of their sense of identity and attitudes will have been formed. Not infrequently couples may talk specifically about their families. The following example is intended to illustrate the types of disclosures that might be made:

Judy: I have lots of fights with my father. We are very similar, we irritate each other. He always gets so irritating, worries about everything. I suppose it's because he's going blind and expects everyone to feel sorry for him and run around after him. My mother tries to avoid saying things to him, not telling him anything because she knows he will create a fuss. She leaves things until the last moment to tell him anything.

Rick: I never knew my father because my mother and father split up when I was two. But my mother told me that he was an artistic man, an actor. Since we had very little money I had to go to work when I was young so I suppose I didn't really have an adolescence. My mother had some very difficult relationships with men and used to tell me about them. I felt sorry for her but also resented it because I felt it was none of my business, I wanted to get on with my own life.

In these kinds of exchanges, which are a frequent part of the development of intimacy in a couple, it is possible to see not only the transmission of concrete information about each other but also an *exchange of constructs* in terms of the explanations they hold about how they came to be the kind of people that they are. Each of them interprets these outpourings in terms of their *own* construct system. In other words the disclosures undergo a translation, selection, sifting, a form of *editing*. Robin Skynner summarizes the constructs that people bring to a relationship from their previous families:

> each family tends to have a particular way of handling emotions. They'll all tend to think some emotions are 'good' and some 'bad'. So they'll be open about some expressing the 'good' ones and very guarded about expressing the 'bad' ones. Or they may keep a stiff upper lip about emotions in general, or a completely floppy one. The result is that each family develops a characteristic set of emotional attitudes, so that members of that family will share the same emotional habits.
>
> (Skynner and Cleese 1983: 20)

As the relationship develops, these understandings about each other start to regulate the relationship, especially in that each partner may refer to this disclosed information in order to explain or negotiate interactions with the other. As an example, Judy may remind Rick that his emotional outbursts are inappropriate and 'unmanly', he wouldn't act that way if he'd had a proper father figure to model himself upon. Rick, on the other hand, might encourage her to be 'more open' with him and not to try and avoid telling him things until the last minute the way that her mother does with her father.

Through these exchanges the couple start to construct a shared history. The way in which an interaction between them was defined on a previous occasion can form the basis for the definition of the current interaction. In Kelly's terms they are learning to anticipate each other's actions and to anticipate the nature of their relationship. At first they may be largely non-verbal in that they may simply 'look forward to having a good time together'. Over time a shared reality is constructed. Pearce and Cronen

(1980) stress that the meanings constructed for previous events and current ones interact in a recursive loop: a renegotiation of a current definition of the relationship can serve to reconstruct the meaning given to prior events, and in turn the new meaning given to prior events can serve to reconstruct the present events. We will return to a discussion of such loops at the end of this chapter. The important point here is that social constructions are located in time, and the past, present and future actively interact so that the past frames the present and vice versa.

Outside perspectives

It is important to distinguish between talking about couples and families from an 'outside' perspective by using constructs that the families may not themselves be using and an 'inside' perspective where we try to identify how they see events. Couples can be seen to face a variety of 'tasks' in negotiating their relationship, and we can examine these briefly before turning specifically to the patterns of beliefs they hold about their relationship.

Kelly emphasized the importance of a reflexive psychology in which researchers and therapists take care to examine their own premises. He stated that the theory should be as applicable to the personal and professional activities of the psychologist as it is to the people they are studying. Likewise when considering family theories, it has to be borne in mind that the models are constructions and may be more or less useful. There are a number of constructs that family therapists have found useful and that will now be used as the starting point for an analysis of interaction in dyads. It has been argued that a number of dimensions – hierarchy, boundary and intimacy in particular – are fundamental or universal to social groups such as families, and there is some anthropological evidence to lend support to this view (Mead 1949, Bateson 1972, Haley 1976). A brief summary is offered of some of the major terms employed by family therapists and how couples might be involved in negotiations to construct their own definitions of these.

Escalations and process
One of the central tasks facing a couple can be seen to be the need to manage the patterns of escalations likely to occur in their relationship, or how to stop situations running out of hand. Bateson employed ideas from cybernetics to describe and explain processes of progressive escalations of actions in couples. He proposed that if we observe two people together, it is possible to classify their interaction according to whether it is showing a symmetrical or complementary process. Watzlawick *et al.* (1964) describe Bateson's distinction as follows:

> In the first pattern the emphasis lies on attempts to establish and maintain equality. It is, therefore, called symmetrical. (The other

pattern is based on the acceptance and enjoyment of difference. It is referred to as complementarity. . . .) In [this] context . . . the term equality refers to the fact that the partners exchange the same sort of behaviour, or, in other words, they *demand* equality through the message characteristic of their behaviour. In this connection, it is quite irrelevant what precisely they are doing; what does matter is that as A relates to B, so B relates to A. If A offers to give, B also offers to give; if A wants to receive, B also wants to receive. If one occupies a position of strength, so does the other, and if one claims helplessness, so does the other. . . .

In a complementary interaction, on the other hand, people exchange behaviour which together forms the same sort of gestalt as day and night, inside and outside, mountain and valley, etc. What this means is that in a complementary relationship, B's behaviour presupposes A's while at the same time it provides reasons and purposes for A's behaviour and vice versa.

A husband might hold a belief that men should make the decisions in a family and women should obey. If his wife shares this construction she may attempt to be obedient and to do what he says. However, the husband might at the same time find her subservience irritating and therefore become more critical. If the wife interprets this as due to a failing on her part to do things 'properly,' then an escalating cycle of complementarity results. People may have some awareness that they are in some kind of an escalating cycle. In therapeutic encounters it is common to hear people say that they seem to be going round and round in circles, getting nowhere, going over the same ground and that things are getting worse. The exact content underlying these intractional patterns may be unique to some extent. At the same time it is important to remember that couples and families exist in a wider social context involving culturally defined ideologies and structures. As a broad sweep it can be suggested that evidence from a variety of sources – anthropology, social psychology and sociology – indicates that boundary, intimacy and power are fundamental dimensions which couples and families, in fact any social group, need to negotiate. The language they use to describe these issues may be idiosyncratic, and they will to some extent create their own system of meanings to cover these.

Hierarchy and power

Though effective relationships seem to involve the ability and the flexibility to alter roles, this does not invariably or easily happen. Bateson pointed out that such cycles, once established, are remarkably resistant to change. Insight or an awareness in a couple that they are caught in such patterns is usually not sufficient to produce any change. Each person presents the other with cues which can be remarkably powerful in eliciting the behaviour despite their attempts to change it. Above all, Bateson made the important point that such struggles are based on a fundamental belief in unilateral power or control of the other. Problems arise, therefore, as a result of attempts to coerce the other or to exert control over them 'whether they like it or not'. Furthermore, he argued that such a belief represents a 'faulty epistemology' in that in any social system it is actually impossible to exert total power without destroying it. Examples of such attempts are child abuse, domestic violence, and other coercive tactics in relationships such as threats, moral blackmail, ultimatums and so on. Just as in biological systems change to any one part has a reciprocal effect in the long term, so too in the long term such unilateral action has an effect in reducing the quality of the relationship. A brutalized wife may appear to 'give in' and do as she is told, but she will not provide any genuine affection or love which her partner may be mistakenly trying to coerce out of her.

There may of course be real differences in resources and the level of power between partners, but the effects that these have on the relationship are, in part, influenced by the constraints that they come to attach to them. In one couple an imbalance of power may lead the subordinate partner to demand and struggle for more power, whereas in another to an acceptance of their position. The constraints they hold will guide how the couple will act towards each other and serve to construct the patterns of interaction that emerge. Watzlawick (1964) uses the construct of 'Up-down' to cover the interactional processes concerning power.

> These positions have variously been described as primary, superior or 'one-up' on the one hand, and secondary, inferior or 'one-down' on the other. . . . They shall be used here with this understanding; primary, superior or 'one-up' refer to the position of that partner in a *complementary* relationship who defines the nature of this relationship, while secondary, inferior or 'one-down' refer to the other partner who accepts and goes along with this definition. As can be seen, this has nothing to do with the respective strength or weakness of the partners per se. Indeed, one partner's weakness can easily be the very element by which he defines the relationship as one in which the other is to protect him.
>
> (Watzlawick 1964: 8)

In contrast, in a *symmetrical* pattern of interaction both of the participants act in similar ways, with both of them competing for the 'up' position, as is seen in arguments or escalations to violence. Alternatively they may compete for the most 'down' position, such as which of them is most ill or had the worst childhood experiences and so on.

A clear example of the two interactional patterns is in the area of conflict and violence. In a symmetrical quarrel, the two participants are likely to mirror each other in body posture, to accuse and blame each other. In a complementary quarrel, one may accuse the other, who responds with passivity, inciting the first to further accusations. And, of course, such patterns of escalation may also be found in more positive examples of interactions, such as friendship formation, falling in love and mutually escalating sexual pleasure.

Boundary

A sense of separation or *boundary* is a central construct in both systems theory and psychodynamic theory (Klein 1932, Fairbairn 1952), where it is suggested that the young child is faced with the task of developing a separate identity and emotional separation from its mother. Existentialist therapists (Laing 1969, Whitaker 1958) have stressed the importance of the development of a sense of self-identity, an awareness of existing as a separate, autonomous being in the world distinct from the parents. In the family therapy literature the concept has been extended by Minuchin (1974) to include the idea of separateness of functioning not just of individuals but of subsystems within the family, such as the extent to which the parents are able to function as an autonomous decision-making, executive unit. With a young couple the issue is often to do with how they develop roles to regulate the extent to which friends, relatives and others enter into their lives, especially how clearly they are able to have their own time together to make decisions and develop their relationship.

Intimacy

Related to the above dimensions, couples and families can be seen as engaged in negotiations about how *intimate* they can or wish to be at different times. At the courtship phase they may wish to spend lots of time together, but inevitably there will be demands on them to separate and engage in work, education and separate leisure activities. They will need to negotiate how close or distant they will be at different times. If they show 'too much' intimacy, they may start to feel stifled or overwhelmed. Alternatively, if there is a threat of too much distance or time apart, then they may feel abandoned and left out in the cold. Byng-Hall (1980) suggests that one of the functions of a symptom displayed by one or the other partner may be to regulate the level of intimacy in the couple. An example may be the bedtime headache which can be employed to avoid unwanted sexual contact. For many couples the issue of separateness versus togetherness is one of the major early hurdles to be resolved in their relationship. It can be extremely difficult even to raise this issue without the other partner feeling rejected, and couples may attempt to negotiate this covertly by making excuses to be away at work and other family commitments.

Symmetrical and complementary patterns offer a pretty bleak picture of the processes in couples. So we need to consider two questions further:

1 What mechanisms operate to regulate these escalating cycles?
2 What beliefs underlie these escalations – what patterns of mutually interlocking constructs are serving to maintain them?

Regarding the first point Bateson suggested that the two patterns alternate so that a period of complementarity would be terminated by an 'enough' marker such as a rebellious outburst or fighting back (symmetrical). Likewise excessive symmetry could be terminated by initially one partner adopting a 'down' position such as turning to tears or show a debilitating symptom of some sort (complementary). The transformation from one pattern to the other might be quite rapid, as when a young boy being bullied by his sister might suddenly flare up and attack her or when, after a period of confrontation, one person might back down and apologize. A number of other variations are possible; even though a relationship may continue in a symmetrical or complementary form, the *meaning* or definition of the behaviour may change. For example, dominance in one context may shift to being regarded as caring protectiveness in another. There may also be changes brought about by accidents of various sorts, such as the dominant partner falling ill and having to be looked after by the other. The relationship may revert on recovery but, alternatively, in some cases it is possible that a discovery is made of how pleasant it can be to be 'looked after' and mothered/fathered.

Couples have the ability to negotiate these issues, and in some couples there can be a reversal of the relationship according to areas of expertise. A typical example is that of the woman taking charge and being in a complementary relationship to her partner with the household and children, and the reverse with practical matters such as repairing the house and the car. In areas which are more neutral to them such as gardening or discussing their social life, they may be involved in a symmetrical relationship.

Escalation and sexuality

Bateson did not attempt to spell out fully how couples can achieve a balanced form of relationship, and there can be relationships where there is a pronounced and long-term imbalance towards one or the other form. However, he offered an important link with psychodynamic theory in the suggestion that escalating processes in relationships resemble the escalation involved in sexual intimacy leading to orgasm, and that, in turn, orgasm can serve to provide a natural release of escalating processes:

> Indeed, all that we know about human beings in various sorts of simple contests would seem to indicate . . . that the conscious or unconscious wish for release of this kind is an important factor which draws the participants on and prevents them from simply withdrawing from contests which would otherwise not commend them to 'common sense'. If there be any basic human characteristic which makes men prone to struggle, it would seem to be this hope of release from tension through total involvement. In the case of war this factor is undoubtedly often important . . . the obvious relationship of these interactive phenomena to climax and orgasm very much strengthens the case for regarding schismogenesis and those cumulative sequences of interaction which lead to love as often psychologically equivalent.
> (Bateson 1972: 111)

It is questionable whether mutual orgasm can be seen to be a *sine qua non* or sufficient in itself to defuse escalating processes in relationships. A wide range of social constructions influence the form and experience of sexuality.

An interesting variation is found in Bateson's (1972) account of Balinese culture, which is imbued with an ethos of balance and where escalative relationships were discouraged at all levels of society:

> In general the lack of climax is characteristic for Balinese music, drama, and other art forms. The music typically has a progression, derived from the logic of its formal structure, and modifications of intensity determined by the duration and progress of the working out of these formal relations. It does not have the sort of rising intensity and climax structure characteristic of modern Occidental music, but rather a formal progression.
>
> (113)

The suggestion is made that Western cultures generally are imbued with an ethos of symmetrical escalation: the shoot out, mutual arguments in couples and, of course, the mutual symmetrical sexual climax. Balinese culture, he argued, emphasizes balance, and he noted that children were discouraged from seeking climax-like escalations in personal relations. He had less to say about sexual behaviour itself, but it is possible that there was less concern with orgasm, perhaps in a similar way to the Indian Tantric Buddhists, who believed in the prolongation of the sexual act to maintain a state of ecstacy.

Sexuality is a primary issue for couples and families, and a range of constructs are generated which regulate sexuality and may in turn interfere with the potentially stablizing release of orgasm. A variety of construction processes both at the interpersonal and the societal level operate to regulate sexuality:

1 One partner may be construed as more 'experienced' and as taking charge of sex in some way.
2 One partner may reach orgasm first, and this may be construed as a sign of weakness or dependence in some way.
3 There may be a negotiated equality to assist each other to reach orgasm in a vareity of ways without necessarily insisting on mutual orgasm.
4 A whole range of social and cultural mores may operate which prescribe how the act should be performed and whether partners are allowed to experience or demonstrate enjoyment.

(Mead 1949)

It is possible to regard sex in relationships as potentially offering a natural force to promote the release of escalating cycles. However, sexuality and psychological issues in couples are reciprocally related, so that a range of relationship issues inevitably underlie 'sexual problems' and vice versa. It is not clear whether Bateson thought that sexual relationships were characteristically complementary. He suggests that this is the case in his description of the Iatmul where the men were characteristically aggressive and the women were expected to be passive sexually. The form of sexuality can be seen to fit more broadly within the organization of any given culture. Again in the Iatmul Bateson describes how two patterns – rigid complementarity between men and women and symmetrical conflict and competitiveness between men – existed side by side. Sexual release between men and women was not enough to accommodate the symmetrical escalations between the men or the complementary escalations between the men and the women. The Naven and other ceremonies were seen to be required in addition to defuse these potentially destructive tensions within the society.

Bateson appears to suggest complementarity is the fundamental form of sexuality. This is based on the anatomical differences between the sexual organs, giving rise to the idea of female accommodation versus male intrusion. However, it must be the case that whatever the form of sexual etiquette or cultural niceties expected, the act is characterized by symmetrical mutual excitation. It is arguable, therefore, that this fact forms the physiological basis of reciprocity in relationships even if a couple are 'playing' at complementarity. Linked to this escalating excitation is the idea of eventual loss of control and diffusion of identity with the sexual partner. However temporary, this loss of control at the moment of orgasm represents a change of form of the relationship.

It would be wrong simply to conclude from this discussion that sexual orgasm is enough to ensure that escalating tensions in a relationship will be released as a consequence. Not only is sexuality located in a set of definitions within the relationship, but, as Foucault (1979) has pointed out, a variety of concepts or 'discourses' regarding sexuality can be found at different periods of history. He cites as an example 'child molesting' as a relatively recent 'discourse', whereas previously in many societies it was seen as acceptable for various members of the family to touch parts of a child's body, even the genitals (see also Mead 1949).

It may also be argued that the expectation of mutual orgasm is likewise a cultural construct. Many couples who attend for sexual therapy appear to be caught up in a set of expectations about what is 'normal', especially the striving for mutual orgasm. A wide range of 'discourses,' including manuals on how to have more satisfying sex, are recent developments which have elevated the level of conscious contemplation regarding sexuality.

Inside perspectives

The concept of escalation gives a picture of how couples engage in predictable patterns of joint actions. We can now look further at some possible ways of explaining, from the 'inside', how the beliefs they hold serve to maintain these escalating cycles.

Watzlawick (1964) suggested that it is possible for a couple to be involved in *meta-complementary* relationships so that one allows the other to be one-up or dominant in some area. This is a vital point which again illustrates that people are involved in forming explanations about each other's actions and intentions and making *choices* based upon them. A partner who is allowing the other to be dominant in some way is making a choice.

Assuming that this is not based on coercion or abuse, (in which case it is not a choice in any real sense), then the couple is basically in a symmetrical or equal relationship with a tacit contract between them that their mutual interests are best served by agreeing to differ in this way.

This agreeing to take different roles appears to be an essential feature of the successful management of relationships. We can see that meta-complementarity may be one of the key ingredients in how couples negotiate sexuality and other areas of intimacy. It could be argued that until recently this was the expected structure of male–female relationships in Western societies, with women expected to show submissive qualities and men dominant ones in their relationship and especially in their sexual contact. Meta-complementarity then introduces the core idea of choice in relationships. Partners do not simply find themselves to be in a particular form of relationship, but have the potential of choosing to accommodate to certain forms in a tactical way. Of course there are cases where one partner may feel coerced into a complementary, one-down or abused position, but this form seems to be related almost inevitably with an unsatisfactory relationship, not only for the one in the one-down position but for the dominant partner as well (Dicks 1967, Crowe 1987).

Striving for agreement

From the outside we can notice similarities and differences between a couple and make inferences about how we think they complement each other or otherwise. This is an everyday activity that people other than therapists also engage in, as in gossip about the extent to which a couple appear to have different personalities and the extent to which they 'suit' each other. We may engage in such comparisons in therapy when we implicitly draw contrasts between the couple we are working with and our own relationship and other couples that we have had contact with.

A second point is that we can see, still from the outside, that couple themselves are engaged in this process of drawing out similarities and differences. A frequent striking example is when the parents start to impute characteristics on to a new-born child. They may remark that the child looks more like the mother than the father, that he has father's eyes or mother's mouth. Grandparents, who have the benefit of a broader perspective on the family, typically make comparisons such as that their granddaughter is the 'spitting image' of her auntie when she was a child. These physical characteristics may form the basis of the core constructs that will come to be employed to describe the child and may in turn later come to be internalized by him. They also serve to embrace a new child within the family history, to give a sense of belonging.

The process of a couple getting to know each other entails them establishing agreement and common ways of seeing events. But, of course, this is too simple a picture. Couples may openly disagree on a variety of issues and, most importantly, may disagree in areas where they think they are in agreement. Watzlawick refers to tendencies in families or couples to engage in 'mind-reading' or one partner assuming that they 'know' what the other thinks. We can see from Kelly's theory that such anticipations are necessary and, second, that couples do strive for agreement or consistency in order to 'validate' their constructs. Predating Kelly's ideas Festinger (1954) and Heider (1946) proposed that we have a *need* for consistency and agreement. Heider argued that inconsistency in one's belief systems is unpleasant and anxiety provoking. Developing this proposition Festinger suggested that a major source of information we use for testing our beliefs is other people. He proposed that we have a drive to evaluate our opinions and abilities and that we use other people in order to do this as long as they do not appear too different or 'strange' to us. In addition we tend to attempt to reduce differences of opinions in groups that we are involved in.

To take an example of a couple, John may feel that he doesn't like Mary's friend Peter. This potentially poses a situation of dissonance for him because he likes Mary but dislikes someone she likes: 'How can she like an idiot like that, etc.?' Heider explained such situations in terms of a theory of balance in the attitudes that two people have towards a third object or person:

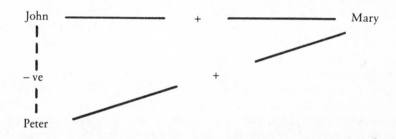

In our example we can see some dissonance which functions to exert some pressure for either a cognitive or a structural change to the relationship. Some possibilities are that John persuades Mary not to like Peter by pointing out his negative qualities, that he is mean, talks about her behind her back, etc. He may even force a structural showdown saying that he feels jealous and doesn't want her to associate with him or he will get angry, or even leave. Alternatively, Mary might try to persuade John to like Peter by attempting to increase his attractiveness to John such as that he likes and respects John. She might also attempt to reduce what she believes to be his negative attributes for John such as claiming that she finds him nice but unattractive.

This analysis goes some way towards introducing the idea that the interplay of beliefs/constructs regulates the actions of the couples. It is important to note that this regulation does not take place in a vacuum but in different social contexts. It is possible that one of the parents may mention that they don't think it is appropriate for Mary to be 'flirtatious' with Peter and that John and she need to spend more time together. It may also occur that one parent subtly encourages this liaison by pointing out that Peter is good looking, etc. Such messages are likely to be delivered to one of the couple. It allows us to see the intrusion of higher order social contexts – in the first instance the family system and, second, the wider cultural situation. The messages from the parents may involve reference to 'accepted' social norms and conventions such as that couples contemplating marriage engage in a process of drawing a boundary around themselves. This requires a negotiation of rules about the choice of friends and the access that friends have to each of them. Minuchin gives some interesting examples of social norms operating in a kibbutz where the youngsters are discouraged from coupling up 'too much' and ignoring the rest of the kibbutz members, as opposed to Western societies where this is encouraged.

Meta-constructs: demands, expectations and actions

The point has been made repeatedly so far that behaviour and constructs are interdependent. It is an error, therefore, to argue that one or the other is dominant or causes the other to occur. The work of Heyman and Shaw (1976) illustrates one approach to exploring the idea of mutually interlocking patterns of demands, expectations and actions in couples. They suggest that participants' interpretations of a relationship both influence and are influenced by the social interaction itself. A theory of social relationships should not seek to define the 'essential' nature, as exchanges or reciprocal obligations for example, but should seek to describe the typical ways in which the actors themselves define their relationship. They argue that many relationship problems and struggles are based upon meta-constructs about how each person regards the relationship. They propose that people employ four main types of constructs or relationship, arguing first, that there may be a limited number of possibilities that are culturally defined as acceptable (this is similar to Pearce and Cronen's (1980) and Harre and Secord's (1972) propositions about Type 1 episodes). Second, they point out that employing a limited number allows generalizations to be made. Last, they propose the interesting analogy from Chomsky (1968) who suggests that from a limited set of language rules, it is possible to generate an infinite number of novel sentences. Likewise, they argue, from a limited set of relationship constructs it may be possible to generate a wide range of construings in relationships, especially when we add meta-constructs or how each person construes the other's constructs. Furthermore, if we add more participants, then the possibilities – even with four basic constructs of relationships – start to expand dramatically.

Their four types of constructs of relationships are briefly as follows:

1 Reciprocity – I have a right to make demands of her and she has a right to make demands of me.
2 Egocentrism – my needs come first.
3 Altercentrism – my duty is to take care of the other, put them first.
4 Exchange – relationships are based on bartering/economics, and you both have a right to get as much as you can out of it.

They base their selection of the constructs in the body of literature from social psychology and Laing's existentialist views regarding self-identity and security. The egocentric and altercentric positions are seen as relating to issues of separateness, similar to Minuchin's concept of boundaries. The egocentric position involves a separateness whereby the rights and feelings of others are denied. The altercentric construct, on the other hand, represents an enmeshment or lack of differentiation of one's own needs from the others. Reciprocity and exchange are associated with a more 'secure' position and an acceptance of the other and the self. They go on to argue that relationships are constrained to these typologies due to the effect of social/cultural factors. They regard their typologies as meta-constructs which are shared at a cultural level.

An interesting part of the scheme concerns the style of the relationship. Each partner may have a preferred construct of the relationship, and they may or may not agree about each other's perspectives:

- *Exchange* – I will do the washing up if you will put the kids to bed.
- *Egocentricism* – I want to develop my career, I think she does too – it's too bad if we don't have much time for each other.
- *Reciprocity* – we both have rights, relationships are based on give and take, sometimes I may be doing more, sometimes she will.
- *Altercentrism* – I just want her to be happy, it doesn't matter about me, and she probably feels the same way.

The following interaction between a couple illustrates the constructs in operation. The woman had experienced sexual abuse by her father in childhood and was unable to enjoy any physical and sexual intimacy with her husband.

Lucy: I was mad about him when we met. I would do anything he wanted. I didn't think about myself at all.

Mike: I'd had lots of girlfriends you know. I didn't care, I would just get them into bed as quickly as possible. Mostly it would just be one night stands. . . . I didn't really love Lucy at first, but she was different to the others. She was a bit different, took a bit longer, not much longer . . . to seduce her.

Lucy: I knew he'd had lots of girlfriends. He was always telling me about them. But I didn't really mind. I'd have done anything for him. I was really in love with him, you see.

Mike: Well, I told Lucy it wouldn't be a rose garden with me.

Lucy: Yes, it was my own fault, I was told...

We can see here a fairly pronounced example of a relationship based around egocentricism–altercentrism. Lucy regarded herself as something of a doormat for Mike. She did not consider her own needs except in terms of trying to please him, and for his part Mike starts off making it clear that he does not care as much for her as she does for him. He also made it fairly clear that he would use her rather than put her needs first or near equal to his.

Inaccuracies in meta-perspectives

Frequently problems in couples reside around misconceptions of each other's perspectives. The partners may have different preferred perspectives and may not initially realize this. For example, one partner may think that his wife should look after him and help him with his career (egocentric) whereas she may think that they should both have careers and he should help her as well (reciprocal):

> Our analysis suggests that the actor construes a relationship in terms of exchange, reciprocity, egocentricism or altercentrism. But since each party defines their interaction in terms of one of the constructs each may consider not only how he construes the relationship, but how the other construes it, and how the other's construct relates to his own construct.
>
> (Heyman and Shaw 1978: 245)

Some examples are offered of *misplaced* differences in perspective where the couple actually do share the same perspective but misinterpret the other's, for example where they both want a relationship based upon reciprocity but see the other as wanting an egocentric relationship.

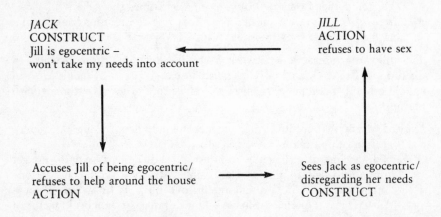

JACK
CONSTRUCT
Jill is egocentric –
won't take my needs into account

JILL
ACTION
refuses to have sex

Accuses Jill of being egocentric/
refuses to help around the house
ACTION

Sees Jack as egocentric/
disregarding her needs
CONSTRUCT

Heyman and Shaw's analysis shows some similarities with Bateson's framework of complementarity and symmetry, in that egocentric and altercentric constructs reflect a complementary up/down relationship, whereas exchange and reciprocity relate to an up/up or down/down symmetrical relationship. Heyman and Shaw conclude that it is important to regard these preferred relationship constructs as part of a dynamic negotiational process. Each partner is likely to generate constructs about the other's preferred position, and these are susceptible to revision as the relationship progresses. Furthermore, the constructs may be revised in the face of specific issues.

Hierarchies of meaning, contexts and loops

An analysis of meta-perspectives is complemented by a consideration of levels of meaning. Each person can be seen to be operating at several levels of meaning: their own construct, their perspective of the other's construct, and their idea of how they think the other person imagines their construct. The work of Pearce and Cronen (1980) emphasizes that at any particular point of time a communication derives its meaning not only from the content of the communication, but also from the context which it is uttered in. In turn, the context is defined by the previous history of the relationship. From the history of their previous interactions a couple have available a repertoire of memories embodying a set of constructs which they employ to anticipate present and future interactions between them. The anticipations about the future may be extremely important, for example a wife may anticipate that her husband will make sexual demands irrespective of her feelings. Her anticipation may set up a self-fulfilling prophecy whereby she responds in a cold and wary way to any signs of overtures of affection from him. Over time they are both likely to anticipate this kind of interaction. Attempts to behave differently or to suggest a different definition of each other's behaviour may be restricted by this context. On the other hand, a warm, more positive context can also serve to disguise or allow a degree of tolerance of certain actions. The following provides a brief illustration:

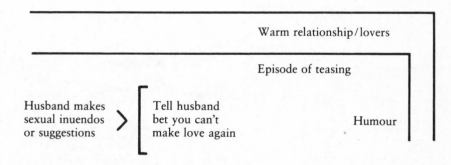

This model represents an elaboration of Bateson's and Watzlawick's concepts of hierarchically ordered levels of meaning. This was discussed earlier in the proposition that any communication can carry several layers of meanings. At any given time one level may be superordinate and provide a context for interpreting the other levels. This idea of contexts as giving meaning to communication is central to Pearce and Cronen's model. They suggested that a communication can be seen as giving meanings at various levels. For example, the remark by the wife above may be seen as an act of teasing in terms of its form—sentence construction and non-verbal cues. This interpretation is made by an interplay of meanings given by the existing definition of the relationship based on a history of experience together. It is also based upon a higher cultural level, such as 'it is good to have a sense of

humour in relationships.' Alternatively in the context of a history of
repeated arguments and cutting remarks, the communication may be
regarded as cruel and deliberately hurtful.

Within the context of a warm relationship, the woman's comments
doubting the man's virility can be construed as implying humour within an
episode of teasing. This adds to the previous analysis and demonstrates how
an overriding preferred construct of the relationship forms a context within
which specific events are given meanings. This view is sympathetic with
Kelly's organization corollary and also with the concept of laddering
developed by Hinkle. Change in a higher order construct has a significant
effect on the lower constructs that are employed to interpret specific events.
As an example we can look at a couple such as the above who are having
difficulties and are both making threats to split up (see Figure 6).

Figure 6 Example of a hierarchy of beliefs held by a family

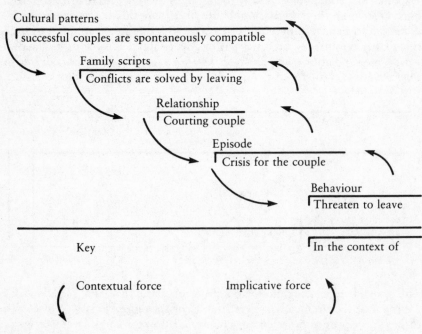

This suggests that any behaviour needs to be understood in the context of
an ascending series of levels. In this example the behaviour of threatening to
leave is to be seen in the context of an episode of 'crisis' in the couple or a
sense that they cannot cope. In turn this episode represents an example of a
relationship conflict. More generally, for this couple there is a family script
based upon previous experiences of relationships and traditions handed on

through their families of origin that conflicts are to be solved by splitting up (both of them come from divorced families). In turn this draws from a wider cultural belief that successful couples are spontaneously compatible, which implies that conflict indicates lack of compatibility and therefore they might as well give up now because it will never work in the long run.

Pearce and Cronen (1980) make the point that there is also an implicative influence from the lower to the higher levels. The previous experience and the current experience of dealing with the situation provide evidence for future decisions. If a family can be persuaded to attempt a different solution, such as that of the parents agreeing to form and uphold some rules of acceptable behaviour for the child, then this can serve to alter the family script. They may come to accept that conflicts can be solved in other ways than attempting to expel one member. Eventually the new solutions attempted in the present can become the context for behaviour in the future.

Strange loops and double-binds

Bateson (1972) and Watzlawick *et al.* (1967) suggested in their theory of double-binds that reflexive loops are generally problematic. This is based on the idea that problems occur when a class of events is employed in such a way as to be included in its own class. Two examples are given below. The first is a statement about a class of statements, all statements in this box. Confusion arises because it also includes itself in the generalization, so that in order to be true it has to be false. Here both levels of meaning are contained in the verbal mode. The second example is much more common, showing a contradiction between the verbal and non-verbal levels of a message. The verbal can supply the context for the non-verbal part and vice versa, but each falsifies the other.

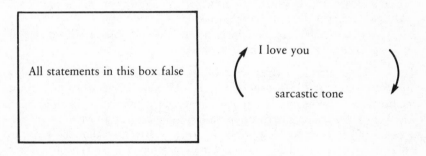

Some authors (Cronen *et al.* 1982, Milton Erickson in Rossi 1980, Bateson 1972) have argued that double-binds need not be harmful but can in fact serve a beneficial and creative function. Examples can be found in humour and game playing of various sorts. I came across one instance which was used by a member of a theatre group attempting to tease the audience into some participation. One of the actors turned to the audience and said, 'Hands up all of you who don't want to participate'. The criterion of whether a double-bind is creative or destructive is whether the underlying context is a positive or negative one. Bateson (1972) emphasized in the early formulations that not only was there a contradiction at the levels of a communication, but there was also an injunction not to leave the relationship enforceable by punishments of various sorts. In order to understand whether a communication operates as a double-bind, it is necessary to know something about the context of the relationship in terms of what has gone on previously and how the participants see each other. Such an analysis of the underlying contexts was lacking in most of the research which attempted to examine double-binds. For example, some researchers (Olson 1972) studied the letters of schizophrenics written to their mothers and used independent raters to assess whether the letters contained more double-binds than letters of normal people. This ignores the significance of the context of the relationship in providing a frame within which messages can be interpreted:

> To know whether a reflexive loop exists, we must have knowledge of contexts not always available or explicit in texts. In part this requires a new research methodology, namely participant observation and idiographic methods which try to access the construct systems of the people in a relationship.
>
> (Cronen *et al*. 1982)

Pearce and Cronen argue that confusing and ambiguous communications exist partly as an effect of a loop in the levels of meaning. For example, a problematic form of reflexivity can exist when a confusing communication, such as 'I do still love you', can serve to define the context as follows:

1 For a relationship defined as good, it can imply that there was some doubt so that it defines the relationship as in doubt.
2 Alternatively if the relationship is seen as bad, this communication can be taken to suggest that it is now better.

The form or structure of the communication gives it an immediate meaning, but at the same time it has superimposed upon it the overall context of the relationship. This is similar to the debates in cognitive psychology as to whether perception is a bottom-up process – built up from small features of a visual object – or whether it is top-down – driven so that the situation offers an overall context within which meanings are given to objects (Neisser 1967). Problems appear to occur when the two parts of the process give contradictory messages. The confusion is fuelled both by the ambiguous nature of the message *itself* and by a history of doubt in the relationship. The partners may not be sure how things are between them and search for meanings in each and every communication to help them. Since all communications are potentially contradictory, though some less so than others, this can become a self-fulfilling endeavour. This offers an operational definition of insecurity: an insecure person (B) is one who has had a history of negative or contradictory experiences and is unable to come to consistent agreement in himself about what any given communication means. This leads to interpersonal problems which serve to fuel his insecurity and inability to decode communications. One outcome may be a depressive state wherein *all* communications are decoded as implying rejection and negativity.

We can see below how a loop can be 'sealed off' at different points. In case A a loop can occur between the definition of the relationship and the particular episode: is this a message of love or contempt, and is our relationship growing or deteriorating? However, the loop need not reverberate at higher levels if the person has had a substantial body of self-confirming, confidence-building experiences prior to this relationship. On the other hand, in case B the loop may reverberate upwards so that this episode and this relationship are taken as evidence that he is a worthless, unlovable person. This is likely because he already has an ambivalent sense of self and this episode can 'tip the balance'. He may frantically attempt, therefore, to extract some validation from this relationship. The loop may reverberate even further in stirring up feelings about the nature of what relationships are like in general.

Figure 7 Sealed (A) vesus open (B) loops

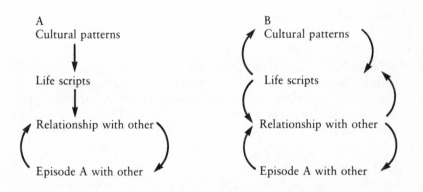

All relationships must be located in time and the definitions of the relationship gradually evolve. So, any given communication at a point in time is both defining the relationship – either to confirm or disconfirm the existing definitions – and defined by the existing context or definition of the relationship. The lower level meaning or communicative act will not inevitably alter the higher level contexts. Life scripts are the characteristic ways that an individual has learned of interpreting events. A reasonable correspondence between these and cultural patterns means that he has some reference point of base upon which to interpret his current interaction. If, however, a person has had experience of confusing or contradictory situations, as Bateson suggested in his theory of double-binds, then he may have no such stable vantage point. As a result he may experience great confusion in any potentially contradictory situations or may even see what to others are fairly unambiguous situations in confusing ways:

> Schizophrenia may be produced because the individual possesses no stable point of focus from which the 'I' in Mead's terms can consider that pattern of interpretations and actions that constitute 'me'. The self may become entangled in a web of shifting perspectives. Bateson has pointed out that if a double-bind can be worked through and pathologically warded off, the experience can promote creativity. Here we offer the speculation that the ability to work through a double-bind depends upon having some stable vantage point from which to operate upon it.
>
> (Cronen *et al.* 1982: 107)

This proposal offers some interesting perspectives on not only schizophrenia but also the general difficulties found by all of us in relationships. And it suggests how a pattern of insecurity can operate in a relationship whereby the person is frequently insecure about what the relationship means and hence what any particular action means. Cronen and his colleagues differentiate these recursively interlocking loops of meanings into 'strange and charmed loops'. A loop may not necessarily be problematic as in the example above. They argue that social interaction involves the creation of meanings and this will necessarily entail some ambiguities or loops. They criticize double-bind theory on the grounds that it assumes

> communication must provide clear accounts for an external untangled reality. The new view is that communication is *not* best conceived of as a vehicle for picturing external reality and conveying undistorted pictures from one person to another. The modern view is that communication is the process by which persons *create* social realities.
>
> (Cronen *et al.* 1982: 95)

Tolerance and permeability

In order to deal with fluctuations from the basic definition of the relationship, the couples' constructs may need to have a degree of slack or tolerance. Kelly's terms for this were looseness and permeability. An overly rigid construct system would ignore any inconsistent communication so that the other partner felt misunderstood or ignored. Alternatively, any deviation would be interpreted as a total threat to the relationship. On the other hand, too much tolerance or looseness would not permit the relationship to be renegotiated and develop as required by various external and internal demands. From this it follows that the kind of constructs we would expect in functional relationships show a tolerance to changes in the behaviour of both partners and to external factors. There is evidence to support this view: Constructs such as 'she's just feeling a bit down today,' 'you've got to have a bit of give and take,' 'things don't always run smoothly' or 'you've got to allow each other a bit of rope,' embody the capacity to tolerate behaviour/communication in the relationship. They could be said to embody a *realistic* view of the relationship, rather than an expectation that things should always be good.

Over a period of time the repeated encounters and communications in a couple or a family serve to build up a set of beliefs and expectations about each other and their relationships. A 'few' negative remarks can be handled within some tolerant frameworks such as 'he is just a bit down today'. However, if the incidents of negativity continue to increase or become dominantly negative (a form of experiential level of statistical significance), the definition of the relationship may undergo a radical shift – 'he is dissatisfied,' 'we are on the rocks.' A new overall frame may emerge.

From the history of the relationship the couple have available a set of memories of incidents between them which can be marshalled to reinforce their constructs or to enter into discussions or arguments when either of them attempts to offer some new definitions. An example of this selective sampling of the joint history in a couple is given below. The woman complained that her husband had on several occasions hit her in a moment of rage. She had become so upset at these incidents that, following the last occurrence of violence, she had left with their children and gone to a refuge for 'battered' women. She was referred to a social worker who made contact with her husband, and the couple agreed to attend for some marital therapy. The following is an extract from the first session with them.

Wife: You are always violent, throwing things, breaking that pot the other day.
Man: I just dropped it. . . .
Wife: No, you didn't, you threw it at me.
Man: No, I didn't mean to . . . (getting angrier, clenching fists and body) It just broke in my hand. . . .
Wife: (To therapist) He can't control his temper. . . . He's all right for a while and then he gets violent again and in one second it's all spoilt. . . . I'm worried all the time that he will lose his rag and will start again. . . . I sometimes feel sorry for him because he had such a bad childhood, but I can't stand his moods and temper. . . . I never know when he is going to explode.
Man: This is all I hear. . . . I might as well go . . . (getting angrier) the trouble is you've got too much mouth. . . .

In this extract we can see a 'struggle' over the definition of a piece of behaviour. Central to this disagreement is a definition of the 'intent' behind the incident of the broken pot. Embodied in the wife's statements are causal attributions in terms of temperament – 'he is just like that' – childhood deprivation and learning, and perhaps that he is deliberately being cruel to her. Each of them is attempting to promote and defend their causal explanations or hypotheses about their relationship. The husband repeatedly attempted to make excuses for his behaviour or to deny that he was angry. Eventually when he does appear to accept his wife's definition that he was angry, he accordingly started to demonstrate his anger in the session. The interaction represents a form of self-fulfilling prophecy in that their constructs about each other were serving to maintain a form of interaction which generated considerable anger between them.

Editing history

In the formation of a relationship it is possible to see a process involving the *editing* of past events which are the shared reservoir of memories that constitute history of a couple. This history can form the basis and content of many relationship struggles and conflicts. Couples typically disclose some significant information about themselves at the start of their relationship, and continue to disclose more as the relationship develops and they come to trust each other more. This can be seen as exchange of each other's construct systems in that they exchange their views about themselves, joint friends, relations and more generally how they see the world. For example, a young man might recount a range of bad experiences that he has experienced in his childhood and relationships with women in a pessimistic tone. This indicates that he generally sees the world in this way and maybe implicitly that he expects their relationship might also become a source of pain to him. Each person translates that they are hearing into their own construct system. This process can be seen as a sort of *editing*. Later on in their relationship the couple may at times remind each other by presenting the stories back in an edited version to suit or support their argument.

An example of this process and the influence of beliefs derived from past events is shown in the case of Mr and Mrs Button, who attended for therapy complaining of a lack of sexual responsiveness on Mrs Button's part. As a part of the intitial assessment they were asked what initially drew them together and what they remembered telling each other.

Mrs Button described how Mr Button had rapidly informed her that he had been promiscuous and that he had been extremely successful sexually with women. One evening he had even given her a shoebox full of letters from his ex-girlfriends to read for 'entertainment' because she looked bored. He had also told her that his mother had been distant from him and he had been brought up by his grandmother. He had also said that the men in his family were expected to be 'hard' (his body was covered in tattoos to demonstrate his hardness to the rest of his family and others).

Mr Button remembered his wife telling him that as a young girl she had been repeatedly sexually abused by her father and that the case had eventually come to court and she had been separated from her family. She had had some previous boyfriends but she had told him that she had not enjoyed sex with any of them.

This example is intended to illustrate how current events are interpreted within the framework or context of the past. We can start to see here how the reality that is being created by this couple imports memories of past events before they had met. These are given meaning and edited in various ways, and come to play a continuing role in ascribing meaning to current events. At the same time the current interpretations and behaviour serve to confirm these previous interpretations or the overall frame. With this couple the explanation of the wife's sexual unresponsiveness was fixed in a very compelling explanation that she was like this because of her experience of abuse in childhood. Unfortunately, this igored the reality of the current relationship, especially the pattern of sexual abuse that had developed between the couple. The husband demanded frequent sex even if the woman did not enjoy it, and even when she felt ill she still regarded it as her duty to comply. Furthermore, the husband's story of his early sexual prowess served to avoid any exploration of his sexual technique and sensitivity to his wife.

Layered on top of this there are also themes about the nature of the male–female relationship in our culture and the nature of these relationships in the family history of both sets of parents. We can see cultural scripts emerging here in the form of explanations such as psychological theories of sexuality and the long term effects of abuse. Mr Button made statements like 'I was terrible then, didn't care about how I treated them . . . but we were all like that weren't we?', which recognized that male ideas about sexuality and attitudes to women had changed since his adolescence. Likewise it is a widely accepted wisdom that early sexual abuse does have a long-term damaging effect. However, both these explanations looked to the past and served to avoid looking at the current processes in their relationship.

In the next chapter the analysis of couples will be developed by examining triads. In a sense this also follows the development of thinking in family therapy, which grew out of a recognition that an understanding of dyads could be clarified by considering their functioning in the context of the dynamics of triads. Incidentally this is sympathetic to Kelly's proposal that the triad is the fundamental structure of cognition, the idea that three elements are necessary to enable a bipolar discrimination to be made. Furthermore we can suggest that a triad is the fundamental structural unit of the family. Both psychodynamic and systems theory agree on this point. At the same time it is important to note that couples are not simply reducible to triads, or to the summation of the individuals. The analyses of couples and triads complement each other, and it is surprising therefore to note that in fact two quite separate therapies appear to have evolved. On the one hand, marital and couples therapy often appears to take very little note of the wider systems involved and triadic relations, and on the other, family therapy sometimes seems to ignore the need to work with the dynamics of a couple.

Chapter 6

Family dynamics, patterns and family beliefs

The *triad* can be seen to be the fundamental building block of family life. A child has two parents and an essential first step in the development of its sense of identity is the emergence of discrimination between these two people. Similarly, in personal construct theory Kelly sees people as forming their fundamental discriminations of their social world on the basis of similarities and differences amongst three people. For a young child the task is to form discriminations in terms of similarities and differences between himself and his parents: in what ways is he more similar to his father than his mother, and in what ways more similar to his mother? An interesting question here is to consider what kinds of discriminations would face a child if we were biologically produced by three or more parents. Or even parents of more than two sexes. This takes us into the realm of science fiction, and it might be possible that such children would develop the ability to employ triadic categories rather than just bipolar ones. Alternatively, they might still use a bipolar category and divide the people using a greater range of constructs.

Triangulation and homeostasis

In the previous chapter the concept of escalation in couples was discussed. The question remains of how this escalation can be contained or diffused so as to maintain an equilibrium or balance. One important development for family theory came from the work of clinicians who were involved with child-focused problems. It was noted that frequently the parents of children who were attending child-guidance and similar clinics for treatment were themselves in considerable conflict. In many cases the parents' marriages were far from harmonious or satisfactory. Clinicians started to formulate the idea that the symptoms displayed by a child, such as tantrums, crying or headaches, were serving the function of distracting or avoiding the conflicts between the parents (Haley 1976, Minuchin 1974). They noted further that in some cases the conflict was 'open' and fairly easy to detect. In other families the conflicts were disguised or denied, and were mainly indicated by the disagreements between the parents about how to deal with the child's problems. The child's function, despite appearing to be the source of the family's problems, was instead seen to be as a 'peace maker'.

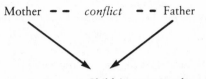

Mother -- *conflict* -- Father

Child (tantrums, plays up, becomes ill, etc.)

The model incorporates Bateson's observations that couples tend to display complementary or symmetrical forms of escalations. One of the ways in which escalation can be contained is through the intervention of a third person. The development of the process of conflict detouring might be similar to a form of 'operant' learning. A young child may experience the stress and tension between his parents and respond to the raised voices, banging of doors or violence by crying, losing his concentration on what he is doing and hurting himself, feeling sick and so on. One or other of these behaviours may be enough to capture the parents' attention and distract them from their struggle to focus on the child. This temporarily produces a cessation of conflict between the parents. Following several repetitions of this process, the child's behaviour or symptoms can become programmed into the family dynamics and function to maintain the homeostasis of the family.

It is possible that this model takes an overly negative and restricted view of family functioning, and Madanes (1981) has emphasized that it is important to see the child as serving a variety of 'benevolent' functions for the family. She suggests that there may not always be conflict between the parents, but nevertheless the child's symptoms can be helpful to the parents. A child may develop symptoms that keeps his mother at home to take care of him, and consequently the mother does not have to face the stress of looking for a job. Alternatively if a father comes home from work tense and frustrated, his son's misbehaviour might serve to distract him from his worries, and in turn offers the mother respite from the potentially wearing task of trying to console her husband. Children, especially if they are young, are unlikely to engage in this 'helpful' function consciously, and it is too simple to suggest that all cases of child problems involve this benevolent function. In some cases the problems presented by a child are due to neglect or abuse, and in others the child has gained such power that it literally terrorizes a family.

An important aspect of triangulation is that it involves the construction of an agreement about the situation in the family. In many cases the parents may disagree about how the child should be treated or even about the causes of his behaviour. However, they are likely to agree that the child is the main cause of the family's current concerns and difficulties. This is essentially similar to Kelly's notion of a construct. The triangulation can embody any of a number of constructs to delineate the differentiation between the child as the 'problem' and the parents (see Figure 7). Any of these or other constructs may serve to define the parents as similar to each other and different from their child in the important sense of the child having the problem.

There are a variety of configurations in which the role of the 'peace maker' may operate in a family. An adolescent son and the father might be in conflict, and the mother's symptoms such as headaches might serve to distract them. Similarly colleagues at work may temporarily shelve their mutual antagonisms and conflicts as they unite in discussing a colleague who is having 'problems.' Likewise the symptomatic colleague can serve to offer a sense of relief and well being in that in contrast they can define themselves as 'well', coping, able to manage their lives, and perhaps also as 'caring' in the assistance they may attempt to provide for her. In families, of course, the personal gains are less clear since the parents may also bear the brunt of the feelings of responsibility for 'causing' the child's problems or for having 'failed' in some way.

Damaging aspects of the process of triangulation are also seen to be related to the *coalitions* that are likely to be formed cutting across generational lines of authority (Haley 1976, Minuchin 1974). The child would be continuously drawn in to taking sides with one parent against the other, thereby disturbing the power structure and making it difficult, if not impossible, for the parents to offer the child any consistent advice or discipline at critical times. Furthermore, Haley described the process of three-generation coalitions whereby a grandmother might take the child's side against the parent's. This was exemplified in problems such as depression where an inexperienced young mother could easily come to feel inadequate as a result of any criticisms voiced by her mother-in-law regarding her abilities as a mother.

A number of writers have emphasized that it is not simply the presence of coalitions which is problematic in families but the presence of *shifting coalitions*, especially in relation to schizophrenia and anorexia (Palazzoli *et al.* 1978). The parents may take it in turn to attempt to draw the child on to their side. One parent may take a 'tough' approach for a period of time,

Secret and shifting coalitions

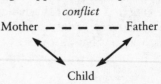

Figure 8 Examples of constructs underlying a process of triangulation in a family

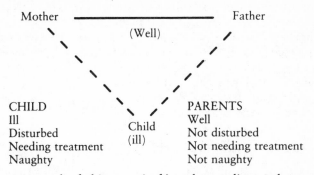

followed by a reversal of this to a 'soft' understanding and sympathetic approach. Meanwhile the other parent will have adopted the reverse position each time. A child experiencing these shifts might start to feel confused, especially when these coalitions are not discussed or when attempts are made to discuss them and they are denied.

This can result in an absence of any consistent sense of reality in the family, and leaves the child with what Laing calls 'ontological insecurity'. One of the few areas of *open* agreement between the parents is likely to be that the child is the cause of the problems. In contrast, one of the few areas of *open* disagreement is likely to be about the causes of the problems and consequently how to deal with the child. The beliefs and the actions based upon them can become self-perpetuating in that since neither parent's solution is applied consistently, therefore nothing seems to work, which convinces the parents that neither of them is right, which leads to more inconsistent parenting.

The model of conflict detouring offers a useful starting point to discuss dynamics of triads, but it has also had some unfortunate consequences for family theory, especially in ignoring the influence of societal factors on the emergence of coalitions in families. Some literature is available which attempts to explore the dynamics of coalitions in families, and we can extend this to examine how these structures are dialectically related to the construings of the family members.

Drawing together the work on the dynamics of dyads, we can note three major processes whereby the escalations are stabilized:

1 Observations of couples suggest that there are periodic changes from one form of relationship to the other. For example, they may both be in the Up position in a complementary (Up–Down) relationship dependent upon whether the content of their interaction falls within their area of expertise. At other times they may be in a symmetrical (Up–Up or Down–Down) relationship when engaged in mutual pleasure giving or mutual complaining about their ailments.

2 The partners may not only bring in 'real' people to attempt to offset their escalation but also draw in a symbolic third person. Jackson (1965) gives

as an example how a woman might employ a tactic such as saying, 'Men tend to do some housework nowadays so don't just leave it all to me'.

3 The most important possibility for our analysis is that people are able to reflect on the processes between them and attempt to avoid excessive escalations. One method noted by Watzlawick (1964) is meta-symmetry or complementarity. For example, a husband might discern that he is being overbearing to his wife and deliberately attempt to take a less dominant position. Again, this reflects a dialectical model offering the possibility that the social reality people create subsequently influences and changes their behaviour.

Coalitions and the family life cycle

A serious problem with the conflict-detouring model is the basic assumption that dyads are less stable than triads. There are important examples of where this is patently not the case. Caplow (1968) points out the case of young couples who may have a reasonable balance of power, especially if the woman is independent as is common during the courtship phase, or where she has a job, her own accommodation and so on. The birth of a child for this couple may result in the woman becoming dependent and in an inferior position leading to a less stable relationship. The stages in the family life cycle can be summarized in terms of power relations governing the potential coalitions:

1 Courtship   Husband = Wife
2 Birth of child $H > W > Child$ and $H > (W + C)$

The woman may start to become aware of her dependence and pull the child into a coalition with her both in order to gain power and influence, and because she is likely to be spending much more time with her child. However, at this stage the child exerts little power, and the coalition with his mother is not likely to be more powerful than the man. Coalitions cannot yet overpower the father.

3 Middle marriage $H > W > C$ but $H < (W + C)$

As the child grows in the family, Caplow argues that it gains in power until the point is reached where the mother and the child working in a coalition can defeat the father in many ways, such as overruling decisions about discipline, use of finances, leisure pursuits and so on. It is also relevant whether the child is male or female, since if it is male he may be expected to spend more time with his father as part of his process of socialization into a male identity. Consequently he may be more (or less) likely to side with his mother against his father.

4 Adolescence

As the child reaches adolescence, the power relations can alter so that it has as much power as the mother; consequently she may be less keen to enter into a coalition where she has little power over the child, and may eventually be at the bottom of the power hierarchy. Caplow suggests that at this stage the mother is tempted to enter into a coalition with the father. This may now be a more attractive proposition for the father, since he too may fear the challenge of the young adult.

This analysis starts to indicate that far from simply being problematic, coalitions are a natural aspect of family life. There are significant cultural variations, though. In some African societies, for example, the father may be so strong that no mother–child coalition can topple him:

> Among the Kgatla, men are held so much more valuable than women that even an adolescent son cannot be dominated by any woman or female coalition. There is no way he can threaten his father's authority, which is based upon both law and custom and supported by the surrounding community. He and his father have considerable need of each other in dealing with the community and in protecting their common interests.
>
> (Caplow 1968: 76)

In general Caplow argues that the position of the father varies across cultures more than that of mothers, since in most cultures women inevitably have more contact with the children and hence are likely to be closer to them, at least to start with. However, the external beliefs, norms and values in a particular culture have a powerful effect on the fundamental structure of coalitions and their changes during the course of the family life cycle. It is important to note that Caplow's analyses, though taking account of cultural variations, tend to ignore the role of daughters and their part in coalition dynamics.

Caplow's theory is based on laboratory-based evidence from game-playing situations and naturalistic observations of primates and humans. He reports evidence of coalition formation in monkeys, such as that of an older, weaker monkey joining the most powerful males and thereby resuming his sexual access to the females. Caplow also examined a variety of evidence from anthropology, sociology and psychodynamic theory. One important conclusion that the draws is to question Freud's Oedipal theory. He suggests that the Oedipal triangle involving a mother–son coalition is *not* the most common. Instead, the coalitions depend on the particular family, the stage in the life cycle, and the culture that the family is operating in.

Coalitions and constructs

Caplow's formulations are expressed mainly in terms of the construct power and power differences within the family. This, of course, has much in common with the feminist critique of systems theory and its lack of attention to gender-based issues of power and inequality. Caplow stated further that a fundamental cognitive factor in coalition theory is the construct *similar–different*. The two people in a coalition are likely to emphasize similarities between them and exaggerate the differences to the third person. For example, a mother and her son may see themselves as similar to being *responsible* as opposed to the *irresponsible* father who drinks too much. Caplow does admit, though, that it is easier for a coalition to be formed and maintained if it runs along basic similarities such as gender. Likewise there are social norms which prescribe that different members of families, such as mothers and daughters, fathers and sons, are expected to engage in certain activities together. These require at least a temporary change in cross-gender coalitions. Freud appears to some extent to have been aware of this in his observations that the Oedipal coalition tends to give way to a father–son or mother–daughter grouping in order for the child to abandon the sexual desires and for socialization to proceed through the process of identification.

So far we have not concentrated on an examination of belief systems, apart from the possibility that people in families act in keeping with their perceptions/construings of external social norms. Also, evidence from research and observations of families in therapy suggest that coalitions have a more dynamic quality than that suggested by Caplow. For example, there may be frequent changes dependent upon a variety of contextual factors such as the influences of other members of the family. A useful starting point for the exploration of triads from the inside is Heider's (1946) theory of cognitive dissonance. This helps us to map the possible patterns of construing in various coalitional configurations (see Figure 9).

In the coalitional situation we can see what Heider describes as a balanced triad. Mother and son are in a positive relationship and both in turn feel negative about father.

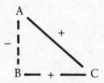

Next we can take a hypothetical situation where mother and father are in conflict but both are close to the child. This represents what Heider describes as an unbalanced triad. For example, the son is in a dissonant state whereby he likes both his mother and his father but they don't like each other. Heider proposes that such situations represent a form of mental tension which motivates people to act in order to reduce the tension. The son likes his mother but she doesn't like his father, whom he also likes. How can he reconcile this? He can try to like one of them less and side with the other. Or, he can try to like both of them less, but unfortunately this leaves everyone disliking everyone else. Although Heider describes this configuration as balanced, it is hardly likely to be a pleasant one to live in

Figure 9   Stable vs Unstable triads

STABLE CONFIGURATIONS

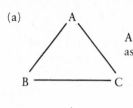

(a)

——— agreement
— — — disagreement

A situation in which all three people are in agreement, as we might expect is a stable arrangement.

(b)

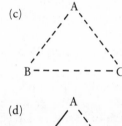

A situation where just one pair is in agreement and each of this pair disagrees with the third person tends to be a stable configuration.

UNSTABLE CONFIGURATIONS

(c)

Not surprisingly, when all three are in disagreement or conflict the triad is likely to be unstable. In order to maintain this triad some agreement is usually attempted.

(d)

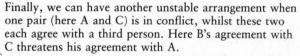

Finally, we can have another unstable arrangement when one pair (here A and C) is in conflict, whilst these two each agree with a third person. Here B's agreement with C threatens his agreement with A.

permanently. We can examine each person in an unbalanced situation and find that they are in a dissonant state. Father likes his son but his son likes his mother, whom he doesn't like and similarly for mother. Such an analysis starts to operationalize what family therapists refer to as the level of generalized stress or anxiety in a family.

The natural triangle

Haley has proposed that cross-generational coalitions are associated with problems in families. However, there have been observations of naturally occurring cross-generational coalitions in various societies in which coalitions appear to serve a positive as opposed to negative function (Freilich 1957). The first serious discussion of such triangle was noted by

Radcliffe-Brown in his observations of the important function of the maternal uncle in some societies. It was later noted that the pattern of coalitions between a friendly adult and authority figure adult can involve various other kin relations. In patrilineal societies the following configurations are found.

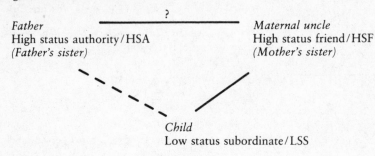

Father
High status authority/HSA
(Father's sister)

Maternal uncle
High status friend/HSF
(Mother's sister)

Child
Low status subordinate/LSS

Freilich describes the triangle as follows:

> The father has jural authority over ego (child): he has the right to give him orders and ego has the obligation to obey them. This relation, between the superior and an inferior, is often marked by formality and considerable restraint, while relations between ego and his mother's brother are characterised by ease and freedom. The mother's brother, though superior in status to ego, often plays the role of intimate friend, adviser and helper.

This pattern was found in many societies such as the Batak, Wik-Munkan, Karadjeri and Tikopia. In some patrilineal societies the roles may be occupied by different kin; for example in the BaThonga of Portuguese East Africa and the Nama Hottentots of South Africa, the HSA is the father's sister and the HSF is mother's sister.

The relationship between the son and the person in the position of authority over him such as the father and father's sister in patrilineal societies, or the mother's brother in matrilineal societies, is prone to complementary schizmogenesis or escalation due to its formal and punitive aspects. It is the job of the authority figure to control and discipline the child, and it can be difficult to combine this with any show of positive feelings between them. An escalation can occur where the authority figure becomes increasingly more punitive and the child increasingly more delinquent. In many societies this process is offset by the development of a coalition between the child and an adult in a 'friend' role. Again who this is depends on the basic structure of the society; in patrilineal societies this is likely to be the maternal uncle, and in matrilineal societies it may be the father. This figure can have the effect of calming or easing the situation of hostility between father and son.

This pattern, which was found in matrilineal families such as the Trobriand Islanders, the Haida, Tinget and the Pende, is dynamically the same but now the HSA role is taken by the mother's brother, while the father plays the role of confidant and friend:

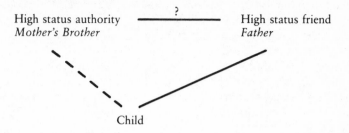

High status authority ———— ? ———— High status friend
Mother's Brother   *Father*

Child

It is suggested that in Western societies these configurations, which can act as a safety valve, have largely disappeared. As a result of the increased isolation of the nuclear family from kinship networks, the child may not have ready access to potential allies in this way. The child may therefore have to rely on the other parent for such emotional support, but this can lead to conflict between the parents when one of them attempts to discipline the child. It has been suggested (Burnham 1986) that various kindly professionals, 'Doctor Homeostasis', can serve this role of High Status Friend. The dangers of this are well known to family therapists in that the parents can in turn unite against the naughty child and professional. Likewise, this analysis indicates difficulties for one-parent families where a mother or father is in the position of trying to fulfil both types of roles. It may be tempting in one-parent families for the parent simply to play the HSF role, and evidence from Wallerstein and Kelly (1980) supports this. They indicate that there can be a tendency in one-parent families for the lone parent to place too large an emotional burden on a child by treating the 'child' as a friend and confidant. The child may become a surrogate husband or wife in that he hears about the parent's emotional problems and comes to feel responsible for their happiness.

The mother-in-law triads

Caplow discusses this triangle as an example of an unworkable or unviable triad which results in a commonly observed fact of 'mother-in-law avoidance.' He gives as the most common version of this the relation between husband-wife and wife's mother.

It is suggested that this triad is largely unviable because two strong

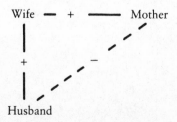

Wife — + —— Mother

+   −

Husband

coalitional tendencies are involved: first, between husband and wife, which is expected and, second, between the daughter and her mother, which again is a function of the daughter's identification with her mother in adolescence. Two coalitions cannot exist side by side in a triad without considerable stress, and hence it is argued that a typical solution is to attempt to limit or avoid this threesome spending much time together. A second argument concerns sexual taboos in that the avoidance precludes the risk of son–mother-in-law sexual involvement. The sexual arguments are rather weak since a similar pattern of avoidance appears to exist between a wife and her mother, a relationship which can be equally tense and prone to avoidance.

It is best to be wary of easy generalizations, and there are reports of many favourable relationships within societies and differences across them with mothers-in-law. Even marriage to a mother-in-law is not universally prohibited. Amongst the Mundugumor, for example, Mead (1949) reports that a man may marry a widow and later marry her daughter. However, she also reports the common incidence of powerful hostility between the woman in this arrangement!

Linked triads

Obviously a triad does not simply exist in isolation but in a wider social context. Caplow suggests that it is possible to think of the relations between larger numbers of people in terms of linked triads. This helps to explain any particular triad's operation. For example, in the case of in-law relations we can see that a coalition between a husband and his mother-in-law poses a whole range of issues for other triads such as husband–mother-in-law–father-in-law. The father-in-law may start to feel jealous, resentful and sexually threatened. Furthermore, there are similarly stressful possibilities with the mother-in-law's other children.

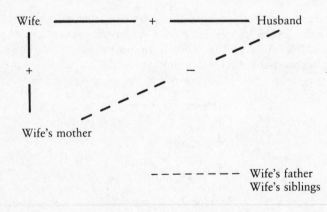

Caplow argues that it is possible to reduce the number of possible triads and coalitions to a relatively few possibilities. In four-person situations he suggests that the following two are the most likely:

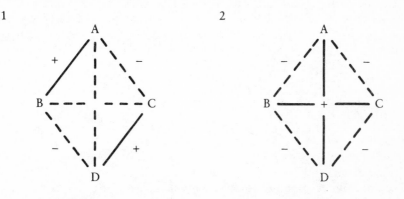

In 1 above we can see an essentially conservative triad (maintaining the status quo of parental authority). The children (C and D) unite together against the parents, who are in turn united against the children. In this pattern the parents can dominate the children, and the children may be able to dominate either parent on their own but not when the parents are united. In the second pattern B/C (mother/son) can dominate father. However, father has little to gain in entering a coalition with his daughter, since this would still be defeated by mother and son. This may be a pattern that is associated with fathers becoming peripheral in the family.

How can we integrate Caplow's work on the basic patterns of coalitions with an analysis of the beliefs held and their relationship to these underlying patterns? Heider's theory suggests that the tendency in the basic family triangle of conflict between the parents is for one or other parent to attempt to pull the child on to their side in order to reduce the dissonance. Likewise, as we have considered, there may also be a tendency for the child to attempt to join one of them in order to reduce his own level of dissonance. This could be that he finds some reasons for thinking that one of them is more right or wrong. Such reasons may, of course, be offered to him by each parent in turn. The concept of cognitive stress therefore provides the motivational fuel for the oscillations that are observed in the basic family configurations. The source of this stress, however, can be seen to extend further than the internal context of the family. As we have seen, different coalitions are more likely in some societies than others. For example, in Western society the most common is for the son to enter into a coalition with his mother against his father. Since mothers usually have somewhat less power but not dramatically less, a mother–son coalition can dominate the father. This allows the son more influence than he would otherwise have over his father and allows mother to gain power. Hence Caplow argues this pattern is predictably common. However, this places father and son in a position of residual dissonance, since fathers and sons in our society are also expected to have some affection for each other as are husbands and wives. For father the position can be that 'I don't get on with my son or my wife but society says that I should if I am a good father.' This is presuming that he has not yet abandoned the wish to be a good father and become totally peripheral.

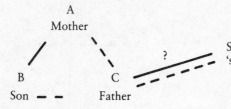

The possibilities are more complex in that a variety of more 'deviant' roles also exist, such as men who opt out of a 'father' role to join a category of disengaged fathers who have little contact with their children. Frequently they may later simply be reabsorbed following remarriage into a nuclear-type family configuration where they play a conventional father role.

Coalitions with social values and norms

What this analysis implies is that what may appear to be a balanced configuration in coalition theory terms can, in fact, still represent a dissonant state for one or more of the members since they live within the influence of a wider set of social constructs, such as the desire to be a good father and husband or to be a respectful son.

Here we touch on an extremely important aspect of family dynamics. There are values in any given society about what it is to be a 'good' father, mother, child, what it is to be a 'good' wife, husband, lover, and what it is to be a 'good' son, daughter and so on. The list of aspects of what is desirable and valued is long and not uniform in a society. There may be real contradictions about what is expected of families. On the one hand, there are prevalent values about the desirability of sons becoming tough and able to take care of themselves, to be aggressive, competitive and physical. On the other hand, there are sanctions about violence or excessive aggressiveness. It is possible to consider these values as representing a plurality or variety of sometimes contradictory values. The task facing families is to make sense of and choose from amongst these values in order to be able to prepare their offspring for life in a world which is different to the one the parents grew up in. There are real rewards and punishments attached to the extent to which families do this more or less successfully. As we saw in Chapters 1 and 2 it is arguably inevitable that childhood experiences form the basis of the belief system that parents later apply, often largely unconsciously, to shape their own children's development. Kelly's idea of 'replication', discussed in Chapter 3, suggests that this process is natural and inevitable. On the other hand, it is emphasized that a key aspect of the parents' task is to come to discriminate between their own past and their children's current circumstances.

Families are also faced with a wide variety of ideas about what is normal in their society – the social *norms*. For example, there are expectations about when it is normal for children to leave home and set up on their own. These may be open or they may be expressed covertly. The single-parent mother of one boy complained that her seven-year-old son was being bullied at school. A conversation with a friend of the boy revealed that he was seen, by other boys, to be a 'mummy's boy', his hair was 'too long' and he was generally seen as a 'effeminate'. These perceptions contain some powerful assumptions about norms and values. It is already regarded by young children that it is 'normal' for a boy to separate himself from his mother, and failure to do so leads to his being punished. It is also a value that he be 'tough' and conform to the values of his peers, and display this by how he dresses and looks. Other children can be seen as being the guardians and officers of society's values and norms. Of course, this does not always work simply to help a child to separation. A frequent reaction of a mother in this situation is to become more rather than less enmeshed with a child, leading to further censure and possibly ostracism from his peers.

Don Jackson (1965) drew attention to the manner in which families are dynamically involved with the wider societal values. Families can be seen to be regulated by rules, as was discussed in Chapter 2, and these represent the norms of the family. In one family hard work and industriousness may be highly valued and in another artistic expression and creativity. These inner norms and values are continually compared with the external societal ones. Families, as we have seen in the discussion of the family life cycle, can experience great conflict at the point of socially prescribed transitional stages. They may acknowledge that they are expected, for example, to allow a young daughter to leave home and start an independent life on her own, but they may be emotionally unable to do so because of her function in preserving the family equilibrium. They may then attempt to invoke contrasting values such as that in 'many' families children do stay at home longer, or they may invoke family traditions (internal value systems) that certain family members stayed at home successfully and so on. In a sense they interact with the external values or ascribe to them tactically.

Jackson suggests that values can represent an extra-familial coalition with religion, society and culture, and they are employed to exert leverage on relationships within the family. As part of the internal family dynamics, values can be seen to be used as interpersonal tactics which affirm or enforce a norm or accepted way of being. He goes on to offer the following example:

Mother and infant, for example, have a strictly complementary relationship (that is, one based on differences which fit together), in which the norm is that the infant is totally dependent on the mother for all gratification. As the child grows older, he may engage in behaviours which abrogate this norm, especially masturbation. Whatever else masturbation may mean to either individual, in this ongoing relationship, it is an indication of self-sufficient pleasure on the part of the child and as such threatens the norm of their relationship, i.e. that the mother controls the child's needs and pleasures. If the mother is unwilling to accept this change in the norm, she may punish the child, and/or she may invoke strong moral injunctions against the 'deviant' behaviour. In this case, her value judgement against his masturbation represents a forceful coalition of mother and society, a coalition which may in fact succeed and perpetuate the complementary norm to absurdity.

(Jackson 1965a: 15)

This analysis bears resemblance to Berger and Luckman's concept of the 'generalized other', which suggests that a child develops a sense of identity initially by becoming aware of what key people that she comes into contact with, such as parents, say about its actions. Gradually the child starts to *internalize* these to form a sense of what these key people are likely to think and what they believe. Later this generalizes to a broader perspective of what society's values and norms are thought to be. In a sense the figure of God the Father represents such an image of a 'generalized other' or 'person' who is referred to in order to help us to reflect upon and evaluate our own actions.

Perhaps nowhere do we have a clearer or more powerful example of the functioning of external values in families than with the changing values that are embodied in the women's movements. A wife is quite likely to invoke these new values in suggesting to her husband that 'most men nowadays assist with the housework, look after the children and allow their wives to develop their own interests and career'. This can be a very powerful tactic, and over a period of time the discussions around these issues can become telegraphic; a shorthand 'isn't that a bit sexist' can be enough to invoke the array of the value set. The response of the man may be quite similar to that if a third actual person was being drawn in. He may attempt to pour scorn on feminists as 'flat chested, frigid lesbians who hate men'. He may also attempt to distance his wife from 'them', perhaps by suggesting that they are unattractive and that his wife isn't, with the veiled suggestion that he will find her unattractive if she becomes more like them. Also, these tactics are played out in the media so that counter-values might be invoked by the man along the lines of statements by anti-feminist women or professionals who do think that the woman's place is in the home. The skilful use of such values, and especially an awareness of the values that one's partner is attached to, can be used to exert influence on them. Some of his analysis is based on clinical observation and represents a relatively unexplored area and possibly a rewarding one for future family researchers!

Psychodynamic theory, ambivalence and coalition theory

Coalition theory, like psychodynamic theory, stresses the idea that people in families, and especially children, may be in a state of ambivalence. As we have seen earlier, children are frequently drawn into coalitions with one parent against the other:

> we can see why ambivalence is a salient feature of most of the family systems that have been observed. A family begins with a parental coalition, and even if its solidarity later declines, that coalition must be revived from time to time in order to cope with emergencies. But the coalition of mother and child is perhaps the fundamental form of human relationship, and thus, though it is weakened as the child matures, it is seldom completely abrogated. The division of labor and the division of sex roles can forth occasions that require the coalitions of males against a female or vice versa. The parental coalition is incompatible with both mother–child and same-sex coalitions. A mother–son coalition is incompatible with a father–son coalition.
>
> (Caplow 1968: 79)

Caplow argues that the situation has become worse in Western society due to the increasing isolation inherent in the nuclear family. This implies that extended families do not become involved in defusing conflicts as in the example of the 'natural coalitions' found in other societies. Second, due to the increasing emphasis on androgeny in parental roles, a parent may find him or herself attempting to play both the authority and nurturing role with a child, which may at times lead to considerable confusion. Caplow may be criticized here for implicitly accepting conventional role definitions in families. On the other hand, he does offer a dynamic and shifting model of family life which emphasizes how parental roles are related to power distributions.

Caplow expresses some important criticisms of Freud's theory of Oedipal conflict in families. He emphasizes that ambivalence is a central feature of family life, but insists that the Oedipal triangle is only one variation of the possible coalitions:

> Yet, unless all factual references made in connection with psycho-analysis are to be given immunity from the rules of scholarly evidence, we must conclude that Freud was mistaken and that the coalitions of mother–son and father–daughter he observed represent no more than a local practice. Cross-cultural studies show no universal leaning towards this pattern. Indeed, it is rather rare. Mother–son coalitions are not uncommon under the appropriate conditions, but they are seldom matched with symmetrical father–daughter coalitions. Mother–daughter coalitions occur frequently, although for different reasons, in both patriarchal and matriarchal families. . . . The libidinal element remains. We cannot deny that the sentiments of

small boys towards their mothers are qualitatively different than those aroused by their fathers, if only because male behaviour is distinguishable from female behaviour in all societies and because the initial relationship of mother and child is closer, more essential, and more crucial for the development of the child than the infant's relationship with his father. But it is not self-evident that the infant's physical attachment to his mother must develop into emotional solidarity with her as he matures, or that sexual impulses of early childhood can distinguish accurately between social categories, or that little girls are less apt than little boys to look to their mothers for sensual satisfactions, or that the father–daughter relationship is a mirror image of the mother–son relationship. The Oedipus concept is a reminder that deep-rooted, unconscious libidinal motives play a large part in the selection of coalition partners and warns us against the attempt to explain family coalitions exclusively in terms of relative power, but the particular coalition patterns that Freud preferred and found whenever he looked for it appear to be only one of many possibilities.

(Caplow 1968: 83)

Consistent with Caplow's critique, similar ideas have been expressed by Nancy Chodorow (1978), who argues that both boys and girls are initially equally attached to their mothers. Boys may later have a more difficult time because they are required to break this attachment and distance themselves from their mother's feminine traits, and deny or repress these feelings learned from her in order to adopt a conventional male identity. It may be this requirement by our society, rather than an attempt to resolve an initial sexual coalition against the father, which also leads boys to become closer to fathers at adolescence.

Family construct psychology

It is possible now to combine the strands in this chapter and explore an integrated model of the functioning of families in terms of their belief systems. The work of Harry Procter (1981) has been one of the few attempts to tackle this by extending PCT to the study of family dynamics. As a first step Procter suggests that it is necessary and possible to propose an extension of Kelly's original corollaries.

The group corollary: to the extent that a person can construe the relationships between members of a group, he may be able to take part in a group process with them.

An essential aspect of relationships in any group or family is that people have a set of constructs about the nature of the *relationships*, not merely the individuals in the system.

Second, a more radical corollary is offered:

The family corollary: for a group of people to remain together over an extended period of time, each must make a choice, within the limitations of his system, to maintain a common construction of the relationships in the group.

He suggests that the family members do not necessarily have to be in agreement. They do, however, *share* a finite set of constructs upon which their choices are made.

The concept of shared construings fits in with a view of each member of a family as developing a set of *anticipations* about how the others will behave. Each person in a family can be seen as potentially free to make his or her own decisions. However, since these impinge on the others in the family, their views must be taken into consideration. Over time, first the couple, and then the couple plus their children, form a web of anticipations, based on their shared experiences, or how the others will react. This is necessary for them to be able to organize their lives and to manage the task of living together. Out of these shared experiences they can be seen to develop a shared construct system which structures, but also constrains, what each person believes to be possible or permissible. This can give a sense of unity and security to everyone in the family. This may be the case, as we will see later, even when the shared construings involve seeing one person as having or being 'the problem.' Procter puts it this way:

The finite number of alternatives in the Family Construct System and their contingent nature explain the phenomena commonly observed by systems theorists: the transfer of illness phenomenon, where another member of the family becomes ill when the identified patient improves, or where severe strain is put on the marriage when a child loses his symptoms or leaves the family. Another clear example is the 'see-saw' shift where for example one spouse is depressed and the other the care giver. From the systems point of view, it does not matter which of the pair occupies the slot. What is maintained is a certain sort of complementary relationship. This is the family's reality; they know of no other way of being together.

It is important to realize that this approach takes us towards a dynamic and dialectical model of family beliefs. In some ways it covers the same ground as theories like Ferreira's family 'myths' and Byng-Hall's 'family scripts'. However, both these approaches are deterministic and tend to assume that the family has got it wrong somehow – that there is an inaccurate or deceptive perception that needs to be corrected. The idea of family constructs is based on a more dynamic view which sees families trying to make the best sense of what is going on and has gone on in the past. Their views are only 'wrong' in the sense that they are unable to move on or develop. However, even this is not seen as different to the processes that happen to everyone and not exclusively to 'problem' families.

Systems theory emphasizes that it is a profound mistake to regard some families as 'sick' or 'wrong' in some kind of way. This is not therapeutically helpful and is more likely bound up with the value systems of the therapist. There is a danger of making precisely this error in applying PCT in a family context, an error which some PCT theorists do in fact appear to make. For example, Ryle says, 'A neurotic patient is like a traveller in unfamiliar country forced to rely upon a deficient or systemically falsified map' (Ryle and Lipshitz 1975: 555–60).

Such statements do in fact follow naturally from Kelly's position that there is a 'reality' out there that we construe. As was argued earlier, this reality, especially in the context of families, does not just sit out there waiting to be construed, but actively constructs and channels our experience and constructions.

Procter's approach avoids many of these pitfalls, but nevertheless it is easy to slip a little towards notions of 'good' and 'bad' functioning:

> Ideally the family has negotiated an FCS that allows each member to make choices that are elaborative. Kelly used the term *propositional* to describe constructs which carry no implications regarding the other realm membership of their elements. The constructs in the FCS of a well functioning family will tend to be propositional. In other words each member's actions and choices will be relatively uncontaminated by the opinions and actions of the other members.

Procter has used his approach in the context of family therapy and makes some important generalizations about the relevance of FCT to family therapy. He describes how it is important for families to generate some clear constructs regarding its boundaries from the outside world and the boundaries between the members. This is essential for people to develop and mature within the family. At the same time it is important for such constructs to be 'permeable' enough to allow change to take place, such as the changes in construings required for a teenager to move from being seen as a 'child' to an 'adult' and as eventually 'independent' of the parents. We need to consider here the possibility that 'rigidity' in the family's construct system may not merely be a 'failure' on their part, but may be related more widely to a rigid, inflexible and constraining social context that the family is in. Ideas regarding change and development will be the subject of the following chapters.

Family constructs and actions

Harry Procter offers an analogy of family construct systems as being like a town with a network of avenues: each avenue represents a construct that family members can move along and they can choose or be persuaded to be at one end of any avenue or another. For example, there may be an avenue which is 'lazy' at one end and 'industrious' at the other. We are potentially free to move along the avenues as we like, but they constrain our movements in that we have only a limited number of avenues that we *believe* we can move along. We also have the potential to construct some new avenues or even to redesign the whole town, but this can be a difficult task. Above all, it is likely that we will put up with the design despite some limitations until some major problems occur. Continuing our analogy, until massive traffic jams or excessive casualties on the roads become common place. In families major demands for restructuring may occur at the family life-cycle transitional stages such as when people arrive or depart from the family. These requirements for change can require massive organizational, emotional and cognitive changes. The FCS provides us with a sense of security, a sense of knowing where we are:

> The FCS governs the sequences of contingent choices that constitute the interaction patterns of the family members. Over the years family members become highly sensitive to each other's reactions and behave together as in a 'dance' of mutual anticipation. Any change in the other's habitually anticipated choices will be experienced as anxiety provoking and threatening. An attempt will therefore be made to change the person back into predictable modes of behaviour. We can thus see how homeostasis will operate amongst any group of people living together over a period of time.
>
> (Procter 1981: 8)

This view of the family helps to explain a number of phenomena such as the way that an ill member of a family may show a tendency to act like a seesaw – improving and then relapsing periodically. Likewise the phenomenon of the 'ill' person in the family being replaced by another member if they leave or improve. The FCS model suggests that what is important is that the slot or role exists, but who occupies it is secondary.

In Chapter 3 the dialectical basis of PCT was outlined. In the context of families we can develop this further in a way consistent with the ideas of constructivists such as Berger and Luckman. The family can be regarded as a microcosm in which the members collaborate in constructing a social reality. This does not mean that they agree on everything; there may be differences in opinion and interests just as there are different interest groups and conflict in any society. They do, however, collaborate, usually unwittingly, and come to set up certain agendas. Foucault (1976) employs the term 'discourses' to describe the constellation of assumptions that underly certain ways of seeing the world at any given time. The processes in families are dialectical in that the social reality that is constructed in turn influences all of the members. It is important to distinguish once more, though, that it does not simply determine what they do or think. Instead, the members interact, they have an interaction with this social reality, and may at times alter or challenge it.

Consider the classic example of the operation of a family construct which is typically found in families with one member who is presenting symptoms. Commonly the construct well–ill will be operating so that the patient is seen as ill and the others are seen as well. Most significantly the patient will typically share this construction and even resist attempts to alter it. Minuchin gives an example of the operation of such a construction at the start of his book *Families and Family Therapy* (1974):

Minuchin: What is the problem? . . . so, who wants to start?
Mr Smith: I think it is my problem. I am the one that has the problem. . . .
Minuchin: Do not be so sure. Never be so sure.

Typically in a family where one member has been in this ill role for an extended period of time, the construction may become extremely rigid. In Kelly's terms the construing processes have become impermeable and pre-emptive: The person is ill and nothing but ill. There may be no permeability or chinks of light through the construct to allow any alternative ways of seeing the person or of interpreting any of his actions as anything but demonstrating how ill and mad he is. Finally, the constructs may have become constellatory so that the ill person is also seen automatically as helpless, difficult and uninteresting.

This only gives us part of the picture, though. We know from observations of families and from Kelly's dichotomy corollary that each person's position in the family is continually negotiated. In a sense there is movement, but movement accompanied by apparent resistance and attempts to return to the status quo. A common example is that movement from the ill slot may be predictably accompanied by a number of other constructs. The person may be seen as *well* and therefore able to work, help around the house and get a job. The consequences in terms of the family's constructions can be seen to underly the predictable patterns of action or circularities described by family therapists. Figure 10 is a case to illustrate this process involving Malcolm, a young man in his twenties, who had been repeatedly hospitalized displaying schizophrenic-type symptoms.

Figure 10   A circularity embodying a psychotic pattern in a family.

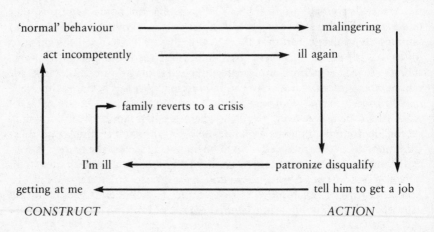

MALCOLM   PARENTS

ACTION   *CONSTRUCT*

'normal' behaviour ────────────────────▶ malingering

act incompetently ────────────────────▶ ill again

family reverts to a crisis

I'm ill ◀──────────────────── patronize disqualify

getting at me ◀──────────────────── tell him to get a job

CONSTRUCT   *ACTION*

When Malcolm shows signs of recovery such as ceasing to act in bizarre ways and saying that he is hearing voices, his parents may start to think and say to him that what he needs to do now is to 'get off his bum' and start to help around the house and find a job. Their intentions may be benevolent but also tinted with some anger at all the 'trouble' that their son has caused them. Malcolm may construe these demands of his parents in a number of predictable ways. He may think that since he is better and acting in adult way, he should not be bossed around. Second, he may still have considerable doubts about his ability to carry out jobs to an acceptable standard. His parents may see this as malingering or laziness, and use it as a vehicle to express some of their underlying anger with their son. Malcolm may construe this correctly as anger, but this may be denied, consistent with the family construct that the expression of emotions is unacceptable.

Jay Haley tells a story of a young man similarly caught in such a cycle with his parents, and illustrates some of the strange communication that can emerge out of these patterns of construings. The parents repeatedly berated their 20-year-old son to find a job. Every day they would wake him up in the morning and look through the papers for him, nag him to go to the employment office and so on. However, their son usually managed to sabotage these efforts on his behalf. One of these incidents is described by Haley:

> One young man reported to his parents that he had been out looking for a job, and went into a store that had a 'help wanted' sign in the window. When the parents asked him what the store owner had said to him about the job, the young man replied that he had not asked anyone about a job. His father said that he could hardly expect to get a job without asking. The young man indignantly said that his father should appreciate the fact that he went out looking and even went into a store where there was a 'help wanted' sign. The more implausible the reason for inaction, the more obvious the fact that other problems, such as difficulties between the parents, are the real issue.
>
> (Haley 1980: 134)

Inside and outside perspectives

FCP helps to extend various aspects of family theory. Rather than simply representing an alternative, it also offers some new ways of embracing and describing concepts in psycho-dynamic family theory and systems theory. One of the most important contributions it makes is to offer an integration of the *outside* and *inside* perspectives in family theory. To take an example, Minuchin (1974) suggests that for a family to function effectively there must be clear boundaries separating it from the outside world, and within the family boundaries separating the parental subsystem from the children. However, this gives us no clue as to how the family members experience this issue of boundaries, whether they consider it at all, and if they do, what constructs they use to do so. In FCP terms the clarity of boundaries depends on there being a set of constructs which discriminate between the subsystems – for example, whether the parents have constructs which differentiate between their activities and those of the children, or a clear set of constructs about who they are as a family. Procter suggests that a number of family therapy constructs can be defined more precisely within a FCP framework. For instance, *enmeshment* may be understood in at least three ways. It may imply that the family constructs are *constellatory*, so that any action the patient makes has a fixed and predictable set of implications for the others. If he forgets something his mother may immediately step in to remember it for him. Second, enmeshment may be regarded in terms of the lack of a set of constructs to differentiate the self from the mother, as is suggested also by Bowen's (1960) concept of undifferentiated ego-mass. It may also be the case that a set of constructs exist, but that they are more appropriate to an earlier life-cycle stage. An example of this can be where an adolescent is kept in a dependent position as a consequence of being construed still as a young child.

The following case of a young girl presenting symptoms of anorexia nervosa serves to illustrate some of these points.

Figure 11   *A circularity embodying symptoms of anorexia in a family*

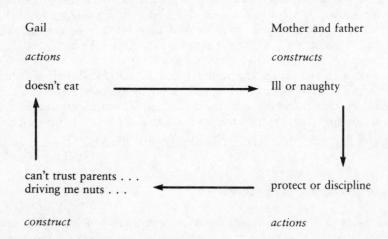

In this example we can see the operation of two core constructs: ill–well or naughty–good. Operating on the basis of these two constructs, the parents alternated between episodes of attempting to enforce some discipline, usually done by father, and attempting to understand what was troubling the girl and be nice to her, which was usually her mother's response. For Gail this appeared to represent a no-win situation since either pole of the construct used to label her actions, ill or naughty, carried negative implications. Furthermore, the two constructs dovetailed to offer a paradoxical situation for the girl: if she was well, it implied that she was naughty to be ill. If she was good she couldn't be ill, but if she wasn't ill she was naughty. With such implications it would be very difficult to experience any validation of her self, however she tried to behave. Further we can see that the process of enmeshment is clarified by an analysis of the construings. In this family the parents were excessively concerned about what Gail was feeling and indicated that they perhaps knew better than she what her body felt like. This was also consistent with viewing her as a child rather than as a young woman with a mind and body of her own. The parents also tended to be overly sensitive to Gail's every action, and would fuss over her or to become panicky if she showed signs of deterioration or improvement.

Also, they did not have a clear set of constructs regarding a boundary around themselves as parents and Gail as their child. For her part Gail reciprocated these constructs in various ways. She tended to stay in and withdrew from her own peers, thereby making it harder for herself and her parents to establish any transitional boundaries, such as seeing herself and being seen as an independent adult. She also encouraged the fussing over her eating habits and the state of her body by eating very little and being extremely finicky about her food. This in turn made it harder for her parents to cease to be continually preoccupied with the state of her body, with the resulting difficulty of Gail gaining a sense of autonomy or 'self' as differentiated from her parents.

Disagreements and misunderstandings

So far the proposition that families construct and share a social reality has tended to emphasize agreements in their construings. This should not be taken to mean that the concept of family constructs implies that people are simply in agreement. There can be disagreement, for example about how to construe a particular action by one of the members, but most likely there will be a meta-agreement about the possible ways that it can be construed. In other words, there will be an agreement about the basic agenda of the family in terms of what issues are seen to be important enough to disagree about. In the previous example we saw how parents might disagree about how to construe the behaviour of their daughter who was not eating, but they were in a meta-agreement that there was only two main alternative ways of seeing her behaviour.

There is a need to distinguish such struggles over how some action is to be defined from cases where there is a misunderstanding or miscommunication. Kelly (1955) and Watzlawick (1984) both discuss the possible ways that misunderstandings can operate, not only negatively but also positively. As we saw in Chapter 3 it is possible to engage in effective interactions with others even though there may be quite profound misunderstandings.

Making assumptions about what the other is thinking without actually checking the basis of our assumptions is like an attempt at 'mind-reading'. It is possible in some instances for a couple to go on for years in a reasonably successful way without really understanding each other very deeply or even harbouring fairly profound misconceptions about each other's constructs.

The question of disagreement and misunderstanding is paramount, as in the earlier extract from Minuchin, when families first enter therapy and are asked about their problems. It is useful at this preliminary stage to ask two types of questions:

1 How each of them sees the problems.
2 How they each explain the problems.

The first question can bring to the surface disagreements about the nature of the problems and sometimes misunderstandings about who is seen to have the problem. The second question consists of asking each person to offer attributional explanations about the causes of the problems. This can again reveal disagreements and, most importantly, some basic misunderstandings. The question about causes can be integrated with questions about what Watzlawick *et al.* (1974) call the *attempted solutions*. The causal explanations have direct implications for how the family thinks that the problems could be solved or treated. It is essential to deal with this before any advice or interventions are offered.

We will return to the therapeutic implications in the next chapters, but we need to note here that misunderstandings are to be expected in families. Kelly suggests, in his sociality corollary, that the constructs that people have about each other need not be totally accurate as long as they are adequate to allow social relationships to occur at the level required. A couple may bumble along until some event forces them to become more intimate or to work together in ways that require them to understand each other in more meaningful ways. The birth of the first child can be an example of the difficulties involved in this. The woman may discover that her man is more of a chauvinist than she thought, or the man that his wife is much less maternal than he expected. Furthermore, we can add, as was discussed in Chapter 3, that there is a tendency in families to engage in linear punctuations or attributions. As we have seen, people tend to make two typical forms of attributions. Dispositional attributions are to do with ascribing causes of behaviour to various internal factors such as personality, mood or childhood influences. The second are situational attributes, which focus on external factors such as stress, context, time of day and so on. What is difficult is to attempt to explain events in circular or interactional ways. Consequently linear attributions may amplify rather than reduce misunderstandings. The following example provides an illustration.

The parents in a family in which their adolescent daughter was acting in a delinquent way construed her behaviour and their possible courses of action in a limited way. They saw her as acting in an immature way and as trying to hurt and upset them. This led them to construe only two main courses of possible action with her. One of these was 'keeping an eye on her' at home, with the consequent tension and distress that this involved. The second unacceptable alternative was to let her lead her own life with the fear that she would 'end up a criminal' and 'ruin her life.' For her part the girl saw her parents as treating her like a 'child' – excessively restrictive, distrustful and not really caring about her, but trying to save being embarrassed by her in their stuffy social circle. She therefore made repeated attempts to assert her independence, and sometimes this involved acting in delinquent ways. The parents' construct system had become rigid and constrained; they focused on the girl's delinquent activities and ignored any signs of 'good' behaviour. This led them to tighten their grip, which in turn infuriated the girl further and led her to increase her delinquent behaviour. Here everyone appeared to be making their own choices based upon their constructions. These, however, were interconnected, and the choices severely constrained their considered possibilities for dealing with their daughter; gradually the 'knot' in the family was tightened, leading to an extremely limited range of 'choices' of action.

Such an analysis starts to offer us the possibility of clarifying some basic family therapy terms. However, the aim is to do more than offer a translation into FCS terms. In the next chapters we will consider how an FCS analysis offers some more powerful and less hit-or-miss ways of going about working with families. The focus will be on working with families in order to reconstruct their construct systems, and in particular to find ways of reframing their constructs in order to enable them to regain their ability to create new constructs and solutions to difficulties as they arise. The next chapter will focus on a scheme for assessing family belief systems, and the final chapter will build on this and give examples of its application to theories of change and clinical practice.

Chapter 7

Exploring family belief systems

Research and therapy: therapy as research

This chapter will examine some implications for the assessment of families. The emphasis will be on therapeutic situations, but the overall theme will be that of systemic or strategic assessment. By this is meant the idea that therapy can be seen as a form of research and likewise that research can function as therapy. This is central to Kelly's thinking and to Bateson's (1972) ecological views. In order to gather any information it is necessary to disturb or change a system, and this may be conducive to change, as when a researcher informs a family that he is interested in getting some information but is not attempting to change them in any way. A powerful intervention may result in that the family may feel under no pressure to change, but some of the subsequent questions asked can result in a 'decision' to examine their ideas and ways of being a family.

Palazzoli *et al.*'s (1978) idea of progressive hypothesizing forms the main theme of this chapter, and it is suggested that this approach is also appropriate for research purposes. It has much in common with ethnomethodological forms of enquiry (Garfinkel 1967) and, of course, George Kelly's approach. We will consider some of the ways in which it is possible for therapists or researchers to examine to construct systems of families and individuals. The aim is to offer some reasonably accessible and useful techniques and a framework for employing them in therapeutic situations. The use of many forms of assessment and record keeping, repertory grids, assessment schedules or check-lists can show a tendency to decline to zero following the end of training courses. Often therapy teams view these assessments with a sense of ambivalence or outright loathing. Partly this is to do with the fact that they are not seen as 'helping' the work but rather as getting in the way. It is not being suggested that we should simply abandon any rigorous assessment, but instead that we try to build a model of analysis and assessment which is compatible with people's natural psychological processes and skills.

A large part of this chapter will be taken up with approaches that derive from the work of George Kelly, who is arguably most popularly known for inventing the repertory grid test – an elegantly simple test which requires only a pencil, paper and some imagination. Volumes of work have been published using the test, and computer programmes have been devleoped to carry out complex statistical calculations and provide measures of the organization of the constructs and elements employed. Kelly later said that one of the regrets in his life was to have developed repertory grids. The grid test has obscured that fact that Kelly's was primarily a humanistic and ethnomethodological approach; simply, he believed that 'talking to people' was a useful way to start to find out what they thought. He believed in 'participating' in encounters with people and 'reflecting' on his own feelings, thoughts, attributions, and then checking whether these made sense to the person he was with. Kelly's interest was in counselling and therapy, and he was most concerned with how the therapist, not unlike other humanists such as Carl Rogers, could increase his or her 'empathy' with clients. He found that sometimes repertory grids could assist with this, especially in offering an element of systematic investigation and rigour, but always within the embracing framework of the development of a close relationship with his client. He likened therapy to the relationship between a researcher and his supervisor in that the two were jointly trying to investigate an area of experience, to share their understandings and to evolve some reasonable degree of understanding between them.

The intention now is to consider the following proposed scheme as a method of analysis which is of use to researchers and is compatible with the 'ordinary' activity of family therapists. A summary of this framework for analysis and synthesis is presented below.

Figure 12   Framework of analysis and synthesis

ANALYSIS: **Preliminary observations**
Information gathering
Listening to the family's language
Family's view of the therapist and expectations,
assumptions and fears about therapy

Behavioural analysis – who does what to whom –
structures and organization

Circularities – process
What appear to be the repetitive patterns of behaviour in
the family

Beliefs/constructs
What are the explanations about the problems or their

relationship that members hold in terms of:
Past – historical explanations
Present – what the current circumstances are seen to be
Future – what likely causal factors they foresee

Attempted solutions
Relating to their attributions, what have they tried to do
to solve their problems or generally manage their
relationship

Meta-perspectives
How do members understand each others perspectives,
attributions – the extent of their empathy or sociality

Reflexive analysis
1 Processes and construings in the therapy team,
researchers
2 Agreements between the families and
therapist/researchers analysis

SYNTHESIS: **Systemic hypotheses**
An interactional model of how the family system is
functioning

Constructs and the behavioural processes
Summary of the circularities in behavioural and construct
terms.

Constructs and contexts
Summary of the relationship between process, constructs
and different social situations – e.g. how do the
relationships, problems differ outside the home and inside

Social analysis
An exploration of how the families' construct system
relates to and is influenced by wider social systems, e.g.
issues of gender, race, class etc.

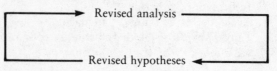

Beliefs: explicit and implicit

One central aspect of this scheme is that a family's set of beliefs, like an
individual's, are not simply explicit and open to analysis. Much of what the
family members believe in may be obtained by simply asking them, but
other aspects will mainly be indicated by what they do and how they do it.
Moreover what they believe is likely to change somewhat from moment to

moment and in different contexts in the family. These changes have a pattern but may not be consciously accessible to individual family members. For this reason the analysis starts with a focus on what people actually do, the patterns of behaviour. It may not be possible, regardless of how long we question a person or encourage them to explore their beliefs, to find out how some of their core beliefs come into play in various situations. Minuchin (1974), for example, will invite a family with an anorexic girl to have lunch in the session. This, more than volumes of talking, can reveal what the underlying beliefs are in the family about the causes of the problem and how to deal with it.

It is debatable whether it is ever possible to be 'objective,' and even in the act of observing behaviours we may be imposing our constructs through selectively attending to certain features more than others. Cognitive theorists (Neisser 1967, Maturana 1981) have suggested that it may be best to think of cognition as a continual interaction between what we expect to see, our unconscious premises or beliefs, and what is actually out there. In other words we do not just construct reality; reality also determines what we see. This seems fairly obvious, for example when we think about the evolutionary survival value of recognizing a tiger pretty fast even if we did not expect to see one. There is a need, even at this early stage of our analysis, to bear in mind that an element of interpretation may be entering into our accounts. For this reason it can be helpful, if time permits, to introduce some 'objective' methods such as counting the incidence of certain types of behaviours or comparing our observations with colleagues.

Analysis and synthesis have been separated in the above model, but it is recognized that the two processes will be naturally occurring simultaneously. Hence, it follows that we can naturally combine these initial behavioural observations into hypotheses about the basic circularities. To see what is occurring in the family in terms of circularities is to impose a pattern or structure on to what is happening. It is important to recognize that this is the start of a process of hypothesizing.

Progressive hypothesizing

An important contribution to family research and therapy is the idea of 'progressive hypothesizing' developed by the Milan team of Palazzoli et al. (1980):

> By hypothesizing we refer to the formulation by the therapist of an hypothesis based upon the information he possesses regarding the family that he is interviewing. The hypothesis establishes a starting point for his investigation as well as his vertification of the validity of that hypothesis based upon scientific methods and skill. If the hypothesis is proven false, the therapist must form a second hypothesis based upon the information gathered during the testing of the first.

The definition of a hypothesis here is faithful to the spirit of the scientific method and has found wide application in clinical psychology in terms of the 'scientist practitioner' model (Shapira 1985). The idea is that the clinician proceeds on the basis of hypotheses about the causes of the problems and is ready to revise these as new data emerge from further investigation or the results of any interventions that she has made. Put simply, this is the same as the ordinary person does: he makes a more or less informed hunch about what he thinks is going on, why it is happening and what to do about it. They go on to suggest two more important advantages of this framework: an hypothesis can 'organise in a few lines a series of empiric facts whose cataloguing might require a entire volume', and secondly, that the functional value of the hypothesis in the family interview is 'substantially of guaranteeing the activity of the therapist'.

The start of therapy can be a confusing affair, and it is easy to feel overwhelmed by the amount of information that a family can present. A hypothesis helps to cut through this chaos and to organize the information into a meaningful structure. Once the therapist has a hypothesis, then he can actively engage the family and ask questions to test the hypothesis, rather than simply flounder about with the risk of getting caught up in or even of unwittingly aggravating the family's problems. This position is similar to Kelly's in the emphasis on *testing*, which consists of examining how useful or effective these hypotheses turn out to be in predicting events. Palazzoli *et al.* (1980) state that 'the hypothesis, as such, is neither true nor false, but rather, *more* or *less useful*'. They go on to offer a definition of what they mean by 'useful': 'The essential function of a hypothesis consists therefore in the guide it furnishes to new information, by which it will be confirmed, refuted, or modified.'

This model of investigation has been influential in family therapy and, as we can see, shares some important features with PCT. However, a number of problems for therapists have arisen from it. The first is the problem of 'impotence'. Frequently therapists know they should be forming a hypothesis, but they are just unable to combine the information into a convincing hypothesis. Second, there is the problem of 'promiscuity': will any hypothesis do? Third, there is the problem of 'satisfaction': how do we know whether one hypothesis was more adequate than another?

A number of possible reasons can be found for these problems, and some tentative solutions can be offered. First, it is suggested that it is necessary to explore not only the family's behaviours and processes but also to explore their belief systems. Watzlawick *et al.* (1974) stress the importance of extracting from families what their attempted solutions have been to a particular problem. This contains by implication how they explain their problem, for example what attributions they hold about the causes and what helps. In the model above, it is suggested that a full analysis of the family's beliefs is conducted in order to fill out the circularities according to how we think their constructs are operating to maintain the situation. Interestingly when we look at Palazzoli's and other family therapists' cases, we often see that what they actually mean by a hypothesis and intervention based upon it 'hitting the target' is when they correctly identify how the family members see things.

In discussing the case of a 13-year-old boy presenting delinquent problems who lived alone with his attractive divorced mother, they state their first hypothesis as: 'the behaviour of the boy could be a way of trying to get the father to come back to the family'. This hypothesis, they state, was rapidly disproved, and they went on to formulate a second hypothesis: 'The mother was an attractive and charming woman, and, perhaps after all these years of maternal dedication, she had met another man, and perhaps her son was jealous and angry and was showing it through his behaviour (Palazzoli *et al.* 1980: 2).

In a sense Palazzoli *et al.* are in fact making hypotheses here about the construings of the mother and the son, but they do *not* emphasize this. An awareness that we inevitably engage in such inferences about others' construings (sociality corollary) is central to this proposed model of assessment method.

Second, a commitment to conducting an analysis of the family's constructs can potentially reduce some of the anxiety about whether our hypothesis is right. It is easier to formulate hypotheses if we feel we know a little more about how people construe events in the family. In turn, rather than seeing the issue as to do with us making a hypothesis, we can regard the formulations more accurately as a process of negotiating a shared reality between the family and the therapist or researcher. To put it another way, we are trying to understand them and they are trying to understand us.

Third, we need to be alert to the idea, as suggested by Kelly, that our construings go through stages of elaboration. So our initial hypotheses may well be fairly simple and based on more or less concrete factors such as how happy or sad people look, who talks the most or interrupts and bosses the others about. As we get to know the family, our construings naturally tend more and more towards Kelly's idea of sociality: we become increasingly aware of how they construe and explain events.

Our analysis should be compatible with any natural social encounter, including a therapeutic one. Haley's (1976) model of the first assessment interview with a family – consisting of the social stage, the problem stage, the interaction stage, defining desired changes, and ending the interview by setting tasks – offers a useful framework. It is normal and polite to get acquainted with people, but this also offers a rich vein of information about a family's general beliefs about the world in terms of what they see as important. First impressions are an inevitable part of this stage, and it is vital for the therapist to reflect on how she feels towards the family and to speculate about how the family sees her and the expectations that they have about therapy. The problem stage encourages a clear definition of the problems in terms of the family's beliefs about what is wrong, and may reveal differences of opinions between family members. The interaction stage encourages a family to discuss issues as they would at home, and this is essential in demonstrating how the beliefs operate in the context of the family's interactional patterns. It can start to show how the behaviours and beliefs are mutually related. In defining the desired changes, the family and therapist enter into some negotiation about what is possible and start to negotiate and construct some new ways of seeing the problems. Finally, some tasks can be set which can provide further information, such as a task to observe events at different times of the day or between different family members. As Haley emphasizes, this ensures the continued involvement of family with the therapist, and increases the likelihood that they continue to think about the session and consequently explore their beliefs further.

Preliminary observations and information gathering

It is usual to have some information about the family before the first session with them. This can form the basis of some initial hypotheses, which can be useful in organizing the collection of preliminary information and in ensuring an active role for the therapist. The initial impressions of the family can also be useful in forming ideas about the family. As Reiss (1980) suggests, the way that a family appears to approach contact with outsiders can reveal some core constructs about how they see the world, themselves and outsiders, and how they anticipate coping with the demands of the situation. Some families may view the therapy situation with considerable apprehension and distrust or alternatively appear 'inappropriately' friendly and light-hearted. These postures can be seen as communications, and the therapist's response to them can quickly set up a pattern which can become persistent and potentially unproductive. It is important to reflect on the therapist's and the team's initial impressions of a family, since if these go unexamined they can lead to self-fulfilling prophecies couched in negative terms such as 'resistant', 'hostile', 'uncooperative', or 'chaotic'. At times it may be useful to open up a discussion about the family's apparent 'resistance', for example by asking whether we have correctly detected that they don't want to attend. Often members differ in their reluctance and can be asked who most and who least wanted to attend.

Listening to the family's vocabulary on constructs

From the start of the session it is helpful to 'listen' for the constructs that people in the family employ to describe themselves and their problems. In the social stage people often reveal constructs about how they see themselves and each other, such as 'just a housewife', 'not very interesting', likes playing with computers' or 'doesn't like going out'. Campbell and Draper (1985) suggest that the therapist and observing team keep a note of phrases the family use repeatedly like 'he loses his rag', 'he gets grumpy', 'he's just stubborn' or 'he just can't be bothered'. These reveal the language of the family and the words that they employ to convey their core constructs regarding their explanations and predictions of each other's behaviour.

Analysis of the videotape following the session can perhaps be used more easily to carry out this logging of the family's phrases.

People also reveal a variety of constructs non-verbally. A mother talking in a slow, monotonous voice may be expressing a construct to the others and the therapist that she 'is' or 'has been defined as' or 'wishes to show that' she is depressed. Palazzoli *et al.* draw an important distinction here between 'connotative' and 'denotative' descriptions:

> For example, if during a heated argument between her husband and her son, Mrs Rossi seemed bored and faraway, it was a mistake to conclude that she really was bored and to discuss and try to discover a reason for her boredom. Instead, we found it more productive to silently observe the effects of her behaviour on the others in the group, ourselves included . . . we can see how the substitution of the verb *to show* for the verb *to be* clarifies the family game . . .
>
> The father, Mr. Franchi, shows, during the session, a veiled erotic interest in the designated patient (his daughter), who for her part, shows hostility and scorn towards him. Mrs Franchi shows an intense jealously towards her husband and daughter, while she shows a strong affection towards her other daughter, who, in turn, shows no sign of reciprocating this affection.
>
> (Palazzoli *et al.* 1978: 28)

Connotative vs denotative language

The distinction made by Palazzoli draws attention to the difference between adopting a constructional view of reality or an objective one. It is almost impossible even at the level of behavioural descriptions to avoid making *inferences* and *interpretations* about what is going on and what the actions mean to the other family members. The substitution of the verb to *show* for the verb *to be* represents a move to a use of descriptions in terms of connotative language. Thus the behaviours are seen as implying certain feelings and intentions rather than denoting in an objective way what something really means. Our task as observers is twofold:

1 We need to consider what the actions imply for us, what we think she means when, for example, mother talks about feeling very tired.
2 We need to think what it means to the family members when she says this. The word tired might arouse quite different connotations for us than it does for the family.

Behavioural analysis: analysis of structures

This analysis is carried out simultaneously with the preliminary logging of the constructs employed. A useful exercise can be to turn the sound off for a while (for the supervision team) or to focus on the patterns of behaviours in the family. A use of some of the basic family dimensions can assist this analysis.

Hierarchy and Subsystems – who usually initiates talking, who does most talking, who appears to make the decisions, who maintains most eye contact or surveys the others watchfully? Patterns of seating and communication can indicate whether the hierarchy is clear and whether the parents work together to enforce it. This can be revealed by behaviour in the session such as who sits next to whom, whether the parents sit together or are separated by the children, the patterns of interruptions, i.e. whether the children interrupt the parents, the children talk among themselves or look at each other more than at the parents.

Boundaries – the patterns of behaviour may start to imply boundaries ranging from:

1 Enmeshed – is there evidence of parents answering for the children, or do the children look to a parent before they answer a question if asked?
2 Rigid – where the rules about contact between the members appear very formal, little in the way of interruptions or any spontaneous activity.

Intimacy – what indications are there about the nature of the emotional contact between the members: who sits close to whom, how much touching is there, what tone of voice is used and so on?

Coalitions and alliances – what are the patterns of side-taking? If one parent starts to criticize one of the children, does the other offer a defence of the child or support the other parent, does another child step into offer support and so on?

It is important to remember that these observations are already mini-hypotheses. The structure as such is our own creation as observers. There may even be agreement amongst the team members or others about the patterns in the family, but this does not mean that there may not be alternative ways of interpreting the behaviours.

Analysis of circularities: patterns in contexts

Just as in the interpretation of structures, the analysis of circularities involves making influences about patterns in a family. Circularities are essentially the rules, usually covert, of the family interactions. They are sequences of predictable actions in a family. The interest in therapy is on behaviours which are associated with the problems. Minuchin, for example, will invite a family in which the daughter is displaying anorexic symptoms to have lunch, and suggest that the parents try and get her to eat. This focuses on the patterns of behaviours relating to the problem and the family's attempts to deal with it. An analysis of circularities need not be restricted to families in therapy, but can be seen to represent the basic rules guiding all interactions in the family.

There are two main ways to collect data on which to base our interpretations about circularities:

1 Direct observation of the family *in vivo*. This can be in the family therapy situation and at home. It is important to try to have at least two settings in which the family has been observed in order to assess the extent to which their behaviour is influenced by different contexts. It can also be helpful to observe the family's reactions to different therapists, for example the way they change if the therapist is a woman as opposed to man, or to the presence of two as opposed to one therapist.

2 Family's accounts of their circularities in other contexts. This consists of questions about the sequences of events surrounding the problems at home and elsewhere. The format can usefully follow a behavioural analysis by focusing on:

Antecedents – what sequence of events precedes the emergence of the problematic behaviour?

Behaviour – what does the person or persons actually do that is the problem? If the problem is a continuous one such as depression, it can be useful to ask at what times it is worse or better, and then enquire about the events preceding and following an episode of it being 'bad' as opposed to 'better'.

Consequences – what are the sequences of events that follow the problem?

Family's constructs, explanations and attributions

The next step in the analysis is to explore how the circularities can be explained in terms of the interaction between the actions and construings of the family members. Interspersed with information about sequences of behaviours, families normally offer a considerable array of explanations and attributions about the causes of the problems and each other's behaviour. Frequently, when each member of the family is asked simply to describe the problem or to describe it in behavioural terms, what happens is that they will start to offer hypotheses such as 'why' they think the problem exists, what the others are thinking, and why they are acting as they do. Not infrequently, they will offer justifications or attempt to defend themselves from anticipated criticisms for causing the problems, or for being a 'bad' family.

This represents an extremely difficult issue for family therapy. In fact the term 'family therapy' is unfortunate, since it inevitably constructs the idea that the family is the primary site of responsibility for the problems presented. There may, however, be a range of other contexts that are responsible: the wider community, social factors, extended family, 'helping' professionals and agencies of various sorts. It has to be remembered also that the very act of collecting data about behaviours and circularities can implicitly convey precisely the message that they are to 'blame'. It may be useful to admit to the family that they probably will feel accused by this analysis. Attempts to reassure them that this is not the case may be seen as false. The family members may well ask themselves why they are being asked all these questions about what they do to each other if they are not to blame. This will be taken up further in the final chapter.

It can be useful to divide the analysis into a number of sections or at least to note the explanations given in three areas:

1 Attributions about the problems – what each person thinks the causes are. These can be further subdivided into:
   a historical factors
   b present circumstances
   c future causes likely to be maintaining the problems
2 Attempted solutions – what has been attempted to assist with the problems and why? This represents a connection between the causes, anticipated consequences of the causes, and indications for future action how to deal with the problem. Kelly stated that constructs consisted of explanations which contained *implications* for action – what to do. This is essentially what attempted solutions are: implications for actions.
3 Meta-perspectives or mutual understandings – Kelly's sociality corollary stresses that people interact on the basis of assumptions about each other's constructs. As we saw in Chapters 5 and 6 this idea is also central to Watzlawick's view that circularities can be maintained by patterns of mutually self-fulfilling constructs. It is important, therefore, to assess the understandings that members hold about each other's constructs. Some information about this may emerge spontaneously in remarks such as 'he seems to think that it's all right for Jimmy to do what he likes' or 'he doesn't realize that I never liked doing that'. At these points it can be useful to check with the other person whether this is in fact how he or she sees things. Alternatively people can be prompted by a number of questions to disclose their meta-constructs:

1 How do you think your X sees Y? e.g. 'How do you think your husband thinks about you going out to work?'
2 Do you think A agrees with you about X? e.g. 'Do you think your husband agrees with you about disciplining the children?'
3 How have A's views changed since time X? e.g. 'How have your wife's views about you changed since you first got married?' or 'When did your wife first start seeing things that way?'

A range of other possible questions can be generated. These can serve as triggers to start the process of exploration of each other's construct systems. This also involves an analysis of *commonality*, or the extent to which family members appear to agree about the way that they see certain events. This produces two types of useful information:

1 Disagreement about how particular events are seen.
2 Misunderstandings about how each person thinks the others see things.

This can involve being wrong about thinking that the other agrees or disagrees. Not infrequently, this reveals information which partners can regard in a positive way, such as the other acting for more benevolent reasons than they had imagined. In short, it reveals information about each person's attributions and motivations. It has to be remembered, however, that this information will be influenced by various contextual factors. The members may want to appear blameless to the therapist, or they may be attempting to draw the therapist or certain members of the family on their side and so on.

Family grids

Palazzoli *et al.* (1980) asked families to rate each other on dimensions that they see as important to the family, such as who appears *least* and *most* worried or upset. Such information can be employed to build up a family grid which can be displayed to the family. The elements can be each member of the family and significant others. The constructs can be the dimensions that have emerged from the family's vocabulary as the session/s has been proceeding (see Figure 13).

Figure 13   Example of a family grid based upon least–most Circular Questioning

1 _____ 2

Happy   _____
Unhappy

Cheer up mother   _____
Make mother sad

Elements (family members)

Construct	Emily	Granny	Father	Brother	Mother	Construct
Happy	3	1	2	4	5	Unhappy
Cheer up mother	2	4	5	1	3	Make mother sad

(Adapted from Palazzoli *et al.* 1980 – ratings shown are illustrative)

Initially this analysis will involve some discussion of who are the significant figures in a system. It might reveal also the presence of significant people not in the room such as boyfriends, ex-spouses, friends, workmates and other relatives. There may be some disagreement about who is included in the grid, and this can reveal differences in people's understandings of who is IN or OUT, or disagreements about who should be IN or OUT, who makes the rules about this issue. In general it can serve to illustrate the family's constructs concerning the erection and maintenance of boundaries and its relation to the outside world.

Second, the words and phrases that the family members have repeatedly articulated up to this point can be offered as possible constructs. The therapist is likely to select what she regards as the *core* constructs of the family, and often these will be constructs covering the symptoms. A common example will be the construct well–ill. The family will probably have used this construct, or other words expressing a similar idea, extensively, with the implication that only the identified patient is the ill one in the family. The exploration of this construct in the grid can start to reveal the extent to which other members are seen to be at risk. Elicitation of further constructs can serve to reveal some of the implications in their core constructs. For example, it might be that ill is used by some members to be synonymous with bad or naughty and by other members as unfortunate or unhappy. This can start to reveal differences in how the members interrelate the core constructs, which can be at the basis of disagreements about how to deal with the problems and attempted solutions. The analysis of the constructs can also indicate how each person in the family is construed and, again, whether there are major disagreements.

The procedure can be to use the grid on a visual display such as a board or large piece of paper. The consensus decisions can be noted along with some disagreements. The negotiation and detailed differences in people's construings can be noted later from the videotape analysis. As each construct is generated, the family members are asked to rate each person on each construct. Once several constructs have been rated, the correlations between the constructs and between elements can be made. This can be carried out using simple calculations and form the basis of further discussion with the family.

Constructs in context

The above analysis, in particular the grid elicitation, starts to offer a way of seeing the family's beliefs in action. There are a variety of ways of mapping the relationships between the family constructs and the range of structural factors discussed. An example might be a construct such as 'pretentious' used to discriminate and draw a boundary between the 'family,' who are 'non-pretentious,' and some or most outsiders, who are seen as 'pretentious'.

It is also possible to analyse the processes in terms of the interdependence between constructs and actions. An example here might be a mapping of a perceived coalition. A mother might be in a coalition with a son who is presenting with a problem of school refusal against a father. It might be that mother and son are seen as similar in that they are both 'patient,' as opposed to the father, who is seen as 'impatient'. Related to this construct may also be a construct of being 'hard' as opposed to 'soft'. The parents may employ this to signify the disagreements and tensions between them enacted through the process involved in how they try to guide and discipline the child.

Mother/Son   — — — — — —   Father

soft   *hard*
patient   *impatient*

The constructs employed by the family and the processes are dialectically related. For example, in the case above the parents showed a pattern of disagreement about how to manage the problem of the school refusal. Mother typically started by complaining about what a strain it was for her to cope with the problem and offering explanations and excuses for the boy, such as he was afraid of being bullied or was being picked on by one of the teachers. At this point the father looked angry and claimed that the boy needed a firm hand and he wouldn't get away with it any longer. This was typcially followed by the boy looking towards his mother, whereupon she would smile reassuringly back at him. Father would look exasperated and turn to the therapist saying, 'She's just too soft with him, I'm getting fed up with it.'

Stories and narratives: development of the FCS and disclosures

Part of the family's construing is the bridging of events over time. Kelly's idea of anticipation contains the idea of predicting future events based upon previous experiences or information. These predictions are often expressed in terms of stories or anecdotes. In the above example there was a story that father had in his childhood suffered at the hands of a 'tough' father and had resented it at the time. Subsequently, though, he had seen friends fall into trouble and had come to attribute his avoidance of trouble to the lessons he learned at the hands of his father.

Disclosures at the start of the marriage

It can be useful to ask couples what they told each other about themselves at the start of their relationship. In one case the wife told of how her husband had told her that he had come from a family where people were always shouting at each other and how he had been compelled to achieve highly. The man remembers his wife telling him that her mother had been hospitalized for schizophrenia and that she had never been able to show her any affection. Fifteen years later, these constructs could be seen to be operating in a significant way in their current situation. The husband was complaining of lack of affection and sexual contact from his wife. She was complaining of living in fear of his violent outbursts and 'loud voice'. Their daughter was refusing to achieve as well as expected at school and had taken an 'overdose' of herbal tablets.

There has been growing interest in psychology in the importance that stories serve in our mental life. Some writers such as Byng-Hall (1980) have talked about the importance of family scripts which can bridge several generations in presenting each generation with a sort of programme of what is likely to happen based upon what has happened in the past. This can lead to a somewhat deterministic view, and it is possible to see the emphasis more in terms of stories as constructions which constrain what family members believe to be possible. Much of our basic cognitive processes may be seen in terms of narratives. As we develop we form our experiences into a story about who we are, our self-identity, in terms of a narrative connecting together past events, the present and the future in a meaningful way. Our memory of events may proceed on the basis of our attempts to recall events from the past by reference to our personal life story. For example, if I try to remember the assassination of John Kennedy, I might be trying to remember what was happening in my life at that time. Developmental models and theories in psychology can be seen to reflect the basic story of life: the stages of man from birth to death. Jung (1959) suggests that such stories are universal and are represented in archetypal stories which cover fundamental human themes such as love, courage, wisdom and death that are transmitted from generation to generation. The stories also convey themes of sexuality, fear and trust wrapped up into moral prescriptions.

An analysis of stories can complement an analysis of constructs. If we examine the family's stories we can see that they contain constructs which are:

1 Connotative – they contain constructs which tell us how to regard certain events, such as that life can be tough and hard.
2 Prescriptive or denotative – they contain constructs about how we should handle certain events and experiences.

As an example in one family there was a story that for several generations the men in the family had tended to chase women, to gamble and to drink. This was told with some veiled admiration – they were attractive men. At the same time, the story went that women had gotten the better of them, and in particular that one father had allowed his second wife to virtually turn out his daughter (her stepdaughter). The second wife was regarded as having no talent; she was essentially a plodding housewife who merely serviced her talented academic husband. This construct, 'weak,' extended to cover the men in the family more generally. They were all seen as men who had talent and abilities, but who above all would fail at the hands of women because of their weakness. The predictions of the story were that the men in future generations would also be weak, and despite apparent success at various stages in their lives they would eventually succumb to this failing.

The story also contained a set of constructs about the nature of male–female relationships, which was essentially to do with it being a power struggle with the survival of the fittest or strongest. Furthermore, there was a paradoxical content around the theme of talent and abilities being imcompatible with strength: 'artists must suffer at the hands of fools'.

Myths and defences

In a similar way to Palazzoli's idea of hypothesizing, the idea of stories serves to make sense of a wide range of events and experiences for a family. It serves an organizing function of helping to make sense of a potentially chaotic world. Ferreira (1963) suggests that 'family myths' as distortions of reality serve the purpose of defending the family members from unacceptable and painful experiences. The idea of myths implies that the families are constructing a distortion of reality, which assumes that there is a 'real' reality out there. An example of this process was provided in Chapter 1 with the account by Pollner and Wikler (1985) of the strategies employed by a family to deny that their child was severely mentally retarded.

Families can appear to formulate explanations which make sense of the world for them but which are divergent from a *consensual* social reality. In many cases we can see this happening when there appears to be large divergence between how the family view their situation and how the therapist and team see it. There can be a danger, though, in assuming that the family have 'got it all wrong' or are seeing it in a 'bad' way. Instead, it can be suggested that the family are seeing the situation in a way which works or is functional in some way for them.

Interface between the family's and societal constructs

The emphasis has mainly been on how families construct a social world for themselves. This carries the implication that they are free to construct any social world, or that what they construct is simply a part of their organization or that it is 'structurally determined'. As Palazzoli *et al.* (1978) argue, 'The family is a self-governing system which controls itself according to rules formed over a period of time through a process of trial and error.'

In this way the family is seen as determining its own course of action from within. However, there are some serious problems with such a view. The first is that there exist within any society structural and ideological realities which inevitably constrain a family's choices. Structural factors can include the economic system, welfare systems, housing and educational opportunities. The possibilities open to a poor family are very different to those available to a rich one. Likewise, the opportunities available for how to organize the family, for example along gender lines, have been constrained in terms of differences in opportunities in the outside world for men and women. Second, the family is subject to ideological constraints. Again, a powerful constraint may be the expectations that are held about what men as opposed to women *should* be like. There are also strong ideological realities about the nature of class, privilege, politics, sexual relationships and expectations, child-rearing and so on which influence families. A powerful example is the change in social attitudes, in Western countries, towards valuing smaller families or even families with no children, as opposed to negative attitudes towards those with large numbers of children, especially amongst the poor. Other areas of change are more contentious; for example, the position of single-parent families is ambivalent as economic support is provided by the state, while social attitudes question whether they are emotionally damaging to the children.

It is important, therefore, to assess how members of a family construe the outside world and themselves. A number of questions can help to focus and explore this issue:

1 How would you describe yourself as a family?
2 In what way are you similar or different to families that you know? Think of two or three families that you know. This can often be set as a task for the family to carry out between sessions.
3 How do you see yourselves as different from your parents' families?
4 What sort of a family would you like to be like? Can you think of a family that you particularly admire?
5 What faults do you think you have as a family? How could things be better?
6 What kinds of ideas do your children have about families? What sort of a family do you think your children will form? How many children will they have? How will they divide up work between the sexes, etc?

These questions are merely illustrative, and it is possible to think of a variety of others to try to assess how a family sees itself, and through this how they interpret the wider social realities that are 'out there'. Of course, there is no one consensual reality but rather a range of perspectives available, and it is a mistake to assume that a family has got it all wrong.

Reflexive analysis

It is important to reflect upon our own constructs regarding the family as the assessment progresses. In addition it is necessary to consider how our views and ideologies may not be consistent with theirs. Examples here might be a family where one or more members appear to the therapist to express what the therapist might consider to be 'racist' sentiments, a 'sexist' view of gender roles or a 'fascist' political view. All therapeutic encounters involve forming a relationship and developing some mutual empathy. It will almost certainly be the case that a therapist 'likes' some families and some members of a family more than others. This might well be based on agreements about political and other views. A danger sign can be when the therapist and the team voice strong negative connotations of a family. This can signal a process of agreement that both parties do not like each other. It might be naive to suggest that it is possible for a therapist to get to like all and any families. Often it is helpful if the therapist and the team reflect on their own construings of the family and try to see things from their point of view. There might nevertheless be times when the ideological differences are so wide that it is better for another therapist to take over. At the same time, persevering with a family that the therapist at first does not like can lead to an elaboration of the therapist's own construct system.

The examination of videotapes of the session can be very helpful in enabling an assessment of the processes between the family and the therapist. This can reveal how a therapist has come to be 'sucked in' or accommodated within the family's construct system, for example a young therapist as a 'scholarly child' to be respectfully tolerated but ultimately disqualified as being 'inexperienced' and 'naive'. The analysis can also help to reveal the impact on certain constructions offered by the therapist and the degree of understanding or misunderstanding between them. Above all, it can help to develop some meta-constructs about the relationship between the therapist and the family and some strategies for how to proceed in the future.

Synthesis: putting it together

The guiding framework for the proposed scheme of analysis is the notion of *progressive hypothesizing*. The point has been made that hypotheses at increasing levels of complexity can be formulated as the assessment progresses. One of the points of this chapter is to emphasize that it is necessary to include an assessment of the family's constructions from the start of contact with a family in order to have this information available to assist the formulation of hypotheses and interventions. This helps us to understand the family's point of view and to explain their reasons for choosing to act as they do. This complements and extends a systemic view which can otherwise appear a deterministic view of people in families.

It is necessary to combine the analysis into a clear, reasonably simple and coherent hypothesis in order to be able to employ it effectively in therapy. The forming of the hypotheses reflects the dialectical processes of construing and action in the family. The hypotheses are the basis for actions and interventions on the therapist's part, and they need to be revised according to their observed effects. The revision will involve gathering some more information and reformulating the information already available. This dialectical process should direct what areas of the family's construing the therapist decides to examine further.

As suggested at the start of this chapter, assessment and therapy are two sides of the same coin, and the process of assessment will have started to set into motion some possibilities for change in the family. The emphasis has been on the first session, but the model assessment of the belief systems and their relationship to the processes in the family will continue into the whole research or therapy. The use of all of the above techniques continues into subsequent sessions, and provides a framework for the methodology not only of the assessment but of the therapy itself. This is consistent with systemic views of continual communication and interaction between and within systems. The analysis will not provide, and should not be used to provide, a frozen or reified picture of a family, but instead always represents one point of time in the relationship with a family. There will, of course, emerge some consistency about how the therapist views the family and how they come to view him, but it is essential to keep in mind the possibility that, even if therapy has been 'successful', further changes may and should occur.

In the next chapter we will look at how this framework of exploration can be employed in therapy. Investigation is seen not as a separate activity but as a part of the continuous process of involvement with a family. The process of assessment in itself starts to promote change. A view of families as composed of people who are similar to 'scientists' implies that they will gain as much, if not more, from the investigation as the therapist or researcher. As we will see in the next chapter, this is not to imply that therapy should simply be aiming to produce 'insights'. However, it is argued that any intervention is accompanied by changes in the family's belief system, and the new permutation of their beliefs will guide their future actions. At times their beliefs will be largely unconscious and might only show themselves more clearly following an intervention. In this sense 'treatment' and interventions and assessment are again two sides of the same coin.

Chapter 8

Therapy and change

The stars up above

R.D. Laing tells a story of a man who comes for therapy complaining that he cannot sleep. He has insomnia and lies awake at night trying desperately hard to get some rest, to get a good night's sleep. But the harder he tries, the more remote the possibility of getting to sleep becomes. He asks the therapist to cure him of this 'problem', if possible without going into all the details of his childhood, potty training and all that.

The therapist pauses and looks at the patient and says: 'Look, you are complaining of not being able to sleep but many people, myself included, have trouble staying awake. In the middle of a lecture, watching television, sitting at home in the evening and trying to play with the children, they just can't stop falling asleep, try as they might to stay awake. But you have this *gift of wakefulness*. You have all those extra hours of consciousness, of ability to experience life to the full. At night you are able, while others are snoring dumbly, to look out and gaze at the *stars above*. Allow yourself to enjoy this gift to the full.'

Throughout this book the emphasis has been on how people create a social reality, a set of beliefs about the world, and how in turn this guides and constrains their actions. The implications for therapy of this view has been referred to at various times, and now we can look at some of the therapeutic implications by examining some cases in a little more detail. The therapeutic approaches broadly divide into two interrelated starting points. First, as in Laing's example above, we can attempt to experiment with people to generate different ways of viewing their 'problem.' This often involves reappraising their initial premises about their 'problem', which typically means questioning 'whose' problem it is and whether it 'really' is a problem or not. Second, our starting point might instead be an emphasis on behaviour. We might start by initially accepting the family's construction of the situation and the 'problem,' and instead work with them to construct some 'experiments' involving new ways of behaving together. These new ways of acting may lead families to form new constructs about themselves and their problems. The choice here reflects the division between strategic and structural family therapy approaches, and as Sluzki (1983) makes clear, they are necessarily related.

A dialectical approach to therapy emphasizes repeatedly that action and construing are inextricably interconnected. Any therapeutic plan has to incorporate both aspects; this point is vital if the therapist is to know where to look in order to assess progress. Change involves a shift at both levels: action and construing. Families start both to act and to talk about their actions in new ways when there has been some fundamental change. We need to be wary when there is only evidence of movement in one area and not the other. It is easy enough to talk about things in a different way and to act in a different way, at least for a while. However, in order for change to be sustained, shifts in both areas are necessary.

Natural and therapeutic change

A focus on families as functioning on the basis of their belief systems provides a therapeutic analysis which respects the ability to families to initiate and make changes. A major change in how a family regards itself and its problems is described in systems theory terms as second-order change. Families make such changes quite naturally in the course of the family life cycle. New ways of seeing themselves emerge normally as a couple decide to start a family and prepare for the arrival of the child. Similarly, new ways of regarding themselves accompany the stage when 'children' move from the family into the outside world as 'adults'. The view that people have the capacity to make creative changes is central to both systems theory and to Kelly's personal construct theory. When families are presenting problems, they can be seen to have become 'stuck' by attempting to apply the same solutions despite the fact that they are no longer working. These attempted solutions are based on their assumptions and beliefs about what is going on and what to do about it.

Again, we need to note that such 'stuckness' is also in a way 'natural'. Kelly refers to the process of 'tightening' and 'loosening' as complementary aspects of the process of creativity. There is a need to find a balance between attempting new ways of seeings events and exploring some of these rigorously. Stuckness can be seen as a form of over-tightening of the belief system. However, families actually have to work quite hard to hold on to a particular construction of events since the world about them is bound to present them with demands for changes. The example from Pollner and Wikler (1985) illustrates how elaborate and demanding some of the actions of a family can become in attempting to maintain a particular 'stuck' and unreal construction of events. On the other hand, excessive 'looseness', as we saw in the work on people displaying thought-disordered schizophrenic symptoms (Bannister 1960), can also be associated with problems. In fact we could say that in some families there is a predictable meta-looseness as they are unable to move towards any consistency and instead continually attempt new but vague solutions.

The inputs from the external world and from inside the family itself exert pressure on families to change. Sometimes these inputs come about in a spontaneous or chance manner. Laing told a story of a young woman who one day found herself suddenly in a catatonic trance. She was frozen in immobility and this experience terrified her. She recounted this experience to Laing for some time in a therapy session, and left feeling a little better but with no major interventions having been attempted. She had merely had some supportive contact and a chance to talk. On the way home she saw some mannequins in a shop window and was struck by the thought that she could get some work as an artist's model. She had intuitively discovered a way of 'reframing' her catatonia and even of utilizing and marketing it. After some weeks of working as an artist's model, she started to feel 'restless' and was no longer troubled by catatonic seizures.

A similar kind of naturally triggered change occurred with a family where the husband had on occasion physically assaulted his wife (see Chapter 5). It turned out that the couple had high standards or expectations about how good their relationship should be. The woman worked hard and was a proud housewife, cooking fresh and good food each day, and was not content to take any short cuts such as serving packaged food. Likewise, the man also worked hard and showed considerable commitment to looking after his family well. It also turned out that the wife had a temper and would throw and smash things in rage at times. Some new ways of framing their relationship were explored using their own constructs – that they had high standards, were passionate about maintaining a 'good' rather than mediocre relationship, but that this led to some frustration which occasionally surfaced. They appeared to have made some progress towards accepting the idea of high standards – the wife put this in their own words by saying 'Yes, we are a hot pudding family' – but on the final session the couple arrived looking particularly pleased and relieved. When asked about these apparent improvements, the man explained that he had been having a conversation with a friend at work who had mentioned *bio-rhythms* to him. They had discussed how changes in one's bio-rhythms are related to fluctuations in emotional states such as anger and depression. From this, the man developed an explanation of his behaviour along these lines. This was acceptable to his wife, and they decided that it would be possible to work out some strategies for dealing with these fluctuations in his moods. This reconstruction fitted with the therapeutic plan, but was in a way more acceptable and genuine in that it was generated from inside the family system. It also indicated that the belief that the man's temper was the problem was still influential, and possibly that we had attempted to move away from this a little too rapidly.

What is at the core of these examples is a *redefinition* or reconstruction of events. Such a reconstruction can occur naturally in a variety of ways. For example, the parents of a six-year-old girl may become embarrassed and worried about her interest in sexual matters. One of them may discuss this with a friend, overhear a conversation or even see a television programme which reinterprets such actions as evidence of normal 'healthy' development, rather than morbid and dangerous habits. Similarly, an uncle, grandparent or friend with adult children may have a powerful effect on parents worried that an adolescent child is going 'off the rails'. He may recount how one of his children acted in 'just that way' but after a period of 'sowing his wild oats' settled down to work and raise a family.

Such redefinitions also occur naturally in the arena of politics and international affairs. On 9 November 1989 the East German government finally took the step of pulling down sections of the Berlin Wall. For over 40 years the belief in the Eastern bloc had been that the wall was necessary to contain the citizens of the East, who would otherwise be lured by the trappings of Western capitalist society. This belief cost several hundred lives of people who were shot attempting to escape, not to mention the unaccountable amount of distress of families who were separated by this monument of our tendency to rigid construing. The move in desperation to a belief that oppression was not the only possible solution, or in fact any longer a viable one, brought fascinating and at times rather sad results. Of course the whole East German population did not desert to the West. Having the choice to go or stay, many East Germans decided that they did not altogether like to look of the West. It was uncaring, superficial in its values, and after a while did not altogether welcome their influx from the East. It almost started to seem that many West Germans, contrary to the years of polemic against the oppression in the East, would have quite liked the wall to have been patched up again! Above all else the paranoid construing of the East was exposed once and for all. The belief that people would abandon socialism if given the choice, could only lead to more repression, which in turn could only produce the self-fulfilling effect that people would do so – because they were so oppressed.

Neutrality and negotiating a new construction or reality

One belief that has handicapped therapy is that the therapist simply does things to change people. Of course this is a simplification, but there is more than a grain of truth in it. Statements in family therapy such as 'we reframed or paradoxed the family', or that a task was set which 'caused some change to happen' are frequent. Ecosystemic models, which look further than the boundary of the family system to include an analysis of how the family relates to other systems (Dell 1982, De Shazer 1982, Keeney 1979), stress the idea that therapy involves a negotiation between the family and the therapist. Further, they add that the therapist and the family become a system whose properties must be considered just as we consider the dynamics of the family itself.

This view is consistent with Kelly's model of therapy. He stated that therapy was to be seen like the relationship between a research student and her supervisor. They are engaged together in an exploration of the 'unknown'. The therapist is a sort of guide who has travelled with others on such explorations but never, of course, this particular journey. She has a few skills to offer such as the ability to form maps as they travel together, to ask some questions at various times, some ideas about who else might be of assistance and about the likely problems and hurdles. However, inevitably some new hurdles will be encountered, and there may be times when the therapist's accumulated wisdom and heuristics for solving problems are actually counterproductive. Above all, if the therapist does not listen, learn and let the family take charge when they come to bits of the journey more familiar to them than the therapist, they will almost certainly fall out with each other and the journey will end disastrously.

Families and therapist, then, are both trying to make sense of what is happening in the therapeutic encounter. Families have their own hypotheses about what is going on and the reasons that it is occurring. Likewise, the therapist forms a set of hypotheses about what he or she thinks is going on. This, as we saw in the last chapter, embodies Palazzoli's ideas of progressive hypothesizing and neutrality. Rather than seeing the therapist as having a better view, we can instead regard therapy as involving a negotiation of two sets of hypotheses, the family's and the therapist's, with neither necessarily being more 'correct' than the other. This is involved in the concept of 'goal setting'. The therapist and the family need to come to a shared agreement about what the purpose of therapy is, with the therapist taking a neutral approach which does not necessarily assume that some goals are better than others.

Underlying this is an endeavour to reach a shared definition of what will count as change (Dallos and Aldridge 1986). Neither the therapist nor the family has a monopoly on this definition. The therapist inevitably brings his own values about what are desirable or acceptable ways of acting and what a 'healthy' family should be like. This might not be anything like the family's view. It is important, therefore, for both sides to understand each other's constructs in order to come to some agreement about what is acceptable. This process of clarification of goals can be one of the major tasks of therapy. As Haley (1971) suggests, this can make the problems solvable once there is a change from a vague general construct about change to manageable and achievable concrete goals. For example, the goals of therapy with a family where the father is suffering from depression become clearer and solvable when the first stage is defined simply as that he and his wife should be able to go out for a walk together once a week rather than a vague notion that he should stop being depressed.

It is not only the family's construction that changes in the course of therapy but the therapist's view of the family. On a training course in introductory family therapy we ask students deliberately to generate negative ways of seeing families as an exercise. This often causes some hilarity, but one frequent observation that students make is how like real referral letters these negative descriptions appear to be. This is not surprising since many problems that families present seem at first sight to be awful. However, as we get to know the family and the way they see the world, our perceptions can change. This is central to Kelly's sociality corollary. I understand, and have empathy with, someone when I can see things from their perspective. Our analysis takes us one step further in that we can also start to understand how the different construings in the family are interlocked.

Elaboration of the family's construct system and circular questioning

The work of Palazzoli's Milan team stresses that exploration of the family's beliefs through the technique of circular questioning can in itself be a powerful therapeutic source of intervention. This is similar to George Kelly's position in that he saw change as occurring through the process of working with people to enable them to examine their construct systems. This process of exploration he felt naturally facilitates some change in allowing people to make new connections and consider new possibilities. A point in common between circular questioning and Kelly's techniques, such as the repertory grid, is that it offers new juxtapositions of the elements in people's lives. In the case of the repertory grid the client is asked to assemble the people that are important to him and combine them in ways that he is unlikely to have experienced them in real life. It is rather like having a party in one's head. For example, I might be asked to compare and contrast my mother, ex-wife and father. This novel juxtaposition can prompt me to explore some of my assumptions because I have never actually encountered these people together, and I am required to reassess some of my assumptions and possibly generate some elaborations.

Palazzoli et al. (1980) suggest in a similar way that questioning can reveal new information as a result of putting together different combinations of family members, and asking questions about how one of them sees the relationship between the other two. This sometimes requests members of a family to comment on relationships that they might not otherwise comment upon. For example, there may be an implicit rule in a family that the children do not comment on the nature of the parent's relationship. Asking the children to do so can challenge this rule and provide some new information. Of course, it is also likely that implicitly challenging the rule in this way may produce some emotional responses from the family such as anger or anxiety. The questioning, therefore, not only produces new information, but also the process of questioning can, indirectly, promote new patterns of behaviour in the family, such as the increased involvement of children. In other words the questioning leads to an elaboration in terms of both possibilities of new construing and new behaviour.

Exploration is, therefore, an active process similar to a form of ethnographic research in that it is accepted that the investigation is, in itself, likely to lead to some change. Families may at some point ask what the therapist is getting at. An honest answer to this is often that the therapist does not really know. He, like the family, is exploring and trying to find out what some of their underlying assumptions and beliefs are and, most importantly, how these construct their patterns of behaviour.

Elaboration of the family construct system builds upon the kind of analysis outlined in Chapter 7. Broadly this suggested that we can outline the pattern of shared beliefs in terms of a set of core constructs held in common by the family members. Second, we need to describe how these construct the patterns of action or circularities which embody the problem or symptoms in a family. Kelly's approach suggests a number of ways we can then proceed to elaborate a person's construct system, and we can find parallels here with some of the techniques that are employed by family therapists, especially the Milan model. Some of the main possibilities are described below.

Relationships between constructs

The underlying belief held by a family in therapy is to do with what is seen to be the problem and how this is defined. A number of ways of elaborating this are possible. First, we can explore the bipolarity in terms of what the opposite to having the problem might be. This can serve to prompt the family to move away from focusing on the problem to focusing on what they want to achieve. Often this is relatively unclear. They may have developed an elaborate set of ideas about what it is to have the problem, but very little about what life might be like without it. Since they have little in the way of constructs about this contrasting positive state of affairs, this means that the potential changes can be quite threatening – 'better the devil we know'. This can also serve to make explicit what te goals are, and to clarify and attempt to resolve disagreements between family members about what the goals are. Second, we can start to explore some of the implications of the problem in terms of how it relates to other beliefs and the family's value system. Again, we can also start to detect disagreements between family members in terms of the implications of the problem. For example, a father might state that his son's school refusal implies that the boy is spoilt, is weak and will inevitably fail in life. Related to this, he may have some constructs covering what should be done, such as the need to give the child some 'firm discipline'. The mother might not agree and insist that the child is not spoilt, but needs some affection and attention. Differences between family members can be raised and discussed in order to clarify what their constructions are, whether they are helpful, and what agreements might be reached.

Our investigation can also reveal the patterns or structure of the family belief system concerned with what they believe to be positive and negative values. The implications of certain strongly held values, such as 'it is important to be hard working', might emerge. Exploring what this actually means in terms of behaviour, and how it relates to other constructs like academic vs manual work and behaviour at home vs outside, can be valuable. In one family this exploration revealed that the parents (both teachers) of a son who was referred because of psychotic symptoms had not valued their son's manual work, and defined him as a failure because he had not been able to follow their footsteps academically. At the same time, they were critical of his reluctance to look for a job without realizing that whatever he would have been able to find would not have been 'good enough'. In this family hard work was related positively only to academic work and success, being clever, being articulate and passing exams. In many other families we could quite easily find the reverse, with academic work being regarded as not 'proper' work and 'unmanly'.

Relationships between elements
Similarities between different members of a family can be noted and considered in more detail. One important source of such similarities can be transgenerational comparisons. Questions can be asked about whom the person with the problem is similar to in the family: 'Whom does David take after?' For example, a wife may state that she sees her alcoholic husband as similar to her grandfather, who died of drink and terrorized her mother. The extent to which such a belief operates as a self-fulfilling prophecy can be examined, and she can be encouraged to differentiate her beliefs regarding the two men. This can serve to disrupt a constrictive set of beliefs and open up more positive ways of seeing the father in the family.

The comparisons between members of a family can also serve to reveal the pattens of alliances and coalitions and the constructs that carry these patterns. Sometimes they are based on concrete attributes such as colour of hair or facial features. They may be linked with psychological constructs such as that a daughter has her mother's looks, her curly hair and dark eyes, and also her volatile, stubborn nature. It can be useful to explore in more detail what characteristics these similarities and differences are based on and develop some further differentiations. In one family such a discussion led to a new view of a troublesome daughter who was seen to be like to 'take after' her mother. After some discussion it was suggested that in fact she had her father's physical strength and his strong will and temper, and further that she was most similar to her father's mother. This opened up some opportunities to construe the girl's behaviour in new ways by eliciting the story of the grandmother who had led a 'successful' life after a stormy adolescence.

Relationships between elements and constructs
This typically is given in the personality descriptions of the different family members that are invariably offered by a family. Descriptions such as 'Jimmy is a shy boy who likes to play with other children but is frightened to approach them' carry a set of contructs which are used by the family to

anticipate each other's actions. Not infrequently, families may offer a generally negative constellatory picture of the person presenting the symptoms, for example that a son is unreliable, weak, troublesome and demanding. If this is pursued, it frequently emerges that there are differences between the members of the family so that some of them will offer positive attributes of the son. This can be used to explore how these different descriptions relate to the patterns of coalitions in the family. The focus can, therefore, move to negotiating some agreement about what is acceptable and what isn't, and clarifying what is expected, whether this is achievable for members of the family, and whether some revised expectations need to be formulated.

Variations over contexts

Frequently a number of core constructs are employed as if they covered all aspects of a person's behaviour in every situation. This is typically revealed in patterns of pre-emptive construing such as that Jimmy is nothing but a troublemaker. This has the effect of sweeping together all the different ways that a person might behave and of obscuring differences. Especially useful here is to ask questions about whether the person behaves in the same way outside the home as inside, whether a son is equally argumentative with friends at school or when socializing. Second, and relating to Palazzoli's technique again, it is useful to enquire whether the person's behaviour differs in different subsystems within the family.

Below is an example of a family where the 13-year-old son was said to be excessively anxious and worried about his school and friends and generally lacking confidence in all areas. As an exercise to explore the differences in behaviour of the family members in the different subsystems, they were asked to think about each possible pairing in the family. They were then each asked to employ the core family construct 'worried–not worried' to compare and contrast the different pairs in the family. Essentially this is a slightly more systematic version of Palazzoli's circular questioning where each person is asked to comment on the relationship between different pairs of family members. This procedure produced some interesting differences in observations. The family consisted of the parents and two children – Sam, the identified patient, and Andrew.

The analysis gave information about how the family members regarded

	Relationship	
Perspective	Most worrying	Least worrying
Mother's	Sam and Andrew	Mother and father
Father's	Mother and Andrew	Mother and father
Sam's*	* Mother and father	Sam and Andrew
Andrew's	Mother and Sam	Andrew and father

* Sam is the identified patient and also most concerned about his parents

the different subsystem contexts representing the relationships in the family. This revealed considerable differences in how people saw these subsystems, and it suggested some of the patterns of side-taking. Most interestingly, of all the people in the family, Sam* is the one to have taken it upon himself to worry about his parents' relationship. It turned out that he had a strong fear that his parents' marriage was in difficulty and they might separate. This was overtly denied by the parents but was suggested by their detached and distant manner with each other in the session.

Variations over time

The family beliefs serve to bridge the past, the present and the future and can operate as if the construct has been valid forever. A useful approach therefore, is to ask about when the problems started and about fluctuations and changes in the problem. This introduces the possibility that the constructs currently in use have not been and need not always be valid or applicable. It also sows the idea that the construction, especially regarding the person with the problem, was originated by one or more members. Again, this implies that it can change. Exploring how the person used to behave can also be employed to make some similarities with the current behaviours. For example, there will often be claims that Jane used to eat properly and was helpful, worked hard and so on. These constructs can be taken out of the bottom drawer, so to speak, dusted off and explored in terms of whether they perhaps still apply. Furthermore, it can be considered what else was happening in the family at the time to convince people that these positive constructs no longer applied.

Constructing new options: reframing and stories

A man was parking his car in a busy street and accidentally bumped into the parked car behind him causing some damage. A number of passers-by stopped to see the outcome of the incident. The man walked over to the damaged car, saw that it was empty and went back to his car. A few moments later he returned with a pen and a piece of paper and, to the satisfaction of the onlookers who probably believed that he was writing down his name and address, he proceeded to write the following message: 'I have bumped into your car and there are some witnesses waiting for me to write my name and address down for you.' He folded the piece of paper, tucked it under the car's windscreen wipers and smiled at the onlookers who returned his smile with approving expressions!

(From Goffman 1974)

We can talk about a set of beliefs which fit together to tell a particular story as a frame or a picture. They are the levels of meaning that we discussed in Chapter 4 and elsewhere. Much of human interaction consists of alternating between these frames or levels, as we have seen. Humour, creativity and story-telling typically make considerable use of unexpected changes between these levels or frames. In the above example we can see some 'playing' at twisting the frames around in that the passers-by expected that a particular frame would apply in that situation. The driver carried out some behaviour which appeared to be consistent with the frame of being 'honest and owning up', but in fact created quite a different frame. In common language such twists are sometimes seen as cheeky. Example of this was a case of a couple who bought a house only to find that all the dimensions of the rooms were about 15 per cent less than had been described on the estate agent's leaflet. The case eventually came to court, whereupon a young representative of the estate agent stated that he understood how the couple felt, but 'there again why not look on the bright side and think of all the money they would save on the fitted carpets!' Almost invariably this kind of unexpected flitting between frames is amusing and interesting; it seems to provide a sort of 'tickling of our consciousness'.

Reframing individuals
A frame in essence is a set of higher-order or superordinate constructs which have implications about how a situation is to be experienced. As in the example for Laing, we can see an over-arching belief held by the man that he had insomnia, that this was a problem, that it was something to be got rid of and so on. A frame, then, is a kind of story about what is going on. The example from Laing illustrates a piece of reframing in that the problem is put in a different, more favourable light.

This piece of reframing offers a more positive and productive way of looking at the situation for the man. There is a need to ask how this might fit into the man's social system. For example, will his wife be pleased to hear that it should be seen as an opportunity to gaze at the stars, or will she be indignant and a bit fed up with him keeping her up all night with his wanderings about the house? For this reason it is usually more helpful to offer a reframe in such a case with other significant people present, to see whether they will also accept it, rather than risk the reframe being dismissed when the client returns home.

From an interactional perspective we realize that problems are not solely to do with one member of a family. At the same time, it is important to realize that frequently the family has a strongly held belief that the problem does reside in one person. To offer a reframe which involves all of them may therefore be unacceptable. This is often apparent in the early stages of therapy. A reframe aimed largely at the individual presenting the problem may be appropriate and fit with the family belief systems, while at the same time creating more flexibility and variety in how the person is seen. For example, a widowed mother saw her adult son suffering with schizophrenic symptoms as generally 'lazy' and preferring to 'stay horizontal in bed' as much as possible. She continually fussed over her son and had insisted on breaking up a relationship with a female patient that she did not approve of, bringing her son back home to live with her. She admitted that at the moment she was very anxious and lonely herself, and her son provided her with some company even though there were conflicts. A reframe suggesting that she and her son were very close and in some ways like a married couple was offered as a way of moving away from her emphasis on his 'sick' role. This appeared to be partly accepted by them, but the mother later defended her actions. She further insisted that he did need looking after, and went on to ask about medication. Consequently the reframe was adjusted to focus back on her son but pointing out how he was showing signs of looking after her, and that she did need him, but of course that he also needed her. This was much more acceptable and become thoroughly incorporated into her vocabulary and descriptions of her son's progress. A number of factors such as the pacing and the importance of a belief in the family's overall construct system have to be considered. Failure to do so can lead us to generate reframes which are rejected and cause entrenchment rather than movement of the belief system.

It is also extremely important to consider our own beliefs about what is appropriate to say as reframes. One assumpion can be that what we say has to be positive or 'nice'. Reframing need not invariably be positive, as Watzlawick demonstrates in the following reframing of the cycle of nagging–withdrawing described in Chapters 2 and 5.

> Her behaviour can be re-labelled as one which, on the one hand, is fully understandable in view of his punitive silence, but which, on the other hand, has the disadvantage of making him look very good to any outsider. This is because the outsider would naively compare his behaviour to hers and would only see his quiet, kind endurance, his forgiveness, the fact that he seems to function so well in spite of the very trying home situation to which he has to return every evening, etc.
>
> (Watzlawick *et al.* 1974: 104)

This reframe focuses on the woman and offers a way of seeing the situation which draws in imaginary outside observers to raise the question of how she would look to others. Watzlawick *et al.* (1974) refer to reframing as a 'gentle art,' and we need to consider carefully what such a reframe assumes. Underlying this reframe we can see two assumptions made about the belief system of the woman. The first is that she cares about *what others think*. Second, it is assumed that she values having *power* in the relationship, since it is stressed that the man's apparent 'goodness' might give him an 'up' position. We might call this a pretty 'realistic' reframe in that the assumptions can be made fairly reliably about most couples. As we saw in Chapter 5 power is a major issue for couples, and we can safely assume that most people do care what others think even if they try to deny it. Having said that, it is necessary to be wary about making such assumptions without having a good grasp of a family's belief system. Watzlawick here has not told part of the story about what he already knew about this couple's belief system, though he does emphasize the need to do so elsewhere:

Successful reframing must lift the problem out of the 'symptom' frame and into another frame that does not carry the implications of unchangeability. Of course, not just any reframe will, but only one that is congenial to the person's way of thinking and of categorising reality.

(Watzlawick *et al*. 1974: 102–3)

We have to be careful to check our assumptions about the way a family or a couple sees things. Watzlawick's reframe is not particularly nice, but it probably does fit the kind of entrenched power struggle that characterizes many relationships. Couples who have been together for a long time almost certainly will reject overly nice stories; some couples almost delight in the fact that they are pretty 'tough' characters and are a match for each other. (A classic example of this is Martha and George in Edward Albee's play, *Who's Afraid of Virginia Woolf?* Parts of the play were used by Watzlawick *et al*. in their influential book, *The Pragmatics of Human Communication*.) A desire to tell a nice or happy story might be more a need on the therapist's part, whereas a more realistic or 'tough' reframe may more likely validate and show acceptance of the family's basic assumptions. This is more likely to lead the family to think 'that man is OK, he understands us', which paves the way for co-operation and creative work in the future with the family.

Reframing the whole or part of a system
Palazzoli *et al*. (1978) suggest that it is necessary and useful to reframe all and not just one member of a family. A step in this direction might be to reframe a subsystem first and to build this up to the whole family. The shift of focus moves to suggesting connections in the family and, especially, emphasizing how the symptoms can serve some positive functions, such as maintaining the family system or contact between parts of it that have been broken.

An example was a case of a young boy who was displaying school phobia. His parents were divorced, but considerable bitterness remained between them. A circularity was in operation so that the mother would wake the boy in the mornings and he would procrastinate and avoid going to school until it was too late. His mother would tolerate this for a few days, but then would phone her ex-husband to come and do something and take some responsibility. He would arrive the next day and angrily take the boy to school; later in the day he might ring and say that he had been no trouble and why didn't she sort herself out and handle him properly. The boy and his brother had seen some fights between the parents and were well aware of the unsolved conflicts, having been called upon to arbitrate on several occasions. It was generally accepted that the boy was 'sensitive' and 'caring' towards both his parents. This was developed into a reframe along the lines that 'it might seem strange to suggest this, but perhaps the boy's school refusal served a positive purpose in getting all of them to come along to sort out their feelings. It was important therefore that he shouldn't go back to school too quickly or this work would not be done.' The family appeared to accept this though they showed a wish to maintain the belief that the boy was a little bit too 'soft'. However, this was quickly absorbed by the view that he needed to spend more time with his father to give him a male role model. At a later stage when the boy was going to school four days out of five, it was suggested that it was now simply up to him whether he wanted to go the extra day, but that there was no need to worry that the therapy would stop. Regardless of whether he went the extra day or not, we would carry on seeing them to talk about their relationships. This was fully accepted by the family, and they continued to attend to discuss issues such as the implications of mother's imminent baby from new boyfriend, and the sale of the old family home.

Again, the reframes need not necessarily be positive. The main requirement is that it should be elaborative in the sense of prompting some development of the belief system. Kelly makes clear that this is more likely to occur if there has been validation. It might be sufficient to offer a reframe which basically validates the existence of the family system. For example, in a family with an anorexic daughter, there was much emphasis on how 'close' they were as a family and how there were no conflicts. It was suggested that, without really understanding why, it seemed to us that her illness served to keep them together and thereby maintain the level of closeness which they had all contributed to building up over the years and which we knew they valued.

One of the reasons that it is easier to move and develop from a point of validation than from a position of invalidation, seems to be that many families appear to carry considerable guilt about their part in causing the problems. They may have heard, for example, explanations which emphasize the parental contribution to children's problems, from a variety of sources, the media, in-laws and friends. Even if not directed specifically at them, such beliefs are likely to be internalized and come to represent a source of internal guilt and fuel for accusations that they regularly direct at each other. Often they will have been trying to explain or justify their actions to themselves and to each other, sometimes for many years. A reframe therefore is not simply another attempt at justification! This will probably have little effect, since families at the same time have become expert at disqualifying such justifications. Instead, the reframe needs to be based in their own belief system and assist them to reorganize their beliefs in ways which lead them to contemplate new choices or potential options and new possibilities for behaviour. Moreover, a successful reframe needs to consider how the explanations are aligned in the family so that a reframe does not appear inadvertently to support one member against another. This is particularly evident where the problems are chronic and the beliefs entrenched, as in cases where a medical model has come to be accepted. A question to ask is who is most and least likely to accept or challenge the reframe that might be suggested. It is very different to deliberately use a reframe to imbalance a family, as opposed to being surprised when one member gets very cross.

An example of the issue of side-taking is shown in the case of Sarah and Barry. The complaint was that Sarah was not interested in sexual intimacy any longer. The couple initially presented a united belief that their relationship was satisfactory and that the only problem they had was a sexual one. Barry explained that he thought the problems were related to the death of Sarah's mother and that she had ceased to be interested since then. Sarah expressed lukewarm support of this explanation. Some preliminary exercises such as massage were suggested in order to re-establish physical contact. However, these were not carried out because Sarah refused. There emerged a very strong pattern of demand–denial in the couple's relationship, with Barry continually asking for sex and Sarah increasingly convinced that that was all he wanted from her. It became clear that she resented Barry's continual harassment for sex, and that in fact all was far from well in their relationship. Initially it was suggested, and agreed, that they could confine sex to one day a week, thereby giving Barry a chance to show, on the remaining days, that he was not just interested in her for sex but still liked her company and valued her as a person. This appeared to be of some value, but Sarah did not show any increased interest in sex, nor did she express much improvement in her feelings towards Barry.

A number of core constructs emerged in the discussion which discriminated between the couple and were the source of conflict. Sarah saw Barry obsessed by sex, energetic, assertive, physical, older and sociable. He worked as a scaffolder and, despite being fifteen years older, was extremely fit. Sarah had a sedentary job in clerical work. These differences were continually emphasized with Sarah expressing willingness to discuss the relationship and Barry expressing increasing reluctance to do so. This drew the therapist into a coalition with Sarah along the verbal pole of the construct physical–verbal. An attempt was made to reframe their relationship as demonstrating a complementarity, and this appeared to be accepted. Sarah agreed that she did not want to be more assertive sexually for example, and Barry comfirmed that he did not wish her to either. Progress was minimal and the couple complained that they were now arguing openly, which they had not done before. It was suggested that this was a sign that they were working things out.

Subsequently Barry came up with a new version of his initial belief, which was that Sarah had been sexually abused in her childhood. He felt that this was the real reason for her reluctance, though again she showed little agreement about this. At this point it was felt that some of Barry's fundamental beliefs were to do with physical or external causes, and these underpinned his reluctance to engage in an analysis of the relationship. Rather than challenging his explanations further, it was suggested that his concern was admirable and that perhaps he and Sarah could look at these issues further themselves. At this point they terminated therapy, and said that things were better and they were continuing to sort things out for themselves.

Dell (1986) makes the point that it is important to recognize that the fate of an intervention should teach us something about what we believe to be true about our clients:

> As therapists we typically respond to the failure of out intervention in one of three ways. We decide that our theory and view of the client is correct, but that (a) 'I did the intervention incorrectly', (b) 'I didn't do it long enough', or (c) 'It should have worked, but there is something wrong with this client' (that is, the client is uncooperative, resistant, pathological, not ready for therapy, and so on). In other words, we are able to interpret or disqualify the data so that our theoretical assumptions are preserved. And, because our theories remain intact, we then continue to make interventions that are specified by those theories. Watzlawick *et al.* (1974) call this the 'more of the same' phenomenon.

Reframes can be developed into stories or narratives. When a family is asked to explain their problems, what is offered is often a kind of a story of their lives. Cecchin (1988) gives an example of a middle-aged couple with an adult son who had been hospitalized with a psychotic breakdown. The couple told a story of how both of them were artistic people but had been unable to realize their ambitions. The father had *sacrificed* his ambitions as a painter for the sake of providing for his family, and had taken up a job in business which he had lost prior to the son's problems. The belief was maintained that they were both strong, talented and capable people, and that father would eventually emerge and be recognized as an artist. The son, on the other hand, was seen in terms of a story about 'week ego strength'. He was seen to be incapable of looking after himself and did not have enough strength and drive. Following some discussion of the circumstances around the son's breakdown, it was revealed that the father had been depressed after losing his job and that this had influenced the whole family. Slowly Cecchin started to weave in a new story along the lines of how protective the son was and how he was now *sacrificing* himself for his parents by becoming ill and distracting them from their own problems. This fitted with a wider story of both parents also making *sacrifices* in not selfishly pursuing their artistic ambitions.

The family did not accept this story whole, but instead there was a to and fro of elaboration, challenging and redrafting the story until it was acceptable to the family. For example, it was maintained that even though father had been depressed, he had handled the loss of the job bravely and tried to protect his family. The couple accepted an embellishment of the story along the lines that they had done a good job in teaching their son also to be stoic and uncomplaining. A new story was jointly woven which was acceptable to all of them. Not just any story will do; it must fit with the family's belief system and offer opportunities for greater choices and movement in the future. A fantasy which is likely to collapse on the first contact with the outside world, for example, is obviously to be avoided.

Neutrality, balance theory and positive connotation

The therapist's position in offering some challenges to a family's belief system has been described by De Shazer (1982) in terms of balance theory and coalition theory. To start with, he suggests that it is possible to represent a symptom as a balanced triadic relation:

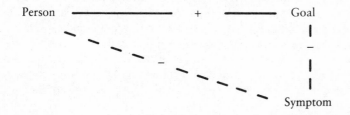

The relation between the person and the goal is positive and that between the symptom and the goal, and the person and the symptom is negative. This represents a balanced triad in that there is no contradiction or tension between having a positive view of the goal and two negative relations between the goal and the symptom, and the person and the symptom. Unfortunately there is also as a consequence very little impetus for change either, except that the symptom will surely become worse as time goes on.

This idea can be extended to show how a therapeutic intervention can be employed to introduce an unbalanced triad, which can have the effect of exerting some pressure on this original triadic relation to change. For example, in a family the parents complained that their two girls were uncontrollable, bickering and constantly rampaging around. The team accepted the parents' predicament uncritically, but offered a tentative positive connotation of their behaviour by praising the girls' inquisitiveness and ability to explore on their own. The situation can broadly be summarized as follows:

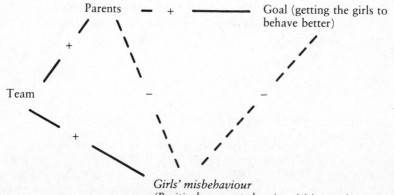

Girls' misbehaviour
(Positively connoted as inquisitiveness)

This situation is summarized in terms of balances and tensions in the system between the therapy team and the family. By adopting a positive, accepting and uncritical position towards the family, the relationship between the therapist and the family is defined as positive. However, the therapist also adopts an uncritical and positive position towards the girls' behaviour by suggesting that it may have some positive aspects. Since the parents have a negative view of this, it puts the triad of family, therapist and complaint in an unbalanced situation – two positive and one negative relations. Following further observation of the family's interactions, it became clear that the parents were unsuccessful in gaining the girls' attention at the start of sequences of misbehaviour, rather than simply in exercising force to stop them. This offered a redefinition of the complaint and allowed some new goals to be set up, such as how to gain the girls' attention.

Tasks can also be set which implicitly offer a redefinition of a problem. In this case the family were told a story of a family with a similar problem to theirs, where the parents solved the problem by buying water pistols and squirting the kids whenever they did not attend to what the parents were asking. The family modified this idea and bought and used a referee's whistle to gain the girls' attention when they started to get too boisterous. Water pistols or whistles are not punishments in the same way that physical force such as spanking is, and it implied that the parents needed to do something a little different to let the children know they meant what they were requesting from them.

De Shazer's ideas clarify the value of an accepting, empathetic and uncritical view of people and their problems. It also helps to show how such a neutral position regarding both the family and the symptoms offers a dissonant situation for the family which can be utilized by exploring new ways of seeing the problems with them and thereby reducing the dissonance. Trust is a vital ingredient of the relationship with the family, and in order to maintain this sense of trust, the interventions offered should not be so excessive or intimidating that they change the positive relations between the family and the therapist. De Shazer calls this being 'isomorphic' with the family's view, prompting a tolerable amount of change which 'fits' with their existing views.

Paradox and creative double-binds

Changes, jumps, twists and plays upon levels of meaning can be amusing and creative. It is this, rather than the idea of paradoxing, that is doing something to a family which is important. De Shazer's use of balance theory is again useful in considering what underlies paradoxical interventions with families. These are characterized by interventions which appear to be a little bit crazy or contrary to common sense. For example, a family may be asked deliberately to maintain the problematic state of affairs, or even to practise and increase a particular symptom or style of interaction. It might be suggested that they attend for therapy but do not talk about their problems, that they carry out a task spontaneously, that they engage in apparently incompatible behaviours such as carrying on with the behaviours but observing them in detail at the same time. In a sense such approaches are usually called upon when more so-called 'common sense' or logical methods have appeared not to work.

It is possible to see these 'paradoxical' interventions as further probes which test out a family belief system that we as yet do not understand. Such explorations into the unknown need to be based on a trusting relationship with a family, since possible negative reactions elicited in a family can otherwise be disastrous. A consideration of the family's belief helps us to realize that in the context of a trusting relationship, a paradoxical intervention can have a positive effect, but in the context of an unsure relationship, it can easily be interpreted in a variety of negative and destructive ways. A paradox is a form of positive double-bind and exists only in the context of a relationship between the therapist and the family (Rossi, 1980). What functions as a constructive paradoxical intervention in one family does not necessarily do so in another.

The basis for paradoxical interventions is the belief that some families have a characteristic transactional style which is contrary or characterized by double-binds. Palazzoli et al. (1978) describe psychotic families as characterized by a meta-rule that all communications are too disqualified, and consequently it is very hard to pin down what anyone actually believes or feels. Underlying such behaviour can be a belief system whwich contains a set of assumptions that revealing what one feels is potentially dangerous and to be avoided. Avoidance cycles are notoriously prone to self-validation, since each time there is a sense of relief attached to avoiding the dreaded issues. And since they are avoided, they become increasingly more dreadful. Faced with such a family, a therapist will have a hard time in extracting any beliefs other than such higher level beliefs about the necessity to avoid emotive issues. The therapist is also likely to find that the family agrees to carry out instructions and assignments, but then returns with a variety of excellent reasons each time for not having done them. In order to validate such a system, a therapist is required to act in a seemingly paradoxical way, for example by saying it is perfectly acceptable not to talk about their problems in therapy but to meet regularly with them to focus on other matters.

The trouble with talking about paradox is that it is very easy to end up in muddles, as many trainee family therapists attempting to use this technique know. The point is that it is not in fact a technique but a form of relationship. As a form of relationship we all know what it is, because we all tease each other, make jokes and use apparently paradoxical techniques on each other. For example, a young mother might say to her child who is playing with her food: 'That's all right, leave it, I don't mind if you get spots and become unhealthy.' Similarly using a joke to defuse a situation, put people at ease, break the ice and so on is a vital social skill. All of us have the ability to make people laugh and the ability to work out what will cause mirth and what will cause offence. We naturally use such playful or paradoxical techniques with each other on the basis of some calculations which take into account how the other person sees me, what I can get away with, and what they think they can get away with, with me.

Cultivating a sense of humour is helpful. In one example of the use of a paradoxical intervention, a family with a young teenage girl who was developing a morbid obsession with her acne, the family were asked to put aside time each day for examining the development of the girl's spots. They were asked not to try to stop her obsession, but if anything to encourage it. The family returned saying that they had attempted to carry out this 'spot department' one evening, but found it so silly that they broke into hysterical laughter. The girl's younger sister pointed out that they had not known whether to include looking for spots on her sister's bum, whereupon the therapy session collapsed into more hysterical laughter.

We can be fairly sure that most families know there is some 'leg pulling' going on when paradoxical interventions are attempted, but this is acceptable if the relationship with the therapist is sound. Of course, families may also tease the therapists. With one couple in which the husband was an assistant publishing editor well used to word games, he tended to make funny faces if therapeutic jargon was used and started to pick up on some reframing ideas. He described how he had attended a play in which his wife had acted recently: 'She was really *high* after the show, joking with her friends and the other players because she had beeen acting in it. I felt really *low* afterwards – I had to sit and watch the play.' Most sessions included this kind of banter, and at one stage it was suggested that the couple displayed some 'fundamental dilemmas of human existence – but unfortunately we had no answers for them'. Another couple remarked that when we returned after the discussion to present the interventions, it was like the jury returning. When we suggested at one stage that there was a difference of opinion between us, they joked, using one of our previous interventions on us, that our disagreement reflected a complementary balance of opinion and we shouldn't worry about it!

Dell offers a powerful critique of the concept of paradoxical intervention, and points out that much of what we regard as paradox has to do with our own belief systems as therapists. He suggests that problems arise because we often have not fully accepted the idea that families do have their own belief systems and that we simply cannot predict how they will act or respond to a suggestion of ours. He calls this the mistaken belief in 'instructive interaction', the idea that we can get people to do things rather than that they inevitably choose how to act based upon the way they are:

> paradoxical interventions are 'paradoxical' because the observer (who considers those particular interventions to be paradoxical) is, at some level, believing that the interventions in question are objective. They

are not. The effect, for example, of telling a person to practice his or her symptom, is determined by that person's structure, not by the supposedly objective or instructive nature of the intervention (which might lead us to think that practicing the symptom would make it worse).

(Dell 1986: 231)

In the next chapter two detailed case studies are offered in order to illustrate the ideas discussed so far.

Chapter 9

Two case studies

The following cases are now offered as illustrations. The examination of belief systems and in particular the application of Kelly's ideas form an important part of these case studies. The analysis is presented in an informal way which is more suitable and applicable to the work with families in therapy. Above all the approach is intended to illustrate how a focus on belief systems makes us more sensitive to the constructs embedded in the explanations that people have about their problems and the language they use to describe them.

Case studies

The Greg family

Harry Greg, at the time in his late twenties, had been hospitalized with psychotic symptoms on over five occasions over a period of eight years. He would display violent outbursts at home, usually towards his mother, engage in bizarre conversations with himself, and embarrass his parents by going out into the street and shouting obscenities in the general direction of his parents' neighbours. More generally he had failed at attempts to finish off his education despite the fact that he was intelligent and articulate at times. He had not had a girlfriend and was sexually inexperienced, though he was reported by his parents, especially his mother, to be increasingly restless and sexually frustrated. Harry did not have any friends apart from other patients that he had associated with in hospital and psychiatric hostels. He had tried some jobs in the past, mainly unskilled activities, and had abandoned these, though he did have an interest in gardening and nature conservation-related activities.

His parents were well-educated and articulate people. His father, now retired, had held a responsible and demanding management position in the chemical industry. Mr Greg now had a part-time job. The parents had met while both of them were working in Kenya, with Mrs Greg at the time working in a secretarial post. They had one other daughter, aged 22, who had left home and was living some way across country with her boyfriend. It was claimed that she was problem free, and the parents did not wish to have her involved in any therapy. Harry was said to get on with his sister, who visited the family fairly regularly.

At the time of involvement with this family Harry had moved back home, following his displaying disruptive behaviour in a residential hostel or half-way house. The move back home was the parents' decision since they were unhappy with Harry's progress at the unit. The return home had been reasonably satisfactory for a while, but now the situation was becoming unbearable due to frequent conflicts, mainly between Harry and his mother. He was said to be abusive towards her and had on several occasions struck her.

The first session

The first impressions of the family were that Harry, rather than appearing to be intimidating as his reported aggressiveness had implied, instead, struck us as a rather frail, prematurely elderly-looking and eccentric man. He was thin, wore glasses and a cap pulled over his eyes, and had a variety of badges ornamenting a sports jacket with distinguished-looking leather patches on the elbows. Mr Greg immediately started the talking and took control of the session, whereas Mrs Greg smiled continually but said little unless prompted. The major theme of the first session was that the family were in agreement that they did not want to be there and were angry at previous attempts at family therapy. When asked which of them was most unhappy about attending, it was agreed that Mr Greg was. The following exchange illustrates the beliefs that the family held, as voiced by Mr Greg, about therapy and also a characteristic interactional sequence that was repeated with minor variations at least a dozen times during the session:

Therapist: Why do you think the sessions weren't of benefit to you and how do you think they could be? What kind of meetings would be of benefit? What was wrong with the previous session?
(Brief silence followed by Mr Greg being elected to speak for the family)

Mr Greg: There was far too much stress as far as I could see on the historical, psychiatric side of why Harry was like he was and a lot of reiteration of questions regarding personalities, differences between the three of us. Whereas Pat (Mrs Greg) and I, I think, felt that there was, certainly in the latter months of his stay at P (unit), since he came off the drugs, that an emphasis on the occupational therapy

side would have been useful. We both used to say, 'He's
not doing anything, he's lying around in bed.' All we can
get from the staff is if he is not self-motivating there is
nothing we can do about it (Mrs Greg nodding in
agreement).

There was no way of being able to motivate him into
doing something when he had in fact come off the drugs,
when we thought that was an ideal time as there was an
obvious change inside him, more energy. Something
should have been done on a more practical side, and we
continued for some time after that on what we felt were
rather irrelevant questions and answers of which most of
the time was spent in Harry doing nothing and me doing
90 per cent of the talking and it really seemed to me that it
wasn't productive.

Therapist: Thank you. Harry, do you want to tell me what, if
anything, would be useful for you here?

Harry: (Silent)

Mrs Greg: (Smiling, whispers) Harry, come on.

Mr Greg: (Joining in crossly) Harry.

Mrs Greg: (Smiling more) Come on.

Mr Greg: Harry, come on. (Crossly)

Mrs Greg: (Turning near to Harry and looking into his face with a
beaming smile) Come out of that trance, Harry.
(Turning to therapist smiling still) He gets like that
sometimes.

Outside analysis

The most striking feature of this family was a tremendous sense of
enmeshment. The number of interruptions made was stunning, and both
parents would take it upon themselves to speak for Harry whenever an
attempt was made to prompt him to voice his views. It seemed clear that
there were extremely powerful anticipations on the parents' part that Harry
would not be able to speak his mind properly, and for his part Harry looked
to his parents to help him answer. He typically started with some mumbled
words and then glanced towards his parents, apparently expecting them to
interrupt him at any second. As they started to do so, he would attempt to
hurry out a few more words. The sequence appeared to be rather like a
children's game of chasing where a child taunts another child to catch her
and runs off at the moment they start to move towards them. The sequence
was so powerful that it was extremely difficult to avoid starting to play into
it and similarly start trying to 'help' Harry get his words out. The session at
times rapidly disintegrated into an incomprehensible babble of interruptions
and people speaking for each other, apart from when Mr Greg proceeded to
offer a monologue, as above.

The second hypothesis from the first sessions centred around the account given by the family of the conflict between Mrs Greg and Harry. In the session Mrs Greg voiced repeated criticisms of Harry's behaviour towards her at home, but this was always disqualified by the manner in which she stated it by displaying a wide, pleasant smile. Mr Greg confirmed that Harry did behave badly but that this usually stopped the moment he returned home. Mrs Greg went on to explain that she felt the 'odd one out' with the two men being very 'close' and having 'a lot in common'. This coalition between the men left her feeling 'very on her own.' Her daughter was a long way away, and though she did have some female friends whom she had previously turned to for support, she was no longer able to do this because she could not drive the car as she had become too 'nervous'. She added that both men were 'strong personalities' and that she often felt that she was 'fighting for her life'. All in all, her life at the moment was not very pleasant, and she had become nervous and depressed. Mr Greg added that he was now worried about leaving Mrs Greg and Harry together on their own when he went out to work.

This pattern suggested the kind of gross disturbance of power described by Haley (1980) and Madanes (1980) in such families. Mrs Greg appeared to have very little power in this system, and it was likley that she felt unable to give any clear messages since she was unsure that Mr Greg would support her. Madanes clarifies how double-bind or contradictory communications exist in the context of such situations where there is a reversal in the expected hierarchy: 'If a parent is simultaneously defined as the person in charge of a family and as tyrannised and exploited by his own child, the family members involved in this situation will communicate in incongruent ways that reflect their incongruent positions in the hierarchy' (p.181).

The evidence from the session suggested the circularity shown in Figure 14. Harry's behaviour appeared to serve the function of keeping his parents together, since Mr Greg's presence was necessary to avoid trouble between Harry and his mother. However, Mr Greg and Harry could go out, but this left Mrs Greg on her own. Since she was nervous and could not drive to see her friends, this implied that she would be lonely and would feel depressed. In turn, then, her symptoms operated also to keep her husband at home, somewhat reluctantly. Mr Greg appeared to be irritated with his wife's symptoms and appeared much more concerned about Harry. The couple did not openly disagree, but they did voice some indirect criticism of each other at times. Mrs Greg said that her husband talked a lot and was aggressive, but again with a smiling expression that served to deny any real expression of anger on her part. Above all, this pattern was serving to maintain Mrs Greg in a subordinate and powerless role in the family.

This pattern was extremely well established, and the family now displayed considerable reluctance to engage in any more therapy. Mr Greg repeatedly spoke for the family in stating that they did not wish to attend any more sessions and simply wanted us to find Harry some suitable accommodation. Their attempted solution was to push Harry out into a psychiatric unit but to avoid any exploration of their dynamics at home.

Figure 14   Circularity depicting a key process of interaction in the Greg family

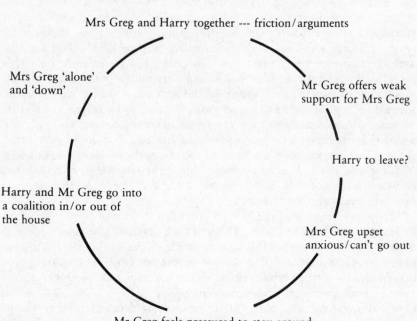

This had taken place several times before, and on each occasion Mr Greg had maintained continuous contact with Harry, visiting him daily and voicing criticism of the staff's ineffectiveness in prompting Harry to get on his feet and do some work instead of lying around in bed all day.

Inside analysis: the family belief system
This revealed the following broad clusters of constructs:

Table 3   Summary of construct clusters in the Greg family.

A	B	C
abusive–non abusive	act stupid–act properly	get on well–don't get on
black moods–good moods	trance–normal	friction–no friction
behave badly–behave well	silly–sensible	close–distant
medication wrong–OK	fool around–make effort	lot in common–little
stimulation–no stimulation	lie in bed–get on	alone–two men together
	lazy–working	
	selfish–responsible	

D	E	F
talkative–quiet	ill–well	go out–at home
aggressive	depressed–not depressed	leave–stay
strong personality–mild	nervous–not nervous	living at home–away
old-fashioned–modern	tense–relaxed	
close–open	no support–support	
	fighting for life–not	

This system of shared constructs in the family could be categorized into six related clusters. A and B: There were a set of constructs which covered the perceptions and anticipations of Harry's behaviour in the family. The cluster A covered the area of his aggressive behaviour, especially towards his mother – 'abusive', 'black moods' and 'behaving badly'. The second set, B, covered the area of his psychotic behaviour and centred around the construct 'acting stupid' and included the constructs 'trance', 'silly', 'fool around' and 'lazy'.

E: represented a cluster covering Mrs Greg's feelings in the family and painted a picture of her as feeling 'ill', 'depressed', 'fighting for her life', 'nervous' and 'alone'.

C: this cluster covered the constructs relating to the relationships and patterns of closeness in the family, and covered the area of the conflict between Mrs Greg and Harry – 'distant', 'don't get on', 'friction' and 'little in common' – and the contrast poles embodied the coalition between Harry and Mr Greg.

D: this cluster covered the differences between the personalities of the family members, and also the hierarchy in the family in that Mr Greg was seen to be 'aggressive', 'talkative' and a 'strong personality'. In contrast Mrs Greg saw herself and was seen as 'quiet' and 'non-aggressive'. However, she also saw herself as a 'strong personality' in a different way to Mr Greg, especially in that she was more capable of being 'open' and was 'more modern' in her outlook and ability to be 'open' to discussing feelings. Harry was seen as like Mr Greg in being 'aggressive' and a 'strong personality', but as more like this mother in being 'quiet' and sensitive to feelings, 'open'.

F: lastly a set of constructs covered the issue of movement in or out of the family – 'leaving–staying', 'going out', 'living at home'. The important issue of whether Harry should be living with them and the issues in finding him a place were covered by this cluster.

Control and parenting

Constructs regarding parenting Harry or working in unison as parents were not very obvious in the family. Instead there was an implicit acceptance of a belief based on the medical model, which included the idea that medication was paramount in controlling Harry. Mr Greg, in particular, voiced repeated criticism of staff who had been involved with Harry for not 'stimulating' him and 'prompting' him to do things.

Embedded here also were a number of contradictory sets of implications between the constructs which were implied confusions about how to deal with Harry, especially how to shape up his 'good' rather than 'bad' behaviour.

Harry Problems – acts stupid, bad behaviour, lazy
     Acts normal – medication OK

This construction made it difficult for Harry ever to assert his independence and prove that he was normal, since any apparent successes could be seen as due to the correct medication rather than efforts on his part. A similarly no-win set of implications covered his anger and black moods.

Harry Black moods – behaving badly
     Behaving well – medication OK

The medical construction served to remove the possibility for Harry to gain any praise or rewards for changes he initiated; in other words, it had become very difficult for him to gain any validation or sense of autonomy and control. It also removed the need to look for any causal factors in other aspects of the family relationships. Typically, the family reverted to the medical model belief system when exploration of interpersonal issues was attempted. A related set of beliefs was based on a form of learning theory. It was suggested by Mr Greg that Harry had become 'selfish' and 'lazy' because the institutions he had lived in did not make any demands upon him, so that he had got into the habit of looking after himself and no one else. This also served to excuse his bad behaviour towards his mother. It denied the coalition between the men and obscured the failure of Mr Greg to support Mrs Greg against Harry's abusive behaviour.

Interventions
The initial strategy with the family revolved around attempting to re-engage them in therapy since they held negative attitudes to previous treatment. It was emphasized that we would be starting anew and that the exploration of psychiatric history had not worked, so it was best to leave that kind of activity behind and simply focus on concrete issues like accommodation and helping Harry to find some work. This was an attempt to validate their belief system and to remove the threat that they would have to examine deep issues again. Interestingly, this had the effect of prompting the family to insist that they did not mind talking about deeper issues, and they hinted that there were marital problems. It was suggested that it might be too early or even inappropriate to explore these issues yet. This message was repeated during a home visit. Second, the emphasis was on effecting some changes in the hierarchy in terms of enabling Mrs Greg to regain a sense of power and control in the family. A deliberate strategy was adopted of giving her time to talk about her problems and consider what ways the parents could work together to exert control over Harry. This was acceptable to Mr Greg since he had indicated in his opening statements that he felt his wife and Harry should have more chance to talk. However, he had to be firmly restrained from interrupting when Mrs Greg did attempt to talk.

The effect of reassuring the parents that they did not have to delve into personal material and the focus on Mrs Greg's position prompted a revelation of the 'family secret', which was that in fact there were major marital problems. The couple both stated that they had not been in love for over 25 years, having discovered that they did not really care for each other when they returned to England shortly after the birth of their daughter. They had both had several affairs and would have left each other except for the need to help Harry and because they were financially tied together. They believed that Harry did not realize any of this, but admitted that at times he may have sensed there was tension between them. This revelation represented a massive breakthrough for the family, since they said that they had never confided this information to anyone before. They believed that it was up to them to sort this out, and there was no point in trying to change their relationship since they were basically 'incompatible'.

The parents apparently believed that Harry had not been aware of any tensions between them, and that his behaviour was not related to their marital situation. To question this belief overtly might have been too threatening, and instead it was suggested that Harry, like other children, probably did worry about them a little bit and wanted to see them getting on reasonably well in themselves and with each other. Therefore they would need to reassure him that they would be OK whatever they decided to do now. It was agreed that they would spend some time talking to me as a couple and would keep Harry informed, but that he would continue to stay close to both of them whatever happened.

Harry was also able to say that his preference was for his parents to stay together but that it was up to them. It was suggested that Harry's statement was an indication of his maturity and adult status; he could be sensible when he wanted to be. The construct child–adult also came up in individual sessions with Harry, where he indicated that he became angry at his father when he treated him like a child. Harry would bottle up his anger and burst out in the black moods described by his parents. Following some discussions Harry agreed to try to assert himself immediately when he felt he was treated as a child or to confront his parents about it when it happened. In the family sessions Mr Greg admitted treating Harry like a child when he behaved like one, but went on to say that he was not acting so childish lately. A reframe was offered along the lines of it being inevitable that he would always be thought of as their child, since of course he was, but that it was important to encourage his adult behaviour since they would not always be around to care for him. He would have to cope by himself as an adult when they were older, and even possibly help look after them. The parents seemed to accept this and started to allow Harry some more autonomy and responsibility.

In discussing their problems the couple talked about the sacrifices that they had made in trying to stay together for Harry, and this was developed to suggest that they now deserved some time on their own without Harry. In order to carry on helping him, they needed to have some time to recharge

their batteries and decide whether to stay together. Harry appeared happy
for his parents to do this. To emphasize his independence (and at the same
time appear to accept the belief system that Harry was the problem), some
time was given to work with him individually. It was recognized that it
would be difficult for the parents to allow time for themselves without
drawing Harry back in, and the following frame was offered to validate
their concern about him and at the same time to allow him some
independence:

> *Therapist*: The price of being conscientious parents is feeling bad,
> upset that places aren't OK. You have high standards so
> wherever Harry goes you will always have some *pain*.
> That is the price of being conscientious parents.
>
> *Mr Greg*: There is *no pain* if he is OK, we just want him to find his
> niche.
>
> *Therapist*: Right, there will be *concern*, a niggle that it's not good
> enough, you will think about him. Conscientious parents
> will never be happy, that the place he is in is OK.

(The use of the word *pain* here does not fit with their construct system
and is rejected. A brief negotiation follows and the word *concern* is
acceptable).

One of the individual sessions with Harry also illustrated the intensity of
the involvement that he still felt with his parents. He had now moved away
from home into a residential unit:

> *Therapist*: So you feel happier about your parents now?
>
> *Harry*:   Yes, they seem happier, especially Mum, she smiles more.
>
> *Therapist*: How many times do you think about your parents?
>
> *Harry*:   I should think about once or twice a day.
>
> *Therapist*: When do you think about them? What times?
>
> *Harry*:   Erm. At night, just before I go to sleep and in the morning
> when I wake up.
>
> *Therapist*: What sort of things do you think about?
>
> *Harry*:   I think about the cat, maybe what it's doing at home.
>
> *Therapist*: Do you think the cat is OK?
>
> *Harry*:   Yes.
>
> *Therapist*: What other kinds of things do you think about?
>
> *Harry*:   I think about nice parts – my Mum's pleasant smile,
> expressive face. My Dad can have a smile but not very
> often, sometimes he behaves like someone very silly but he
> sometimes behaves like a good bloke. . . .

(Note that Harry uses the same construct 'silly' applied to him to describe
his father and indicates the coalition and lack of separation between them.)

The major direction of therapy has been to create a new story or set of
beliefs with the family. Harry is now seen and sees himself as an adult and
as able to offer his parents some advice. The construction that the parents
are only staying together for Harry has been exposed as now no longer

viable, since Harry has been reframed as adult and getting on with his own life. His parents have decided to stay together for fairly realistic reasons: 'we have rubbed along for so long now' and 'who else would have us', 'we can't afford financially to split up'. A task was agreed with the couple for them to observe some other couples and compare and contrast their relationship with them. From this they decided that 'we are no worse', and some reframes, such as that they were a 'modern' couple who had been able to experiment with an open marriage and still stay friends, were considered. Mr Greg during this described himself as a 'lovable bastard', a sentiment with which Mrs Greg agreed and laughed. Harry in the meanwhile has developed a good friendship, his visits home are pleasurable, and he is thinking about finding a girlfriend. The changes are modest, but it seems likely that the family has moved away from a belief that he is irreparably ill, which previously fitted with his parents' needs. There is still a danger that Harry may be pulled back, by Mr Greg in particular, in an attempt to avoid further marital changes and intimacy. Contact with the family through review sessions suggests that the parents are beginning to enjoy their increased independence from Harry and are having more of a social life of their own.

Dorothy and George

This couple were in their mid-thirties. Dorothy had been married previously and had two daughters aged 13 and 7, from her previous marriage. The older girl had decided to live with her father and the younger, Carol, with her. The problem was that Dorothy had repeatedly had sexual relations with other men and this caused George great distress. She also suffered from bulimia and had been sexually abused by a relative as a child. Dorothy had not engaged in affairs in her first marriage until the very end. She had done the rounds of the psychiatric services having been treated by a psychiatrist, attended a sexually abused women's centre and received some individual counselling. Relations with her family, who were Jehovah's Witnesses, were bad; Dorothy had been ostracized by them because she had had a divorce and an abortion. Apart from the housework she had very little stimulation, though she had worked for brief periods previously. These invariably resulted in her having sex with her employer or a colleague, whereupon George would force her to leave the job. Even this confinement to the house was not sufficient because she had engaged in sex with workmen who came to the house. She had become pregnant six months previously, but because George was not sure if the child was his, he had insisted that she have an abortion and she had complied with this.

George had not been married before and was close to Carol, Dorothy's daughter. He had a responsible job in local government, a good car and they owned a pleasant house. The couple had met at the local badminton club while Dorothy was still married. The story of this meeting was that George had been interested in meeting her and Dorothy simply went along with his initiatives, as she did with any man who showed an interest in her.

He was apparently shy and she had made the first direct moves: she teased him by looking up his shorts when he climbed a ladder to adjust the badminton net, and later asked him, 'Well, are you going to kiss me or not?'

Initial assessment
The differences in manner, style and appearance were striking in the couple. Dorothy was extremely open, energetic, extrovertly dressed and did virtually all of the talking. She also wore a lot of perfume which pervaded the room. George, on the other hand, was quiet, retiring, thin and dressed unobtrusively. George rapidly disclosed that he felt the problem was Dorothy's affairs with other men, and at the same time offered the explanation that she went with any man who showed any interest in her simply because she wanted the attention. Dorothy initially agreed that it was all her fault, but then started to discuss George's nervousness and inability to eat.

On asking what they knew about each other's family background George emphasized the sexual abuse that Dorothy had suffered; he attributed her current problems to the need for acceptance and attention that this had caused her because she did not value herself. Dorothy described George's background as 'stable' but 'stifling', and said that he had been a 'mother's boy' who allowed his parents to thwart his ambitions, especially an early wish to become a racing driver. She felt that he emerged from his family as 'weak'. Dorothy added that her own mother had 'ruled the roost' and that she was like her in this way, having dominated not only George but also Terry, her first husband.

The first circularity revealed in their interactions was that Dorothy, on the one hand, accepted and, on the other, strongly retaliated against these accusations. She launched into a counter-complaint of how her husband never ate the dinners that she proudly prepared for him. She wanted him to be a *man* with a *real man's* appetite instead of 'struggling to eat a bowl of soup'. This attack generalized into a statement that she had realized that he was not very manly when they had first met, but had hoped that she could '*change him into more of a man*'. She added that he also had a variety of 'hangups' such as feeling insecure at any social gathering. The following illustrates their interactional style:

> *Dorothy*: I am getting all this help, I am doing my utmost to change. As far as affairs go, I haven't been out with anyone for several months now. I feel that I am doing my damnedest but he is doing absolutely nothing towards solving his problem.
>
> *Therapist*: Are you just talking about his eating problem; he has been to hospitals for examination, hasn't he? What other aspects would you like to see changed?
>
> *Dorothy*: I wish he could be more sociable, not be so neurotic about people looking at him. You know if he goes into a room

> with a lot of people he has to sit in the corner, he can't bear anyone behind him.
>
> George: I'm very self-conscious. She's always telling me how puny I look, I can't bear to look in the mirror, how can you not be self-conscious?
>
> Dorothy: I'm only telling you the truth, you tell me to say what I see and feel.
>
> George: Yes, but there is no need to say it and put the boot in as well.
>
> Dorothy: He's the nicest man in the world, really, he's just got so many hangups – well I can't say nothing.

The main theme here seemed to be a contest about the respective definitions of what it was to be 'male' and 'female'. Dorothy expressed the classic paradox in terms of her statement that 'I thought I could change him into more of a man.' For his part George refused to accept what she was trying to offer him – good, hot food. Both of them had serious complaints regarding the other and were insisting that the other change. George wanted his wife to stop having affairs and she wanted him to be more of a man. These constructs were extremely powerful and illustrate the role of external value systems. Dorothy explained that she felt 'ashamed' when she went out with George because he was so 'unmanly' both in his looks and his behaviour. She could 'feel' other people looking at them and felt 'ashamed'. These descriptions were reminiscent of teenagers who talk about their dates and are extremely conscious of maintaining their image. It also emerged that Dorothy's first husband had insisted on constant sex and had on occasions forced her to comply.

The initial hypothesis was as follows. First, the couple were locked in a power struggle which at first glance seemed to be in Dorothy's favour, but on closer examination was possibly one-sided in George's favour. The balance of power appeared to be:

Dorothy	George
Sexually attractive	Good job
Affairs	Economic independence
Good housewife	Car and house
Potential to have a child	Supportive family
'for George'	Stable background – no psychiatric history
Ridiculing George	Dorothy might lose Carol if they split up
	More social contact – work, etc.

Second it was possible that the couple had made a choice in selecting each other which was a temporarily effective solution to their needs. Dorothy wanted a man who would not abuse her as her first husband had done. She was perhaps attempting to move away from the cycle of abuse that had become a part of her self-concept. On the other hand, George wanted to move away from home to stop being a 'mother's boy'. Unfortunately, in the longer term this was not working too well since Dorothy had become dissatisfied with him and was seeking sexual excitement elsewhere. However, this had given George the opportunity to demonstrate some masculine and assertive behaviour, since he would eventually put his foot down and see her men off by confronting them and telling them to leave his wife alone. Dorothy accepted this and did not insist on seeing the men after a confrontation had occurred. Her affairs were in a sense now functioning to activate George to demonstrate some of the behaviours she wanted.

A combination of the two parts of the hypothesis was that the power struggle was becoming even more extreme. As a result of the affairs George was so resentful that he would not change in any way, and attempted to solve the problem by metaphorically keeping her chained in a 'chastity belt' at home. This increased Dorothy's powerlessness, and she retaliated by generally ridiculing George or having affairs.

An interaction in one of the early sessions illustrates the analysis and shows an interesting juxtaposition of food, sexuality and power struggles. Dorothy said that her idea of going out was to go to a restaurant and be with a man who ate heartily. This had powerful sexual overtones and served to attack George's masculinity. However, when it was suggested that Dorothy might stop cooking, George said that despite his claim that he physically could not eat very much, he liked having his dinner ready. It was possible that this was partly so that he would be able to get back at his wife by refusing to eat it. However, contrary to the second hypothesis, Dorothy stated that George was sexually competent and she was not dissatisfied with him. At the same time she partly disqualified this by saying that she had 'taught him a lot'. Similarly she only partially reassured George by saying that she had only gone with other men to please them; she had not derived pleasure from it and had never had an orgasm with them . . . except once'.

The constructs regulating the relationship appeared to be as follows:

Table 4 Summary of construct clusters for Dorothy and George

A	B
eating–finicky	affairs–no affairs
manly–puny	no control–control
man–mother's boy	needing attention–not needing
abusing–not abusing	abused–not abused
hangups–OK	responsible–not responsible
sociable–shy	breaking trust–trustable
normal–abnormal	
proud of–ashamed of	

C	D
good wife–bad	frustrated–content
cooking–not	ambitions–fulfilled
house cared for–not	appreciation–no appreciation
hard working–lazy	wanting other to change–not
guilty–guilt free	want other to change–don't
wicked–good	angry–not angry

The construct cluster broadly divided as follows. A: these constructs covered the perceptions of George and were used to give a generally negative picture around the construct 'not manly', 'puny', 'mother's boy', 'hangups' and 'ashamed of'.

B: a reciprocal set of negative constructions applied to Dorothy. She was seen as having 'broken trust' by virtue of 'having affairs'. At the same time this action was seen in terms of her having 'no control' and a pathological 'need for attention' because of having been 'abused'.

C: this set of constructs mapped the beliefs about what a wife or husband should be. Mostly they covered the area of Dorothy's activity in the house, and she set great store on being a 'good wife' in the sense of 'cooking' and 'taking care of the house'. Both of them regarded themselves and each other as 'hard-working' rather than 'lazy'. Most importantly this set covered the area of religion and guilt. Based upon her religious background Dorothy felt guilty and responsible for the sexual abuse she had suffered as a child. She felt that God was punishing her because she was basically 'wicked' and that she had also caused the problems in her marriage.

D: lastly a set of constructs covered the area of their dissatisfactions with each other, themselves and the relationship. A core construct of hers was 'wanting the other to change'. Both of them were extremely dissatisfied with aspects of each other's behaviour. For George this was specifically to do with her affairs, whereas for her it was a more general dissatisfaction that he was not 'manly'.

The constructs appeared to have some powerful, mutually interlocked implications. George wanted his wife to stop having affairs and was obviously angry about this but largely denied his anger. Dorothy attempted to appease him following her affairs, for example by cooking for him. However, George used this as an opportunity to demonstrate his anger and rejected these offerings. Over time Dorothy had also become angry and anticipated these rejections, and therefore used the dinners in an ambivalent way to punish him for not being a 'proper man' who eats wholeheartedly. A similar pattern appeared to exist regarding socializing; Dorothy said that she liked going out but was angry that George would simply sit in the corner when they did. For his part he anticipated that she would flirt and use the occasion to show him up again as 'unmanly'. This was self-fulfilling since Dorothy would interpret his behaviour as showing that he was 'unmanly', 'shy' and also not caring enough to want her to enjoy herself. Partly in anger, and partly possibly because it was 'fun', she would be quite likely to flirt, thereby convincing George that he was right. His subsequent further retreat and sulkiness would serve to encourage Dorothy to flirt. Their current solution was to avoid socializing, so they never went out. This was also, of course, frustrating for Dorothy and her solution was occasionally to 'escape' and find a 'man'.

A circularity describing this self-fulfilling cycle, appeared to be roughly as follows:

Figure 15 Circularity depicting a key process of interaction between
George and Dorothy

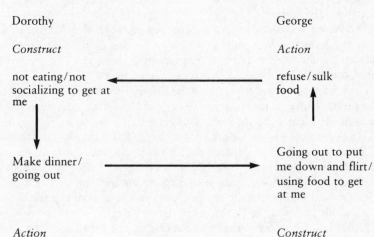

The construct 'responsible–not responsible' also appeared to be central to
the relationship, and was used to deny that their respective actions–not
eating and having affairs–were deliberate. George explained her behaviour
in terms of her being not responsible due to her childhood abuse. This
served to excuse her behaviour and remove the implication that she was
'getting at him' or was dissatisfied with him. This belief was held despite the
fact she did continually 'put him down' as 'unmanly'. Likewise, George was
seen as not being responsible in that he did not eat her dinners because there
was something wrong with him. One implication of accepting responsibility
for both of them would have been that their relationship was no longer
viable and perhaps they should split up. However, as it was they could both
engage in activities such as getting at each other and having affairs without
having to take responsibility for them. The explanations had the quality of
'myths' in that they were distortions and denials of the reality that they were
both dissatisfied and angry with each other and were deliberately acting in
ways which they knew would upset the other.

Interventions
The first major intervention was based on the preliminary hypothesis
regarding the power struggle between the couple as displayed around the
issue of food. It was suggested that Dorothy continue to make wholesome
and large amounts of hot food for George; however, he was also to buy an
expensive surprise present for her. When he came home with it she could
have the option of throwing it into the bin, and he also could have the
option of throwing the food into the bin. The intentions were that this
might paradoxically help disrupt the cycle of conflict over food and make

their mutual anger with each other more overt. A second, related intervention was directed at their mutual negative views of each other, which fuelled their incessant mutual demands to change the other. The following intervention was given as an attempt to reframe these critical and negatively loaded demands:

> There are obviously some things that you would both like to change in each other. That feeling is fundamental to all couples, and if that wanting each other to change disappears, then you might as well pack up and call it a day. As soon as that urge to change each other goes, then there is nothing left of the relationship. So it is actually a healthy sign. If you stop wanting each other to change, what it means is that you have stopped caring about each other. Wanting each other to change as intensely as you do means that deep down there is still quite a lot of feeling for each other.

The intention was to shift the emphasis from a struggle about whether either of them was going to change, more or less or before the other, to an emphasis on how potentially positive this wish for change was. There was an apparent acceptance of the reframe, except that it was followed by an attempt on Dorothy's part to negate it by returning to the well-established frame that it really was all her fault and she needed to change. Without overtly challenging this, the proposition was put that she was protecting him by saying this.

Some further renegotiation of the rigid belief that George was 'unmanly' and that Dorothy had 'no control' comprised the main thrust of the treatment. Some observational tasks designed to encourage elaboration of their constructs about themselves and each other's actions were agreed. Previously the couple had spontaneously attempted a form of 'systematic desensitization', going out to less threatening places such as the theatre to desensitize George's anxiety, though the potential success of this was foiled by Dorothy inevitably insisting that they go for a meal afterwards. Consequently they had argued over eating and the outings had ceased, so that the couple no longer went out together socially or otherwise. Their attempts at 'systematic desensitization' were validated and reconstituted with the proviso that they omit going for a meal afterwards in order to move away from the battle zone of food. The outings encouraged some reconstruction to occur regarding the perceptions of George's social anxiety and Dorothy's anger with his social incompetence. The couple were encouraged to observe carefully what cues triggered and confirmed George's anxieties and Dorothy's sense of frustration and irritation with him. Simultaneously, they were asked to consider what aspects of each other's behaviour confirmed their mutual anticipations or beliefs that these feelings in each other were occurring.

The issue of George's unmanliness pervaded these discussions and coloured the observations from the tasks. A reframe was suggested which attempted to incorporate some of their core constructs:

The two of you have created a powerful myth or fantasy that George is 'unmanly' and 'unattractive'. We are puzzled by why you need to hold on to this myth when it denies the reality. One of our female colleagues says she can easily see how women would be interested in him. In fact, she had a fantasy about him sitting on the bonnet of a racing car, surrounded by attractive women and swilling champagne having just won a race. We think that it is possible that he is colluding with this myth because he feels a need to protect you from feelings of jealousy and insecurity if the truth was faced that other women might desire him.

Following this statement, Dorothy burst out laughing. She then checked herself and said that in fact they had talked about this the other day and perhaps there was some truth in it. Further work along these lines helped the couple to make some reconstructions of their beliefs about each other and their relationship. George started to develop in confidence and the focus turned to Dorothy's beliefs about herself. It emerged that she held a set of beliefs relating to her religion which implied that she saw the future as bleak because she had sinned, and likewise she wanted to escape from the past because of the abuses she had suffered. It was suggested that her impulsive and uncontrolled actions in the past were to do with her 'choosing to live only for the present . . . that she was a woman with no past and no future only existing in the present . . . but this was resulting in her taking some decisions which were later a source of problems for both of them.'

Dorothy was very receptive to this frame, especially in that it helped to accommodate the belief that she had often acted in a powerless way, as she did in her casual sexual affairs. She said she did not derive much sexual pleasure but only did it to please the men. However, at this point in the treatment it was felt that the balance of power may have swung too much towards George. She was no longer ridiculing him and she had ceased having affairs. However, she looked depressed and George was increasingly insistent that she have a child by him. She was contemplating 'giving in' to this demand even though she felt she would be totally 'trapped' as a result. The usual pattern in their interaction was that she would passively comply, then complain and attack George in a variety of ways. This focus on the future was also developed to consider how Dorothy could develop as a person, for example by advancing her education in a way which did not threaten George. The couple decided to take German classes together.

An important aspect of the therapy was that it started to offer a story of a woman making choices, rather than suffering from some form of pathology resulting from her childhood experiences which had been the story at the start of treatment. The conflict over the choice of having a child was dealt with more openly, as was the question of whether they would stay together. Simply, the use of symptoms as a way of negotiating the relationship gradually disappeared, and the couple were able to discuss whether they wished to stay together.

Conclusions

The intention in the last two chapters has been to illustrate some of the ways in which the various theoretical approaches to the study of family belief systems can be combined together within a systemic approach to form a way of working with families. The aim is not to produce yet another brand of therapy but instead, consistent with Kelly's ideas, to offer a framework which is elaborative. This does not attempt to remove all of the problems indicated by each family, but to assist them to regain their abilities to solve the inevitable problems that they will face. Above all the intention has been to emphasize how people in families are involved in a search for meanings. They want to understand what is going on in their family, what other families are like, what kind of a life together they should aim for, and how the world about them is changing. Not to take their understandings and beliefs into account tends to be reductionist, and can lead to a mechanistic model of families which sees them as simply operating in terms of homeostasis, determined by structures and stuck like some kind of a faulty clock.

A mechanistic analysis is inadequate for a number of reasons, not least because we would not be happy to describe our own families and our own rich sensations of family life in such a way. That is not to say such concepts aren't helpful, but that any theory which only accounts for a part of the terrain is necessarily limited. Behaviourism failed to account for cognitions and psychodynamic theory for the social realities and dynamics outside of the individual psyche. Hopefully, what has been suggested in this book goes some way towards offering a framework for developing a little further models about the beliefs and understandings constructed by families. Certainly the integration of systems theory and personal construct theory seems to offer fertile ground for further cultivation.

In the examples of therapeutic work the intention has been to indicate how an exploration of belief systems can be easily integrated into normal clinical practice. It does not require large amounts of paperwork or additional assessment. The core idea is that we continually reflect on the assumptions that we inevitably make about what the family members are thinking. This is what Kelly calls sociality, namely the process of forming constructs about what the other person's constructs might be. This is not something we need to learn to do. It is as inevitable as the fact that we breathe and eat to stay alive. In order to work with families or any person/s, we have to have some notion of how they see the world. Hopefully, this book provides a few tips about how to utilize this natural activity as much as possible in work with families.

Bibliography

Argyle, M. (1969). *Social Interaction*. London, Methuen.

Asch, S.E. (1956). 'Studies of independence and conformity: a minority of one against a unanimous majority' *Psychological Monographs*, 76, no. 9 (whole no. 416).

Bannister, D. (1960). 'Conceptual structure in thought disordered schizophrenics', *Journal of Acta Psychologia*, 20, 104–20.

Bannister, D. and Fransella, F. (1986). *Inquiring Man*. Harmondsworth, Penguin.

Bartlett, F.F. (1932). *Remembering: A study in Experimental Social Psychology*. Cambridge University Press.

Bateson, G. (1958). *Naven*. Palo Alto, Stanford University Press.

Bateson, G. (1972). *Steps to an Ecology of Mind*. New York, Ballantine Books.

Bateson, G. (1980). *Mind and Nature: A Necessary Unity*. London, Fontana/Collins.

Brazelton, T.B. (1974). *Monographs of Society for Research into Child Development*. University of Chicago Press.

Beck, A.T. (1967). *Depression: Clinical, Experiential and Theoretical Aspects*. New York, Harper and Row.

Berger, P.L. and Kellner, H. (1964). 'Marriage and the construction of reality', *Diogenes*, 64, 1–25.

Berger, P.L. and Luckman, T. (1973). *The Social Construction of Reality*. Harmondsworth, Penguin.

Black, D. (1987). 'Handicap and family therapy', in A. Bentovin, G.C. Barnes and A. Cocklin (eds) *Family Therapy: Complementary Frameworks of Theory and Practice*. London, Academic Press.

Boszromenji-Nagy, I. (1973). *Invisible Loyalties*. New York, Harper and Row.

Bowen, M. (1960). 'A family concept of schizophrenia,' in D.D. Jackson (ed.) *The Etiology of Schizophrenia*. New York, Basic Books.

Burnham, J. (1986). *Family Therapy*. London, Tavistock Publications.

Byng-Hall, J. (1980). 'Symptom-bearer as marital distance regulator: clinical implications', *Family Process*, 19, 355–67.

Byng-Hall, J. (1985). 'The family script: a useful bridge between theory and practice,' *Journal of Family Therapy*, 7, 301–7.

Campbell, D. and Draper R. (eds) (1985). *Applications of Systemic Therapy: The Milan Method*. London, Academic Press.

Caplow, T. (1968). *Two Against One: Coalition in Triads*, Englewood Cliffs, Prentice Hall.

Carter, E. and McGoldrick, M. (1980). *The Family Life-Cycle: A Framework for Family Therapy*. New York, Gardner.

Cartwright, C. and Harrary, F. (1956). 'Structural balance: a generalisation of Heider's theory', *Psychological Review*, 63, 277–93.

Castenada, C. (1974). *Journey to Ixlam*. Harmondsworth, Penguin.

Cecchin, G. (1988). 'Old wine in new bottles: hypothesising, neutrality and circulation revisited', Paper presented at the Annual Conference of the British Assocation for Family Therapy, York.

Chodorow, N. (1978). *The Reproduction of Mothering: Psychoanalysis and the Sociology of Gender*. Berkeley, University of California Press.

Chomsky, N. (1986). *Language and Mind*. New York, Harcourt Brace Jovanovich.

Cicourel, A.V. (1967). *Cognitive Sociology*. Harmondsworth, Penguin.

Cronen, V. Johnson, K.M. and Lannaman, J.W. (1982). 'Paradoxes and reflexive loops: an alternative theoretical perspective' *Family Process*, 21, 91–112.

Crowe, M. (1987). 'The treatment of marital sexual problems,' in A. Bentovin, G.C. Barnes and A. Cocklin (eds) *Family Therapy: Complementary Frameworks of Theory and Practice*. London, Academic Press.

Dallos, R., and Procter, H. (1984). *Family Processes*. Milton Keynes, Open University.

Dallos, R, and Aldridge, D. (1986). 'Change: how do we recognise it?' *Journal of Family Therapy*, 8.

Dallos, R. and Aldridge, D. (1987). 'Handing it on: family constructs, symptoms and choice; *Journal of Family Therapy*, 39–58.

De Ath, E. (1984). *Stepfamilies in Great Britain*. National Step Family Association, Information Sheet no. 1.

De Shazer, S. (1982). *Patterns of Brief Therapy: An Ecosystemic Approach*. New York, Guildford Press.

Dell, P.F. (1982). 'Beyond homeostasis: towards a concept of coherence', *Family Process*, 21, 1, 21–41.

Dell, P.F. (1986). 'Why do we still call them paradoxes'. *Family Process*, 25, 2, 223–5.

Dicks, H.V. (1967). *Marital Tensions*, London, Routledge and Kegan Paul.

Duck, S.W. (1975). 'Personality, similarity and friendship choices by adolescents', *European Journal of Social Psychology*, 5, 70–83.

Duvall, E. (1977). *Marriage and Family Development*. Philadelphia, Lippincott.

Fairbairn, W.R.D. (1952). *Psychoanalytic Studies of the Personality*. London, Routledge and Kegan Paul.

Ferreira, A.J. (1963). 'Family myths and homeostasis', *Archives of General Psychiatry*, 9, 457–63.

Festinger, L. (1954). 'A theory of social comparison processes', *Human Relations*, 7, 117–40.

Foucault, M. (1976). *The History of Sexuality*. Peregrine.

Freilich, M. (1957). 'The natural triad in kinship and complex systems', *American Sociological Review*, 29, 529–40.

Garfinkel, D. (1967). *Studies in Ethnomethodology*. Englewood Cliffs, Prentice Hall.

Goffman, E. (1971). *Asylums*. Harmondsworth, Penguin.

Goffman, E. (1974). *Frame Analysis: An Essay on the Organisation of Experience*. Harmondsworth, Penguin.

Haley, J. (1959). 'The family of the schizophrenic: a model system', *Journal of Nervous Mental Disorder*, 29, 357–74.

Haley, J. (1976). *Problem Solving Therapy*. New York, Harper and Row.

Haley, J. (1980). *Leaving Home*. New York, McGraw Hill.

Haley, J. (1981). *Uncommon Therapy*. New York, Norton.

Harre, R. (1979). *Social Being: A Theory for Social Psychology*. Oxford, Blackwell.

Harre, R. and Secord, P. (1972). *The Explanation of Social Behaviour*. Oxford, Blackwell.

Heider, F. (1946). 'Attitudes and cognitive organisation', *Journal of Psychology*, 2, 107–12.

Heyman, B. and Shaw, M. (1978) 'Constructs of relationships', *Journal for the Theory of Social Behaviour*, 8, 3, 231–62.

Hinkle, D. (1965). 'The change of personal constructs from the viewpoint of a theory of construct implications'. Unpublished Ph.D. thesis, Ohio State University.

Hoffman, L. (1981). *Foundations of Family Therapy*. New York, Basic Books.

Jackson, D.D. (1957). 'The question of family homeostasis', *Psychiatry Quarterly Supplement*, 31, 79–99.

Jackson, D.D. (1965a). 'The study of the family', *Family Process*, 4, 1–20.

Jackson, D.D. (1965b). 'Family rules: marital quid pro quo', *Archives of General Psychiatry*, 12, 589–94.

Johns, M. and Dallos, R. (1984). *The Development of Understanding*, Milton Keynes, Open University.

Jung, C. (1959). *Archetypes and the Collective Unconscious*. London, Routledge and Kegan Paul.

Karnst, T.O. and Groutt, J.W.E. (1977). 'Inside mystical heads: shared personal constructs in a commune with some implications for a personal construct theory social psychology', in D. Bannister (ed.) *New Perspectives in Personal Construct Psychology*. London, Academic Press.

Keeney, R. (1979). 'Ecosystemic epistemology: an alternative paradigm for diagnosis', *Family Process*, 18, 117–29.

Kelley, H.H. (1967). 'Attribution theory in social psychology,' *Nebraska Symposium on Motivation*, 15, 192–238.

Kelly, G. (1955). *The Psychology of Personal Constructs*. New York, Norton.

Kelly, G.A. (1963). *A Theory of Personality: The Psychology of Personal Constructs*. New York, Norton.

Klein, M. (1932). *The Psychoanalysis of Children*. London, Hogarth Press.

Klein, M. (1945). 'The Oedipus Complex in the light of early anxieties', *International Journal of Psycho Analysis*, 26, 11–33.

Kuhn, T.S. (1970). *The Structure of Scientific Revolutions*. University of Chicago Press.

Laing, R.D. (1969). *The Politics of the Family and Other Essays*. London, Tavistock Publications.

Laing, R.D., Philipson, H. and Lee, A.P. (1966). *Interpersonal Perception*. New York, Harper and Row.

Lasegue, C. and Falret, J. (1877). 'La Folie a deux, ou folie communiquee?,' *Annals Medico-Psychologiques*, 18, November 1877. English translation by R. Michard (1961) in *American Journal Of Psychiatry*, supp. to vol. 121, 4, 2–18.

Leach, N. (1977). 'Social anthropology', in N. Pole (ed.) *Environmental Solutions*. Cambridge University Press.

Lewin, K. (1958). 'Group decisions and social change,' in E.E. Maccoby, M. Newcombe and E.L. Hartley (eds.) *Readings in Social Psychology*. 3rd edn, New York, Holt, Rinehart and Winston.

McCall, G.J. and Simmons, S.L. (1966). *Identities and Interaction*. New York, Free Press.

Madanes, C. (1980). 'The prevention of rehospitalisation of adolescents and young adults', *Family Process*, 19, 2, 179–93.

Madanes, C. (1981). *Strategic Family Therapy*. San Francisco, Jossey Bass.

Malinowski, B. (1960). *Sex and Repression in Savage Societies*. London, Routledge and Kegan Paul.

Maturana, H. (1981). *Autopoiesis and Cognition*. London, Reidel.

Maturana, H. and Varela, F.J. (1980). *Autopoeisis and Cognition. The Realization of Living*. Boston, Reidal Publishing Co.

Mead, M. (1949). *Male and Female*. Harmondsworth, Penguin. (First pub. 1949; Pelican 1964)

Miller, G.A., Gallanter, E. and Pribram, K.H. (1960). *Plans and the Structure of Behaviour*. New York, Holt, Rinehart and Winston.

Minuchin, S. (1974). *Families and Family Therapy*. London, Tavistock Publications.

Minuchin, S., Rosman, B.L. and Baker, L. (1978). *Psychosomatic Families: Anorexia Nervosa in Context*. Cambridge, Harvard University Press.

Mitchell, J. (1971). *Women's Estate*. Harmondsworth, Penguin.

Moscovici, S. and Zavalloni, M. (1969). 'The group as a polariser of attitudes,' *Journal of Personality and Social Psychology*, 12, 125–33.

Neisser, U. (1967). *Cognitive Psychology*. New York, Appleton-Century-Crofts.

Nisbett, R.E., Caputo, C., Legant, P. and Maracik, J. (1973). 'Behaviour as seen by the actor and as seen by the observer', *Journal of Personality and Social Psychology*, 27, 154–164.

Olson, D.H. (1972) 'Empirically unbinding the double-bind: review of research and conceptual formulations', *Family Process*, 10, 69–94.

Palazzoli, M.S. (1974). *Self-Starvation: From the Intrapsychic to the Transpersonal Approach to Anorexia Nervosa*. London, Chaucer.

Palazzoli, M.S., Boscolo, L., Sechim, G. and Prata, G. (1980). 'Hypothesising-circularity-neutrality: three guidelines for the conductor of the session'. *Family Process*, 19, 3–12.

Palazzoli, M.S., Cecchin, G., Prata, G. and Boscolo, L. (1978). *Paradox and Counterparadox*. New York, Jason Aronson.

Parsons, T. and Bales, R.F. (1956). *Family: Socialisation and Interaction Process*. London, R.K.P.

Pearce, W.B. and Cronen, V.E. (1980). *Communication, Action and Meaning*. New York, Praeger.

Piaget, J. (1955). *The Child's Construction of Reality*. London, Routledge and Kegan Paul.

Piaget, J. (1977). *The Grasp of Consciousness: Action and Concept in the Young Child*. Trans. S. Wedgewood, London, Routledge and Kegan Paul.

Pole, N. (ed.) (1972). *Environmental Solutions*. Cambridge University Press.

Pollner, M. and Wikler, L. (1985). 'The social construction of unreality', *Family Process*, 24, 2, 241–59.

Poster, M. (1978). *Critical Theory of the Family*. London, Pluto Press.

Procter, H. (1978). 'Personal construct theory and the family: a theoretical and methodological study.' Unpublished Ph.D. thesis, University of Bristol.

Procter, H. (1981). 'Family construct psychology', in S. Walrond-Skinner (ed.) *Family Therapy and Approaches*. London, Routledge and Kegan Paul.

Reiss, D. (1980). *The Family's Construction of Reality*. Cambridge, Harvard University Press.

Rogers, C. (1955). *Client Centred Therapy*. New York, Houghton Mifflin.

Rosenthal, R. and Jacobson, L. (1986). *Pygmalion in the Classroom: Teacher's Expectations and Pupil's Intellectual Development*. New York, Holt, Rinehart and Winston.

Rossi, E.L. (ed.) (1980). *The Collected Papers of Milton H. Erickson*. Vol. 1, New York, Irvington Publications.

Ruesch, J. and Bateson, G. (1968). *Communication: The Social Matrix of Psychiatry*. New York, Norton.

Ryle, A. (1975). *Frames and Cages: A Repertory Grid Approach to Human Understanding*. London, Chato and Windus.

Ryle, A. and Lipshitz, S. (1975). 'Recording change in marital therapy with the reconstruction grid', *British Journal of Medical Psychology*. 48, 39–48.

Salmon, P., Bramley, J. and Presley, A.S. (1967). 'The word-in-context test as a measure of conceptualisation in schizophrenics with and without thought disorder', *British Journal of Medical Psychology*, 40, 253–9.

Scanzoni, J. and Palonka, K. (1980). 'A conceptual approach to explicit marital negotiation', *Journal of Marriage and the Family*. Feb. 31–44.

Schachter, S. and Singer, J.E. (1962). 'Cognitive, social and psychological determinants of emotional state', *Psychological Review*, 69, 379–99.

Shah, I. (1968). *The Way of the Sufi*. London, Jonathan Cape.

Shapiro, M.B. (1985). 'A reassessment of clinical psychology as an applied science', *British Journal of Clinical Psychology*, 24, 1, 1–13.

Sherif, M. (1966). *Group Conflict and Cooperation: Their Social Psychology*. London, Routledge and Kegan Paul.

Shorter, E. (1975). *The Making of the Modern Family*. Glasgow, William Collins Sons & Co Ltd. Basic Books.

Skynner, R. and Cleese, J. (1983). *Families and How to Survive Them*. London, Methuen.

Sluzki, C. (1983). 'Process, structure and world views: towards an integrated view of systemic models in family therapy', *Family Process*, 22, 469–76.

Stone, L. (1977). *The Family, Sex and Marriage in England, 1500–1800*. London, Weidenfeld and Nicolson.

Stoner, J.A.F. (1965). 'A comparison of individual and group decisions involving risk', in R. Brown (ed.) (1965) *Social Psychology*. New York, Free Press.

Storms, M.D. (1973). 'Videotape and the attribution process: reversing actor's and observer's points of view', *Journal of Personality and Social Psychology*, 27, 165–75.

Wallerstein, J.S. and Kelly, J.B. (1980). *Surviving the Break-Up*. London, Grant MacIntyre.

Watson, J.P. (1970). 'A repertory grid method of studying groups', *British Journal of Psychology*, 117, 309–318.

Watts, A. (1961). *Psychotherapy East and West*. Harmondsworth, Penguin.

Watzlawick, P. (1964). *An Anthology of Human Communication*. Palo Alto, Science and Behaviour Books.

Watzlawick, P. (1984). *The Invented Reality*. New York, Norton.

Watzlawick, P., Beavin, J.H. and Jackson, D.D. (1967). *Pragmatics of Human Communication*. New York, Norton.

Watzlawick, P., Weakland, L. and Fisch, R. (1974). *Change: Principles of Problem Formation and Problem Resolution*. New York, Norton.

Whitaker, C.A. (ed.) (1958). *Psychotherapy of Chronic Schizophrenic Patients*. Boston, Little Brown.

Whitaker, C.A. and Keith, D.V. (1981). 'Symbolic-experiential family therapy,' in A.S. Gurman and D.P. Kniskern (eds) *Handbook of Family Therapy*. New York, Bruner-Mazel.

Whorf, B., (1957). *Language, Thought and Reality*, Cambridge, MIT Press.
Winch, R.F. (1958). *Mate Selection*. New York, Basic Books.
Wittgenstein, L. (1951). *Tractatus Logico-Philosophicus*. New York, Humanities
    Press.

Index